MW00784399

VAMPIRELLA®

BITES

Nick Barrucci, CEO / Publisher
Juan Collado, President / COO
Rich Young, Director Business Development
Keith Davidsen, Marketing Manager

Joe Rybandt, Senior Editor
Hannah Gorfinkel, Associate Editor
Josh Green, Traffic Coordinator
Molly Mahan, Assistant Editor

Josh Johnson, Art Director
Jason Ullmeyer, Senior Graphic Designer
Katie Hidalgo, Graphic Designer
Chris Caniano, Production Assistant

Visit us online at www.DYNAMITE.com
Follow us on Twitter @dynamitecomics
Like us on Facebook /Dynamitecomics
Watch us on YouTube /Dynamitecomics

ISBN-10: 1-60690-522-8   ISBN-13: 978-1-60690-522-7   First Printing   10 9 8 7 6 5 4 3 2 1

VAMPIRELLA® BITES, VOLUME ONE. This volume collects material originally published in Vampirella Annual #2 (2012), Vampirella vs. Fluffy (2012), Vampirella: NuBlood (2013), and Vampirella Annual 2013. Published by Dynamite Entertainment. 113 Gaither Dr., STE 205, Mt. Laurel, NJ 08054. Vampirella is ® & © 2014 Dynamite. All Rights Reserved. DYNAMITE, DYNAMITE ENTERTAINMENT and its logo are © & ® 2014 Dynamite. All rights reserved. All names, characters, events, and locales in this publication are entirely fictional. Any resemblance to actual persons (living or dead), events or places, without satiric intent, is coincidental. No portion of this book may be reproduced by any means (digital or print) without the written permission of Dynamite Entertainment except for review purposes. The scanning, uploading and distribution of this book via the Internet or via any other means without the permission of the publisher is illegal and punishable by law. Please purchase only authorized electronic editions, and do not participate in or encourage electronic piracy of copyrighted materials. Printed in China

For information regarding press, media rights, foreign rights, licensing, promotions, and advertising e-mail: marketing@dynamite.com

ALL STORIES WRITTEN BY

MARK RAHNER

VAMPIRELLA ANNUAL #2:
BLOODSUCKER DUSK (2012)

ILLUSTRATED BY ILIAS KYRIAZIS

LETTERED BY MARSHALL DILLON

COLORED BY MAE HO

VAMPIRELLA vs. FLUFFY THE
VAMPIRE KILLER (2012)

ILLUSTRATED BY CEZAR RAZEK

LETTERED BY MARSHALL DILLON

COLORED BY INLIGHT STUDIO

VAMPIRELLA: NuBLOOD (2013)

ILLUSTRATED BY CEZAR RAZEK

LETTERED BY MARSHALL DILLON

COLORED BY VINICIUS TOWNSEND

VAMPIRELLA ANNUAL 2013:
VAMPIRELLA MEETS BAXTER

ILLUSTRATED BY RANDY VALIENTE

LETTERED BY MARSHALL DILLON

COLORED BY VIVIANE SOUZA

COVER BY JOSEPH MICHAEL LINSNER

VAMPIRELLA ANNUAL #2: BLOODSUCKER DUSK

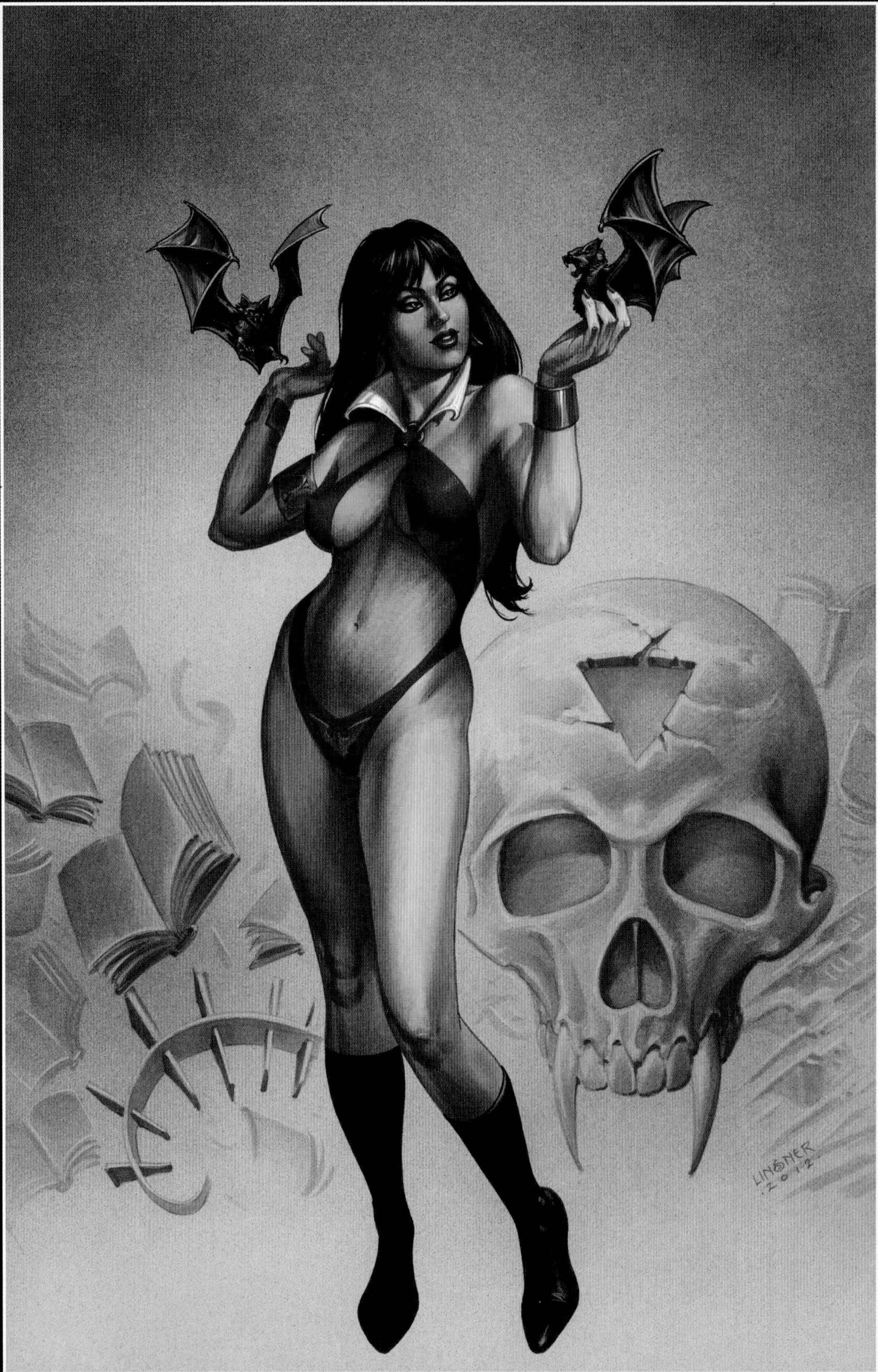
LINSNER
2012

cover art by JOSEPH MICHAEL LINSNER

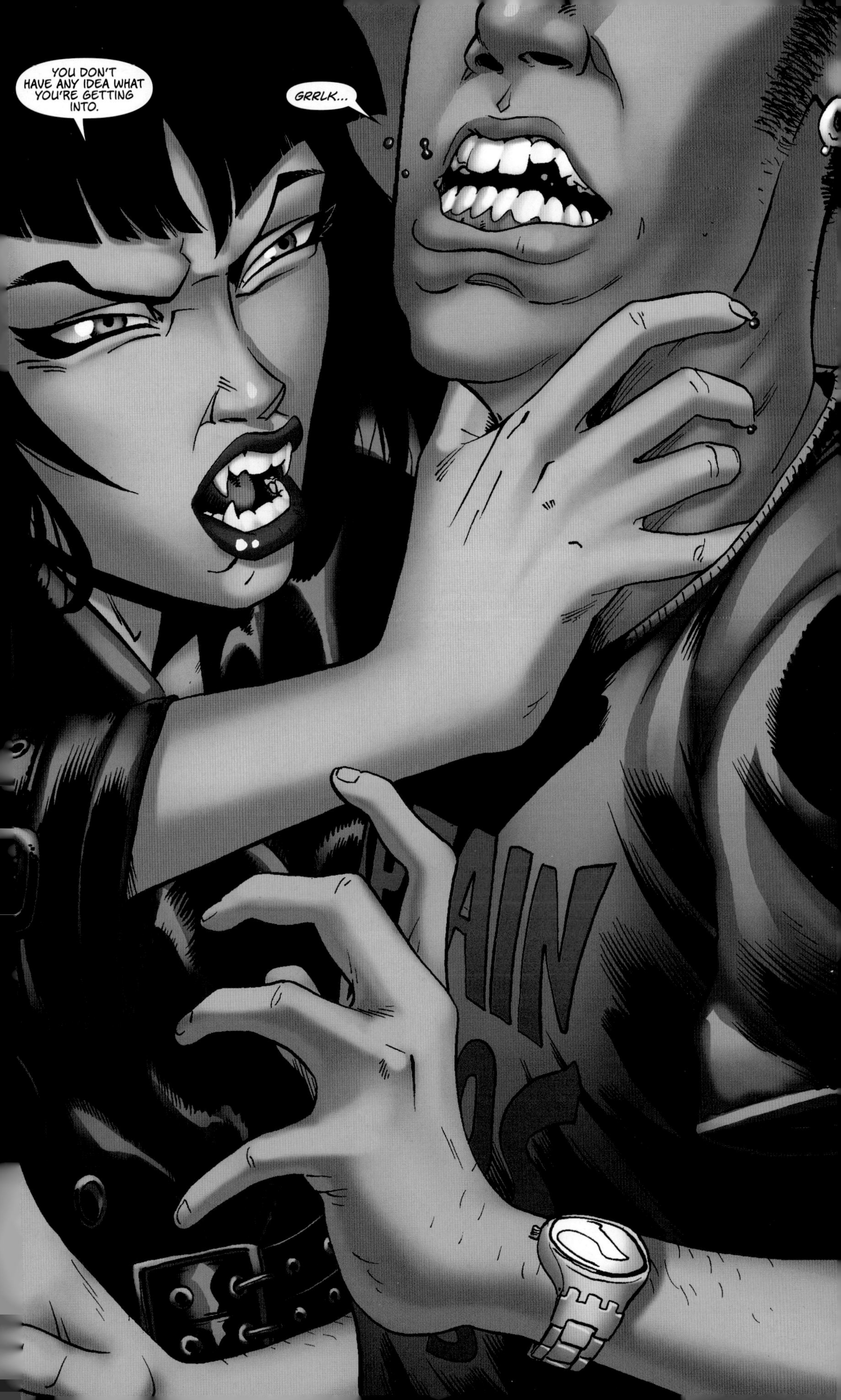
YOU DON'T HAVE ANY IDEA WHAT YOU'RE GETTING INTO.
GRRLK...

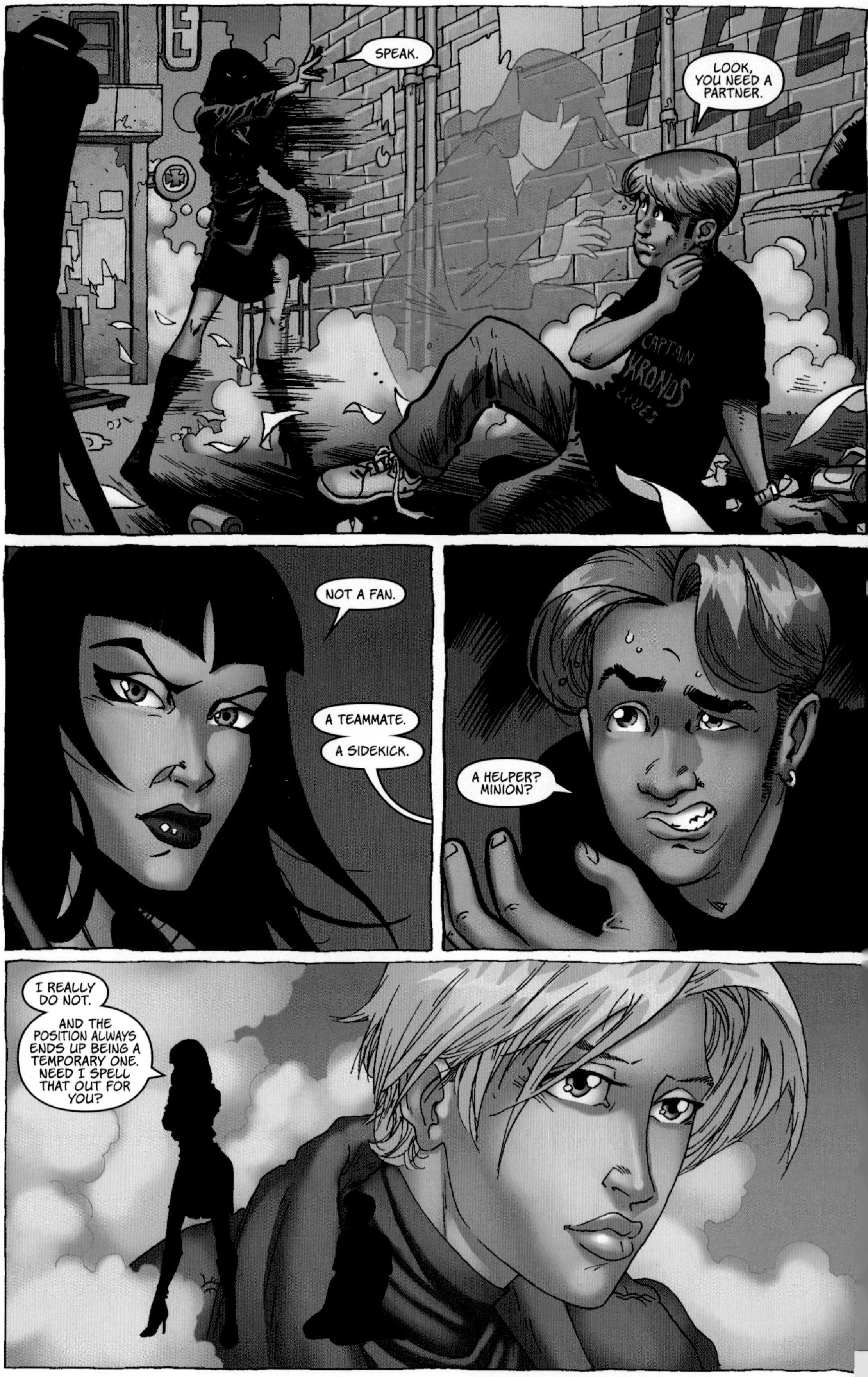
SPEAK.
LOOK, YOU NEED A PARTNER.
CAPTAIN KRONOS LIVES
NOT A FAN.
A TEAMMATE.
A SIDEKICK.
A HELPER? MINION?
I REALLY DO NOT.
AND THE POSITION ALWAYS ENDS UP BEING A TEMPORARY ONE. NEED I SPELL THAT OUT FOR YOU?

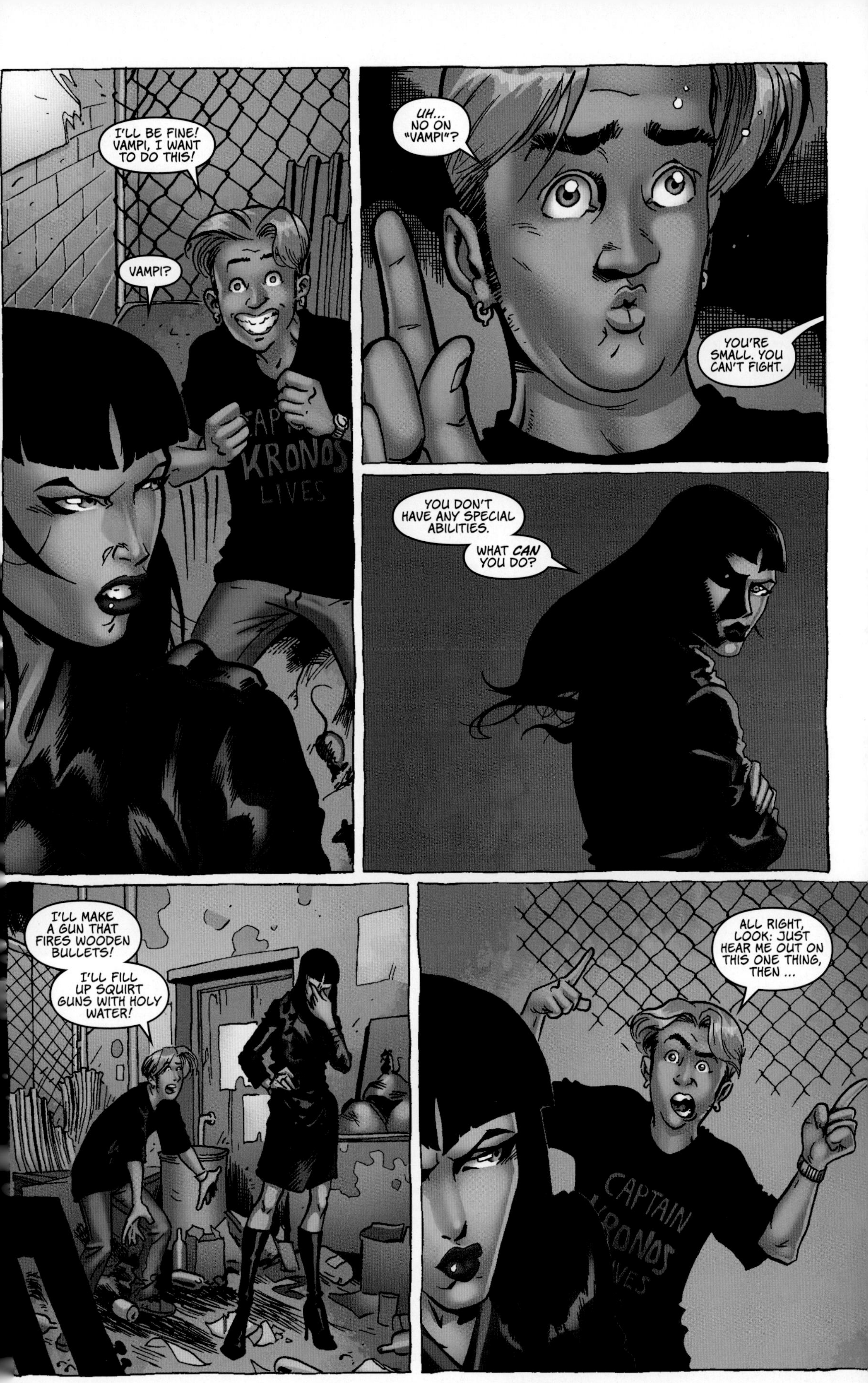
I'LL BE FINE! VAMPI, I WANT TO DO THIS!
VAMPI?
CAPTAIN KRONOS LIVES
UH... NO ON "VAMPI"?
YOU'RE SMALL. YOU CAN'T FIGHT.
YOU DON'T HAVE ANY SPECIAL ABILITIES.
WHAT CAN YOU DO?
I'LL MAKE A GUN THAT FIRES WOODEN BULLETS!
I'LL FILL UP SQUIRT GUNS WITH HOLY WATER!
ALL RIGHT, LOOK: JUST HEAR ME OUT ON THIS ONE THING, THEN ...

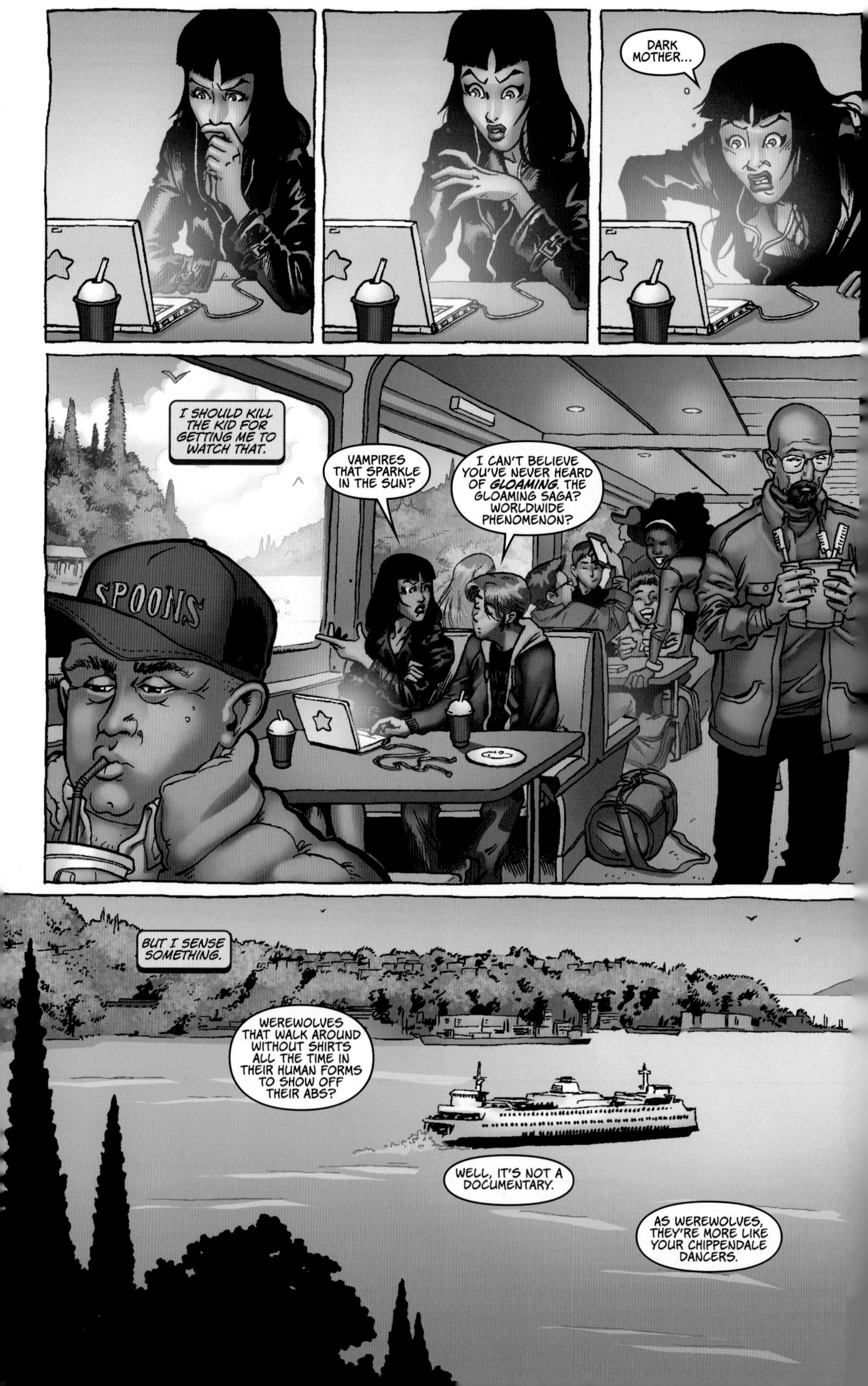
DARK MOTHER...
I SHOULD KILL THE KID FOR GETTING ME TO WATCH THAT.
VAMPIRES THAT SPARKLE IN THE SUN?
I CAN'T BELIEVE YOU'VE NEVER HEARD OF GLOAMING. THE GLOAMING SAGA? WORLDWIDE PHENOMENON?
SPOONS
BUT I SENSE SOMETHING.
WEREWOLVES THAT WALK AROUND WITHOUT SHIRTS ALL THE TIME IN THEIR HUMAN FORMS TO SHOW OFF THEIR ABS?
WELL, IT'S NOT A DOCUMENTARY.
AS WEREWOLVES, THEY'RE MORE LIKE YOUR CHIPPENDALE DANCERS.

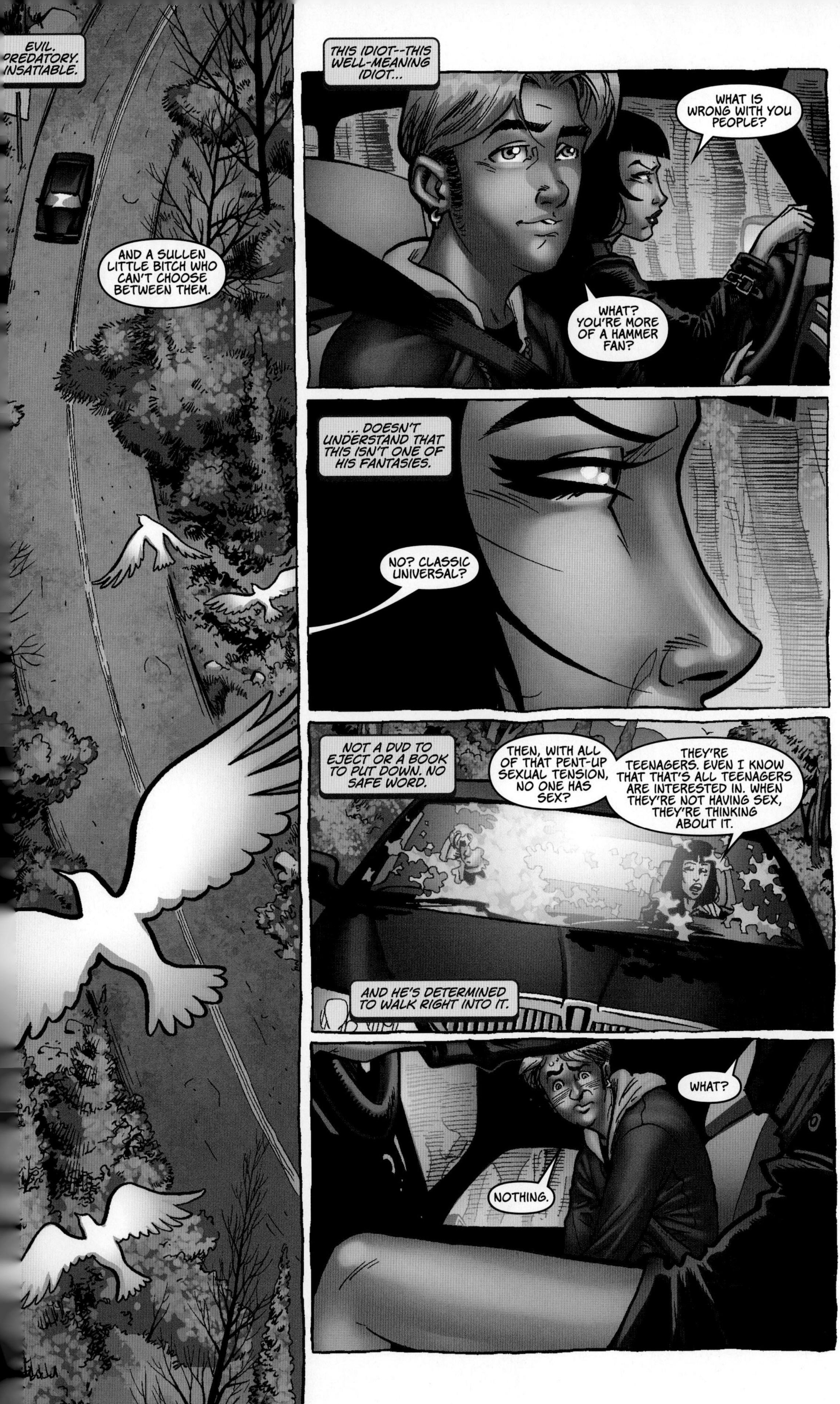
EVIL. PREDATORY. INSATIABLE.
AND A SULLEN LITTLE BITCH WHO CAN'T CHOOSE BETWEEN THEM.
THIS IDIOT--THIS WELL-MEANING IDIOT...
WHAT IS WRONG WITH YOU PEOPLE?
WHAT? YOU'RE MORE OF A HAMMER FAN?
... DOESN'T UNDERSTAND THAT THIS ISN'T ONE OF HIS FANTASIES.
NO? CLASSIC UNIVERSAL?
NOT A DVD TO EJECT OR A BOOK TO PUT DOWN. NO SAFE WORD.
THEN, WITH ALL OF THAT PENT-UP SEXUAL TENSION, NO ONE HAS SEX?
THEY'RE TEENAGERS. EVEN I KNOW THAT THAT'S ALL TEENAGERS ARE INTERESTED IN. WHEN THEY'RE NOT HAVING SEX, THEY'RE THINKING ABOUT IT.
AND HE'S DETERMINED TO WALK RIGHT INTO IT.
WHAT?
NOTHING.

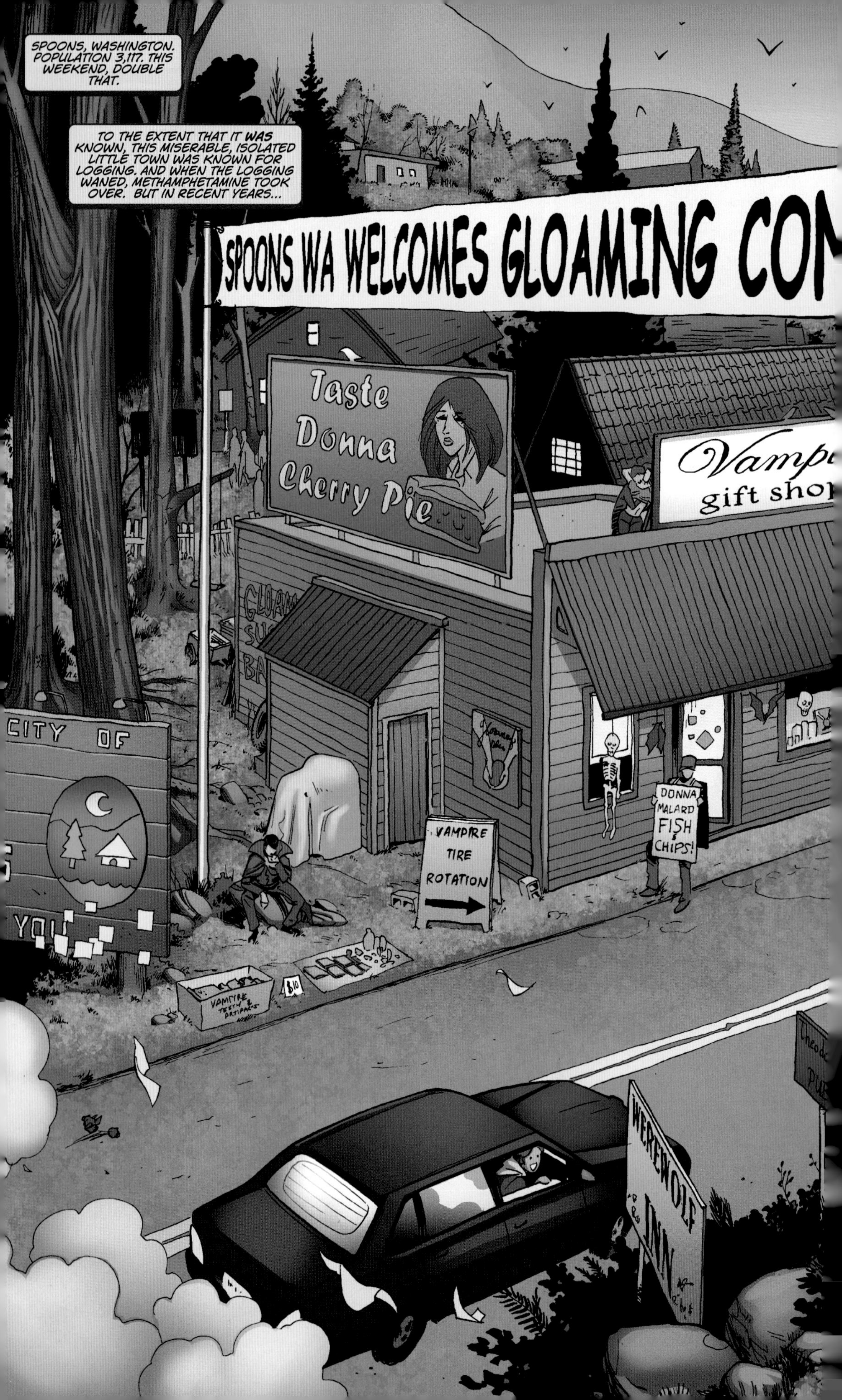

SPOONS, WASHINGTON. POPULATION 3,117. THIS WEEKEND, DOUBLE THAT.
TO THE EXTENT THAT IT WAS KNOWN, THIS MISERABLE, ISOLATED LITTLE TOWN WAS KNOWN FOR LOGGING. AND WHEN THE LOGGING WANED, METHAMPHETAMINE TOOK OVER. BUT IN RECENT YEARS...
SPOONS WA WELCOMES GLOAMING CON
Taste Donna Cherry Pie
Vamp
gift shop
CITY OF
YOU
VAMPIRE TIRE ROTATION
DONNA MALARD FISH & CHIPS!
$10
VAMPIRE TEETH & ARTIFACTS
WEREWOLF INN

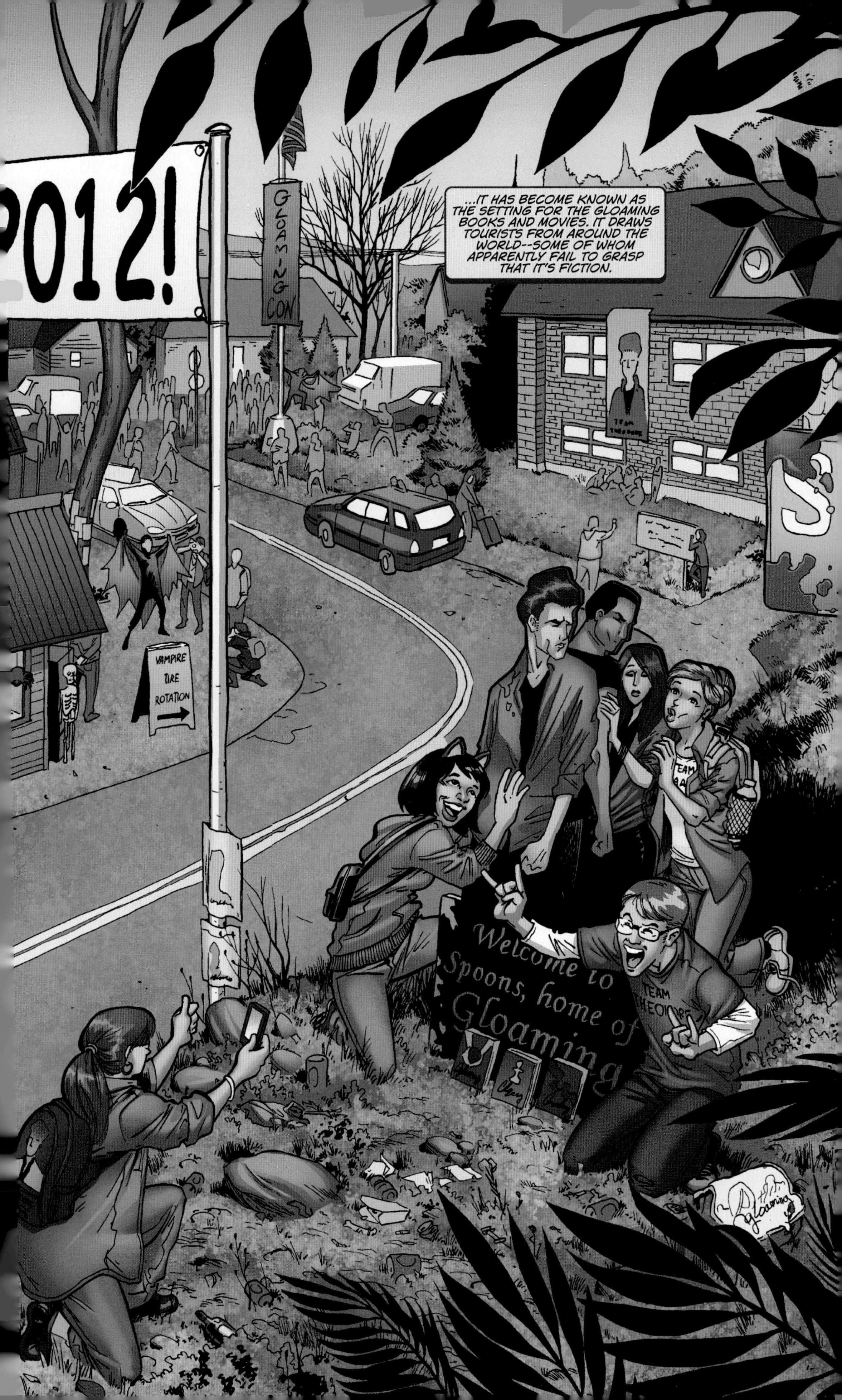

2012!
GLOAMING CON
...IT HAS BECOME KNOWN AS THE SETTING FOR THE GLOAMING BOOKS AND MOVIES. IT DRAWS TOURISTS FROM AROUND THE WORLD--SOME OF WHOM APPARENTLY FAIL TO GRASP THAT IT'S FICTION.
VAMPIRE TIRE ROTATION
Welcome to Spoons, home of Gloaming
TEAM THEODORE

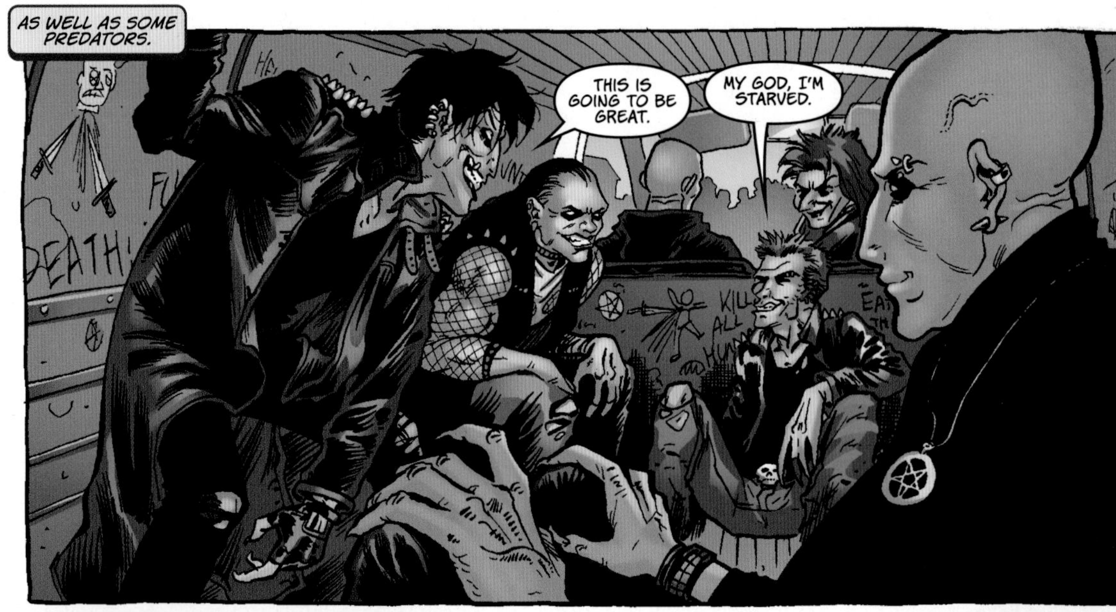
AS WELL AS SOME PREDATORS.
THIS IS GOING TO BE GREAT.
MY GOD, I'M STARVED.
DEATH!

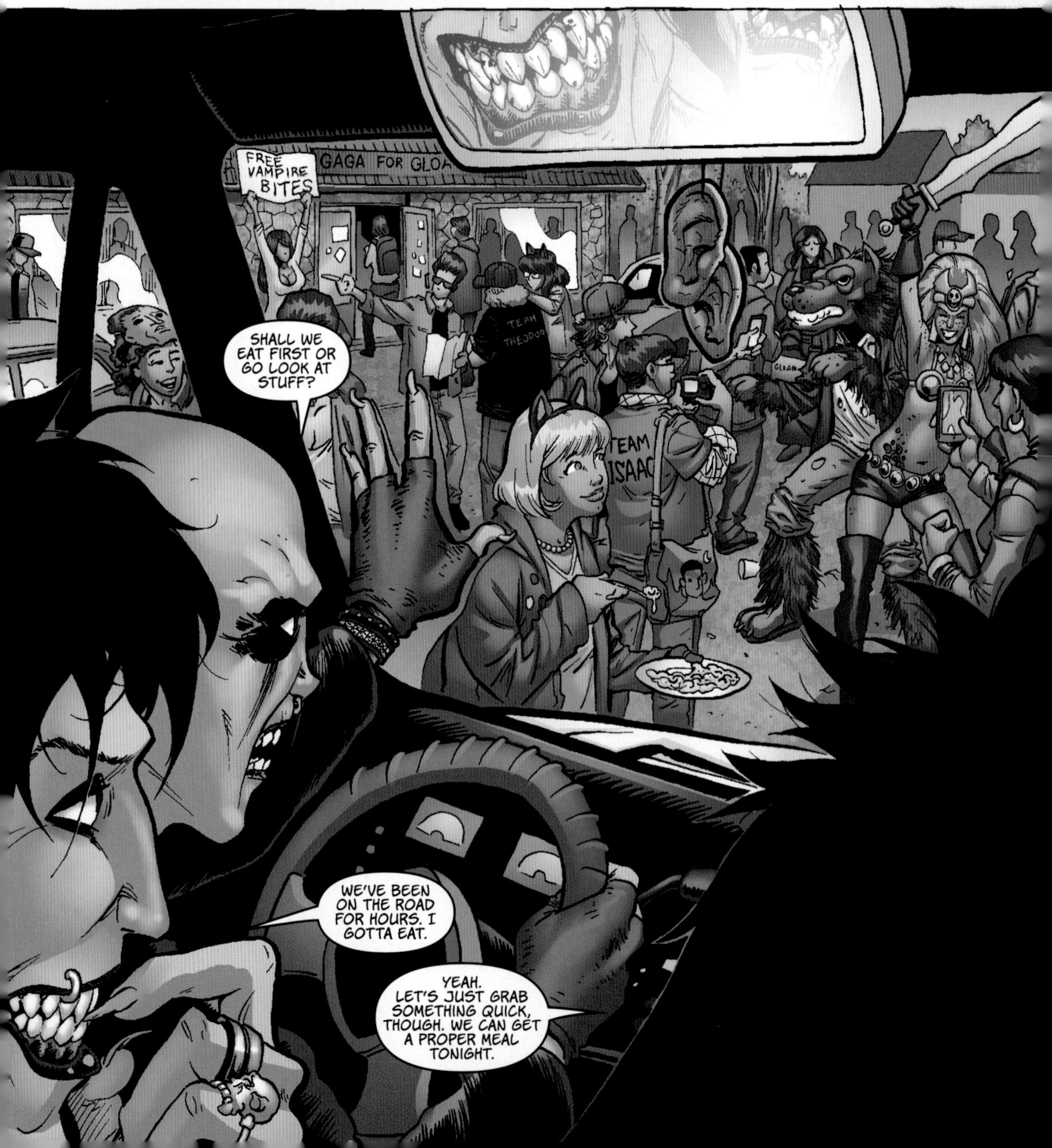
FREE VAMPIRE BITES
SHALL WE EAT FIRST OR GO LOOK AT STUFF?
WE'VE BEEN ON THE ROAD FOR HOURS. I GOTTA EAT.
YEAH. LET'S JUST GRAB SOMETHING QUICK, THOUGH. WE CAN GET A PROPER MEAL TONIGHT.

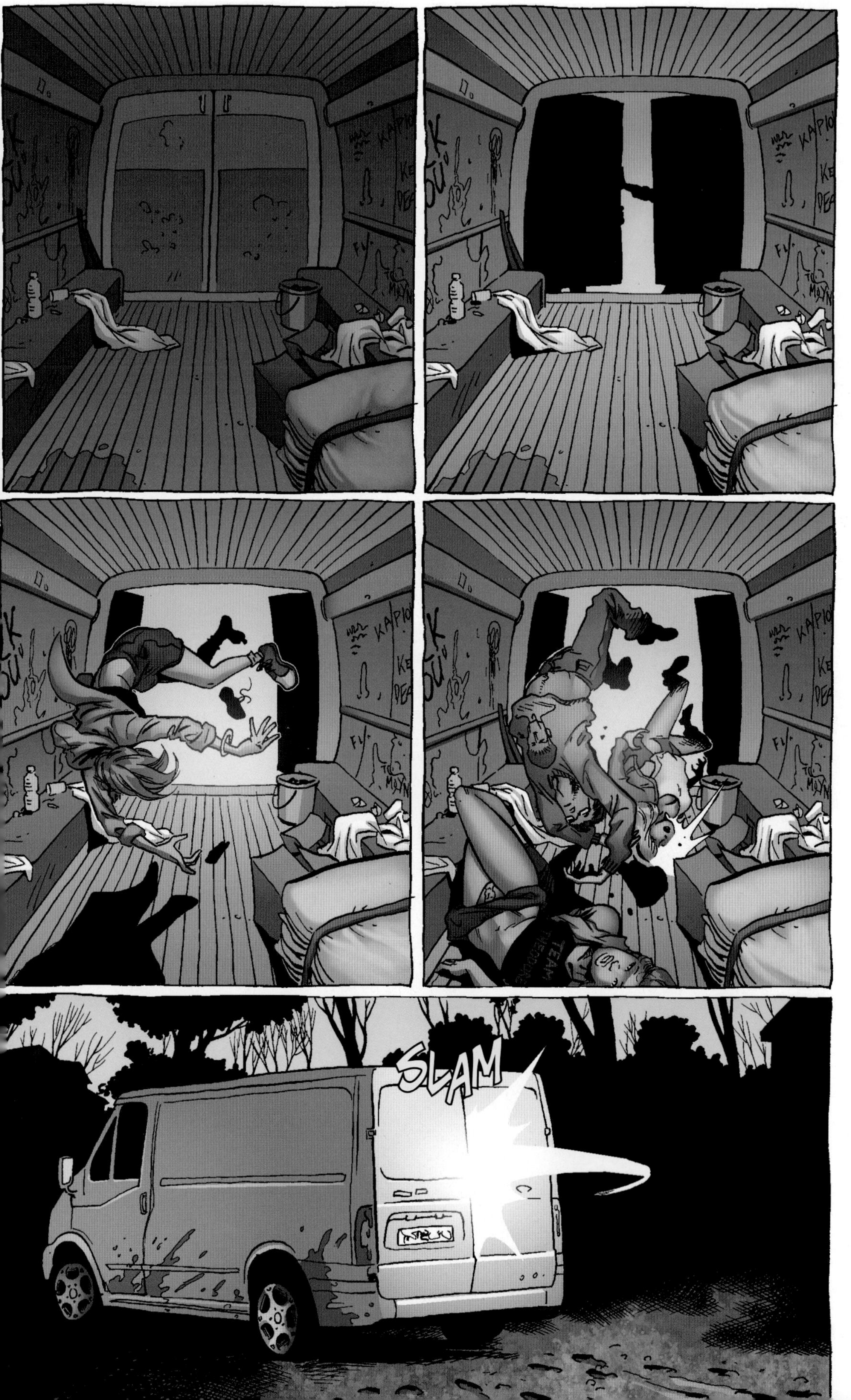
SLAM

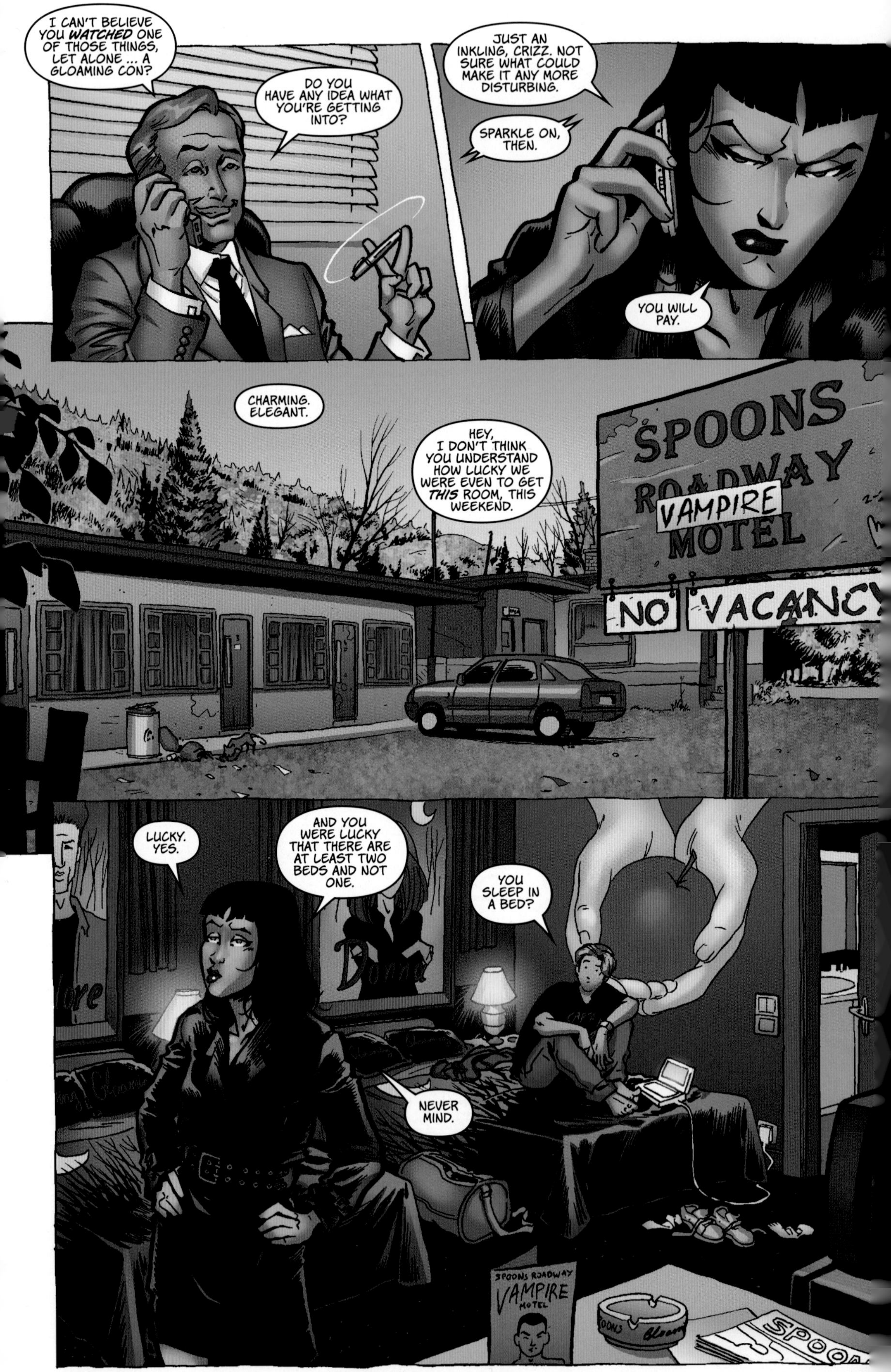
I CAN'T BELIEVE YOU *WATCHED* ONE OF THOSE THINGS, LET ALONE ... A GLOAMING CON?
DO YOU HAVE ANY IDEA WHAT YOU'RE GETTING INTO?
JUST AN INKLING, CRIZZ. NOT SURE WHAT COULD MAKE IT ANY MORE DISTURBING.
SPARKLE ON, THEN.
YOU WILL PAY.
CHARMING. ELEGANT.
HEY, I DON'T THINK YOU UNDERSTAND HOW LUCKY WE WERE EVEN TO GET *THIS* ROOM, THIS WEEKEND.
SPOONS ROADWAY VAMPIRE MOTEL
NO VACANCY
LUCKY. YES.
AND YOU WERE LUCKY THAT THERE ARE AT LEAST TWO BEDS AND NOT ONE.
YOU SLEEP IN A BED?
NEVER MIND.
SPOONS ROADWAY VAMPIRE MOTEL

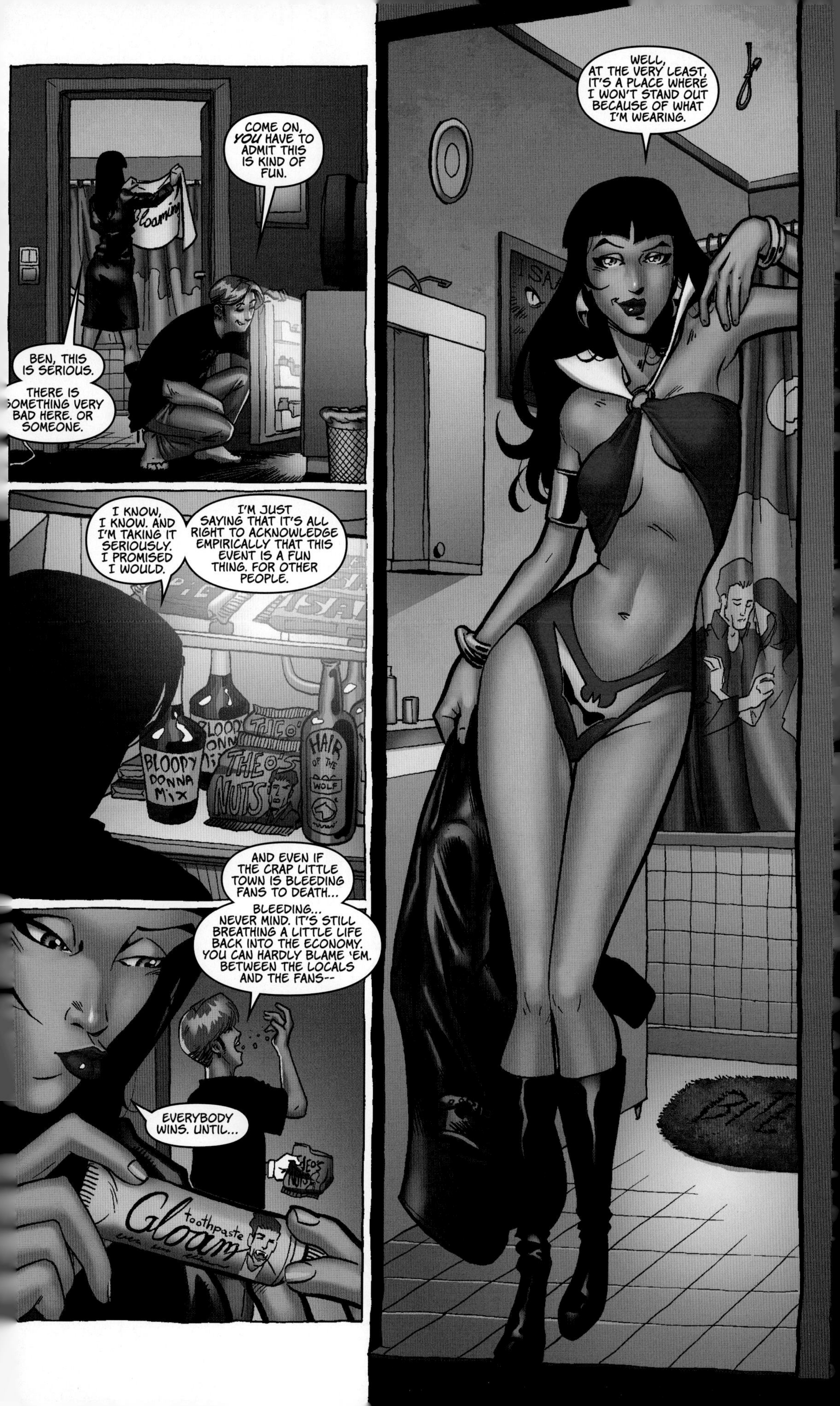
COME ON, YOU HAVE TO ADMIT THIS IS KIND OF FUN.
BEN, THIS IS SERIOUS.
THERE IS SOMETHING VERY BAD HERE. OR SOMEONE.
WELL, AT THE VERY LEAST, IT'S A PLACE WHERE I WON'T STAND OUT BECAUSE OF WHAT I'M WEARING.
I KNOW, I KNOW. AND I'M TAKING IT SERIOUSLY. I PROMISED I WOULD.
I'M JUST SAYING THAT IT'S ALL RIGHT TO ACKNOWLEDGE EMPIRICALLY THAT THIS EVENT IS A FUN THING. FOR OTHER PEOPLE.
BLOODY DONNA MIX
THE O'S NUTS
HAIR OF THE WOLF
AND EVEN IF THE CRAP LITTLE TOWN IS BLEEDING FANS TO DEATH...
BLEEDING... NEVER MIND. IT'S STILL BREATHING A LITTLE LIFE BACK INTO THE ECONOMY. YOU CAN HARDLY BLAME 'EM. BETWEEN THE LOCALS AND THE FANS--
EVERYBODY WINS. UNTIL...
Gloam toothpaste

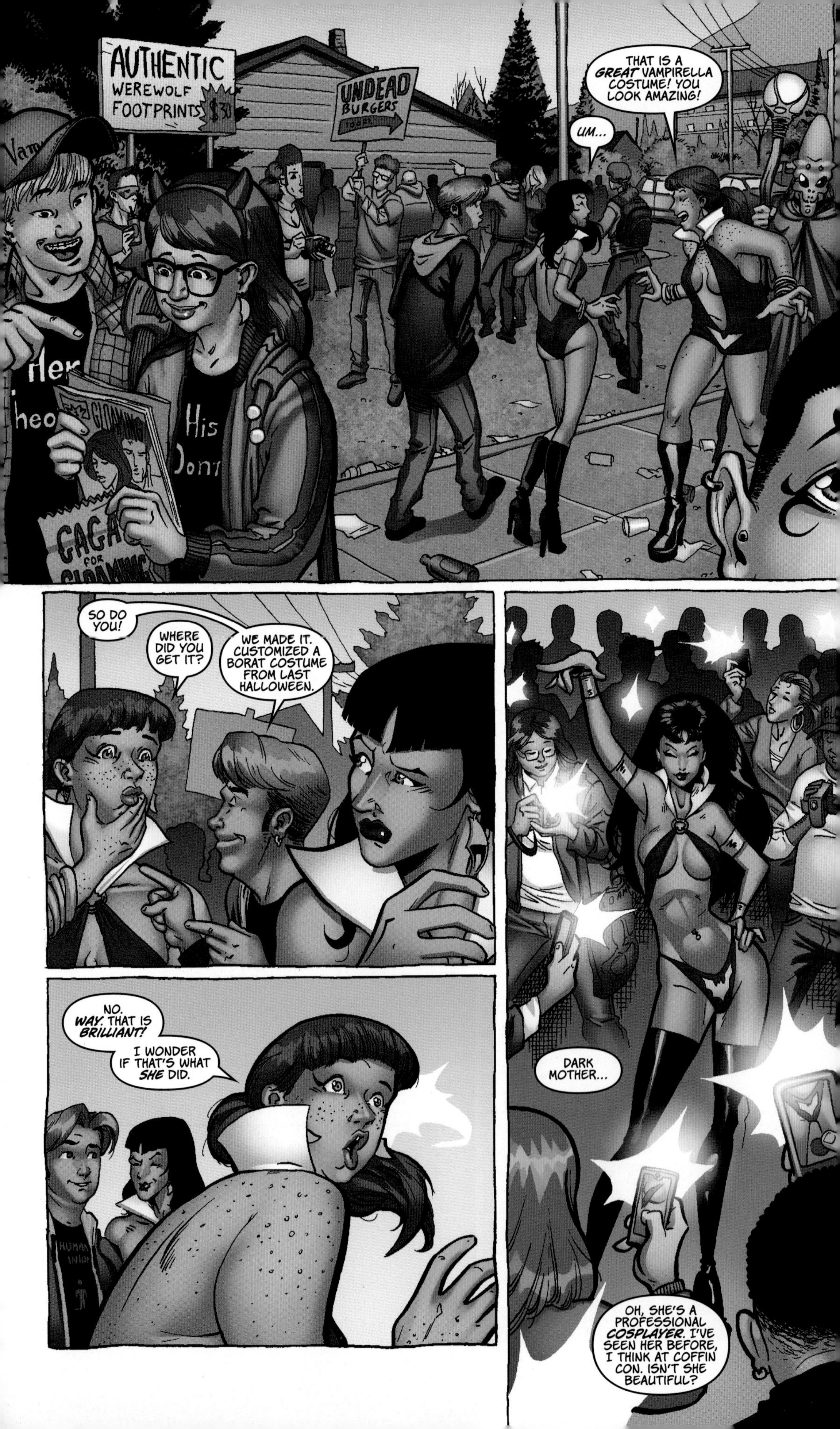
AUTHENTIC WEREWOLF FOOTPRINTS $30
UNDEAD BURGERS
THAT IS A **GREAT** VAMPIRELLA COSTUME! YOU LOOK AMAZING!
UM...
SO DO YOU!
WHERE DID YOU GET IT?
WE MADE IT. CUSTOMIZED A BORAT COSTUME FROM LAST HALLOWEEN.
NO. **WAY**. THAT IS **BRILLIANT!**
I WONDER IF THAT'S WHAT **SHE** DID.
DARK MOTHER...
OH, SHE'S A PROFESSIONAL **COSPLAYER**. I'VE SEEN HER BEFORE, I THINK AT COFFIN CON. ISN'T SHE BEAUTIFUL?

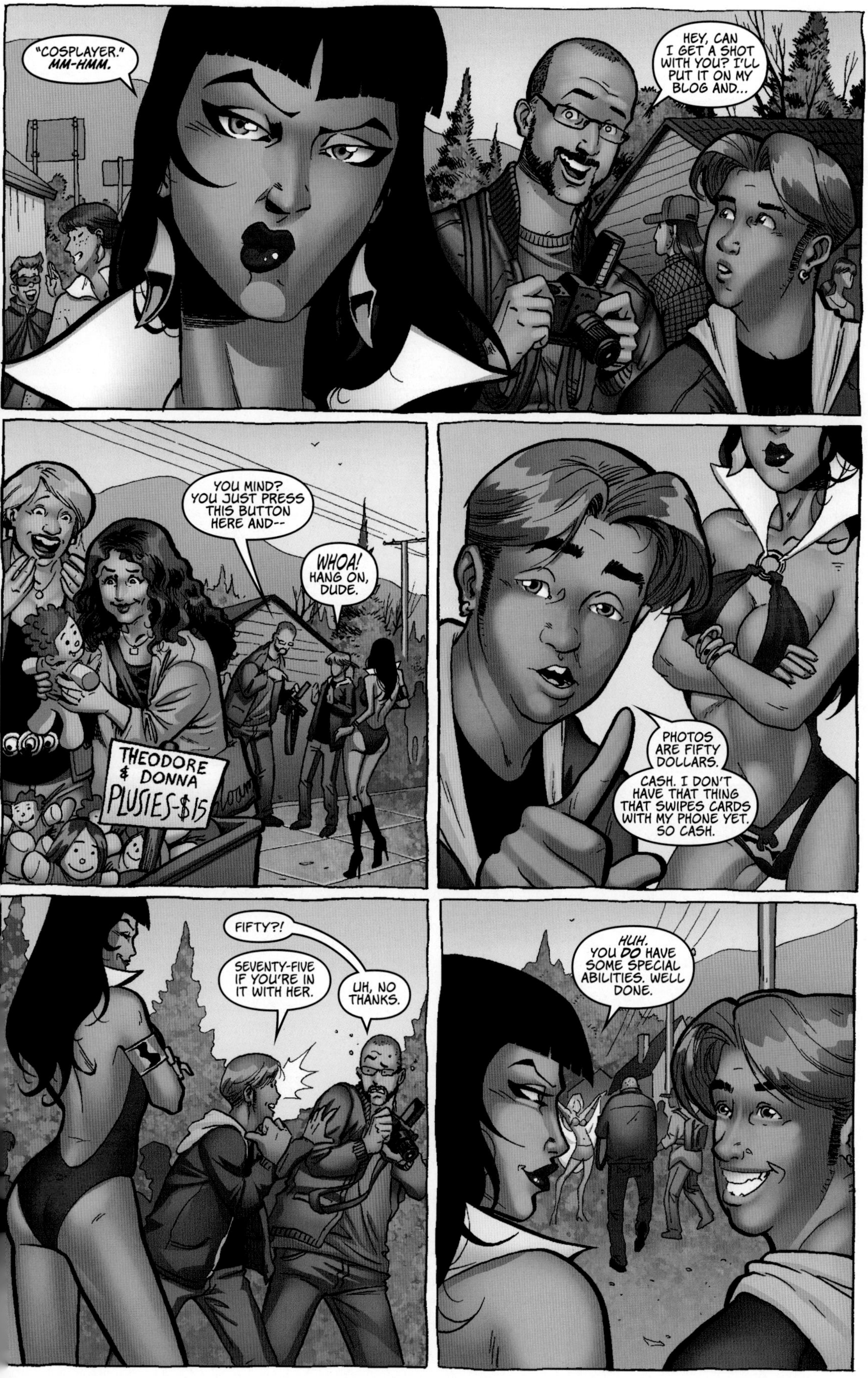
"COSPLAYER." MM-HMM.
HEY, CAN I GET A SHOT WITH YOU? I'LL PUT IT ON MY BLOG AND...
YOU MIND? YOU JUST PRESS THIS BUTTON HERE AND--
WHOA! HANG ON, DUDE.
THEODORE & DONNA PLUSIES-$15
PHOTOS ARE FIFTY DOLLARS.
CASH. I DON'T HAVE THAT THING THAT SWIPES CARDS WITH MY PHONE YET. SO CASH.
FIFTY?!
SEVENTY-FIVE IF YOU'RE IN IT WITH HER.
UH, NO THANKS.
HUH. YOU DO HAVE SOME SPECIAL ABILITIES. WELL DONE.

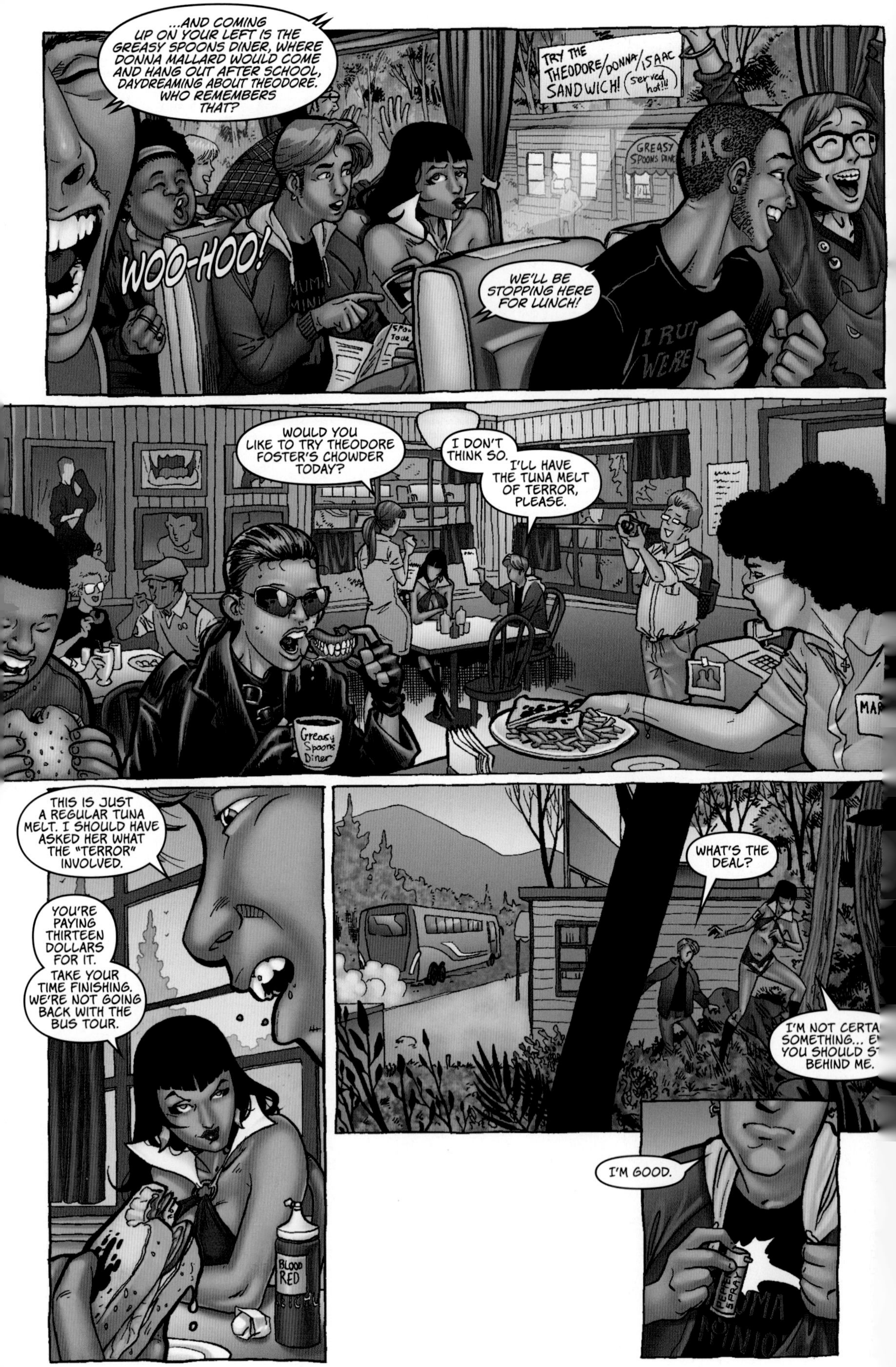
...AND COMING UP ON YOUR LEFT IS THE GREASY SPOONS DINER, WHERE DONNA MALLARD WOULD COME AND HANG OUT AFTER SCHOOL, DAYDREAMING ABOUT THEODORE. WHO REMEMBERS THAT?
TRY THE THEODORE/DONNA/ISAAC SANDWICH! (served hot!!)
GREASY SPOONS DINER
WOO-HOO!
WE'LL BE STOPPING HERE FOR LUNCH!
WOULD YOU LIKE TO TRY THEODORE FOSTER'S CHOWDER TODAY?
I DON'T THINK SO.
I'LL HAVE THE TUNA MELT OF TERROR, PLEASE.
Greasy Spoons Diner
THIS IS JUST A REGULAR TUNA MELT. I SHOULD HAVE ASKED HER WHAT THE "TERROR" INVOLVED.
YOU'RE PAYING THIRTEEN DOLLARS FOR IT.
TAKE YOUR TIME FINISHING. WE'RE NOT GOING BACK WITH THE BUS TOUR.
BLOOD RED
WHAT'S THE DEAL?
I'M NOT CERTA SOMETHING... E YOU SHOULD S BEHIND ME.
I'M GOOD.
PEPPER SPRAY

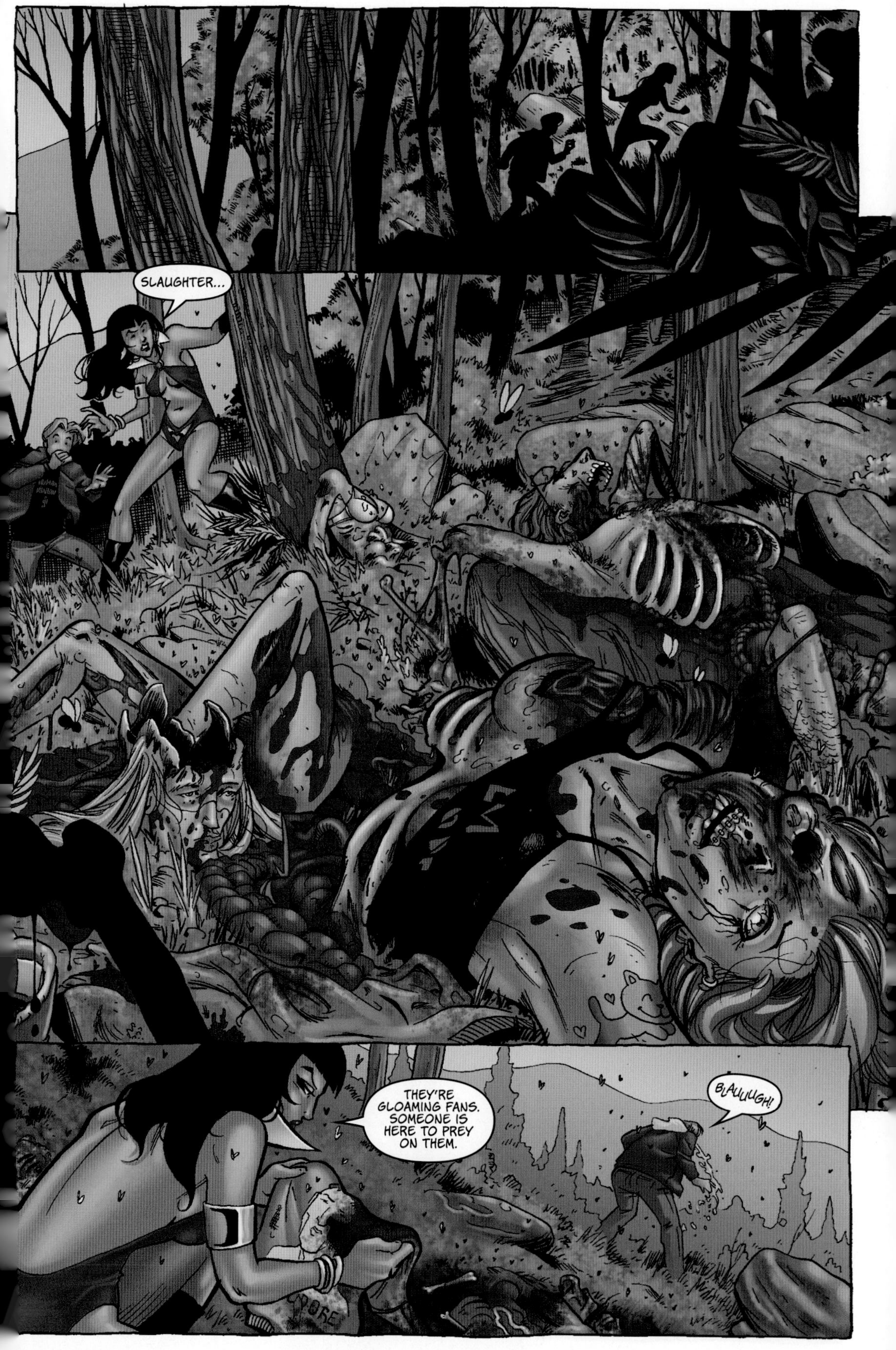
SLAUGHTER...
THEY'RE GLOAMING FANS. SOMEONE IS HERE TO PREY ON THEM.
BLAUUUGH!

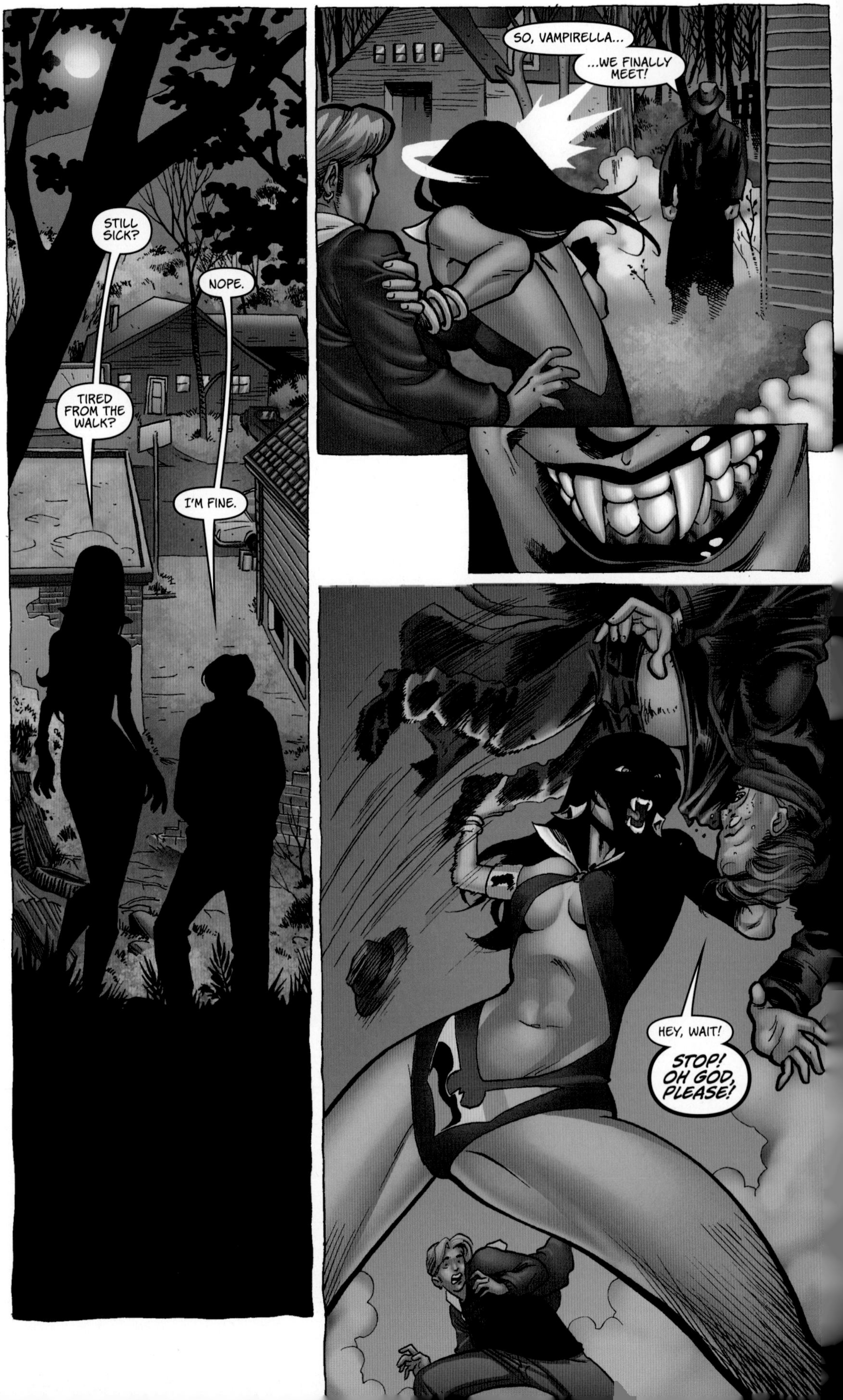
STILL SICK?
NOPE.
TIRED FROM THE WALK?
I'M FINE.
SO, VAMPIRELLA...
...WE FINALLY MEET!
HEY, WAIT!
STOP! OH GOD, PLEASE!

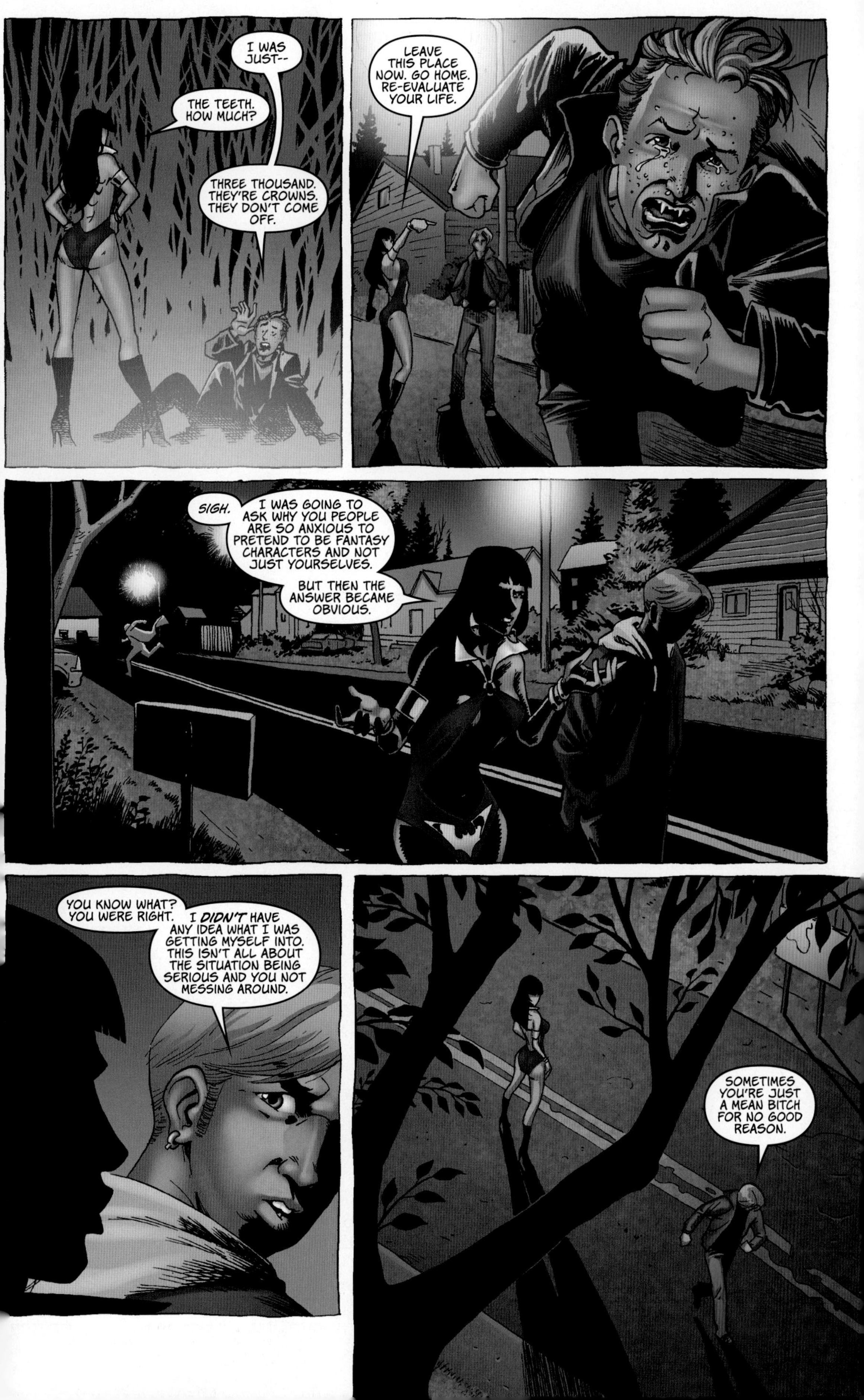
I WAS JUST--
THE TEETH. HOW MUCH?
THREE THOUSAND. THEY'RE CROWNS. THEY DON'T COME OFF.
LEAVE THIS PLACE NOW. GO HOME. RE-EVALUATE YOUR LIFE.
SIGH.
I WAS GOING TO ASK WHY YOU PEOPLE ARE SO ANXIOUS TO PRETEND TO BE FANTASY CHARACTERS AND NOT JUST YOURSELVES.
BUT THEN THE ANSWER BECAME OBVIOUS.
YOU KNOW WHAT? YOU WERE RIGHT.
I *DIDN'T* HAVE ANY IDEA WHAT I WAS GETTING MYSELF INTO. THIS ISN'T ALL ABOUT THE SITUATION BEING SERIOUS AND YOU NOT MESSING AROUND.
SOMETIMES YOU'RE JUST A MEAN BITCH FOR NO GOOD REASON.

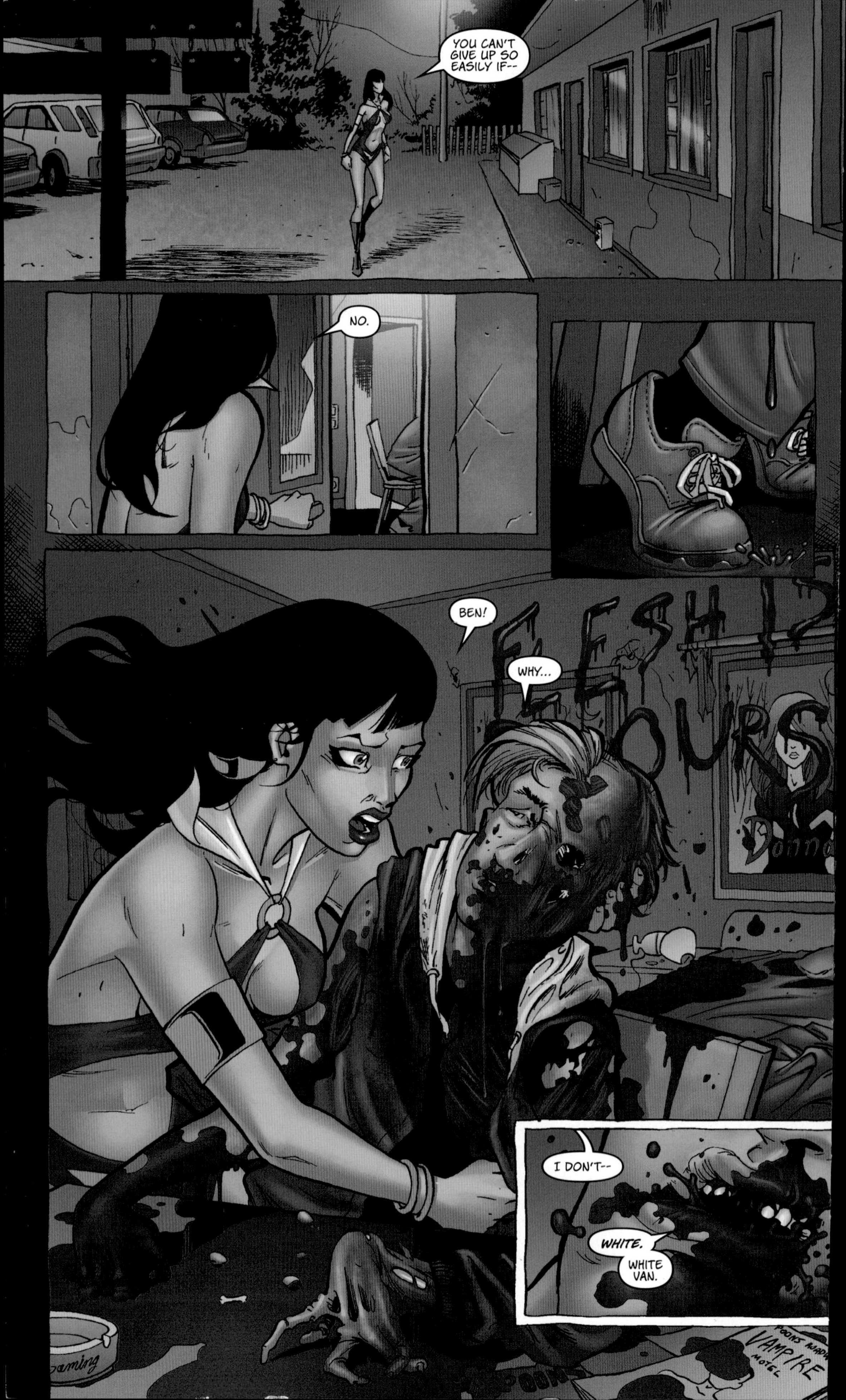
YOU CAN'T GIVE UP SO EASILY IF--
NO.
BEN!
WHY...
I DON'T--
WHITE.
WHITE VAN.

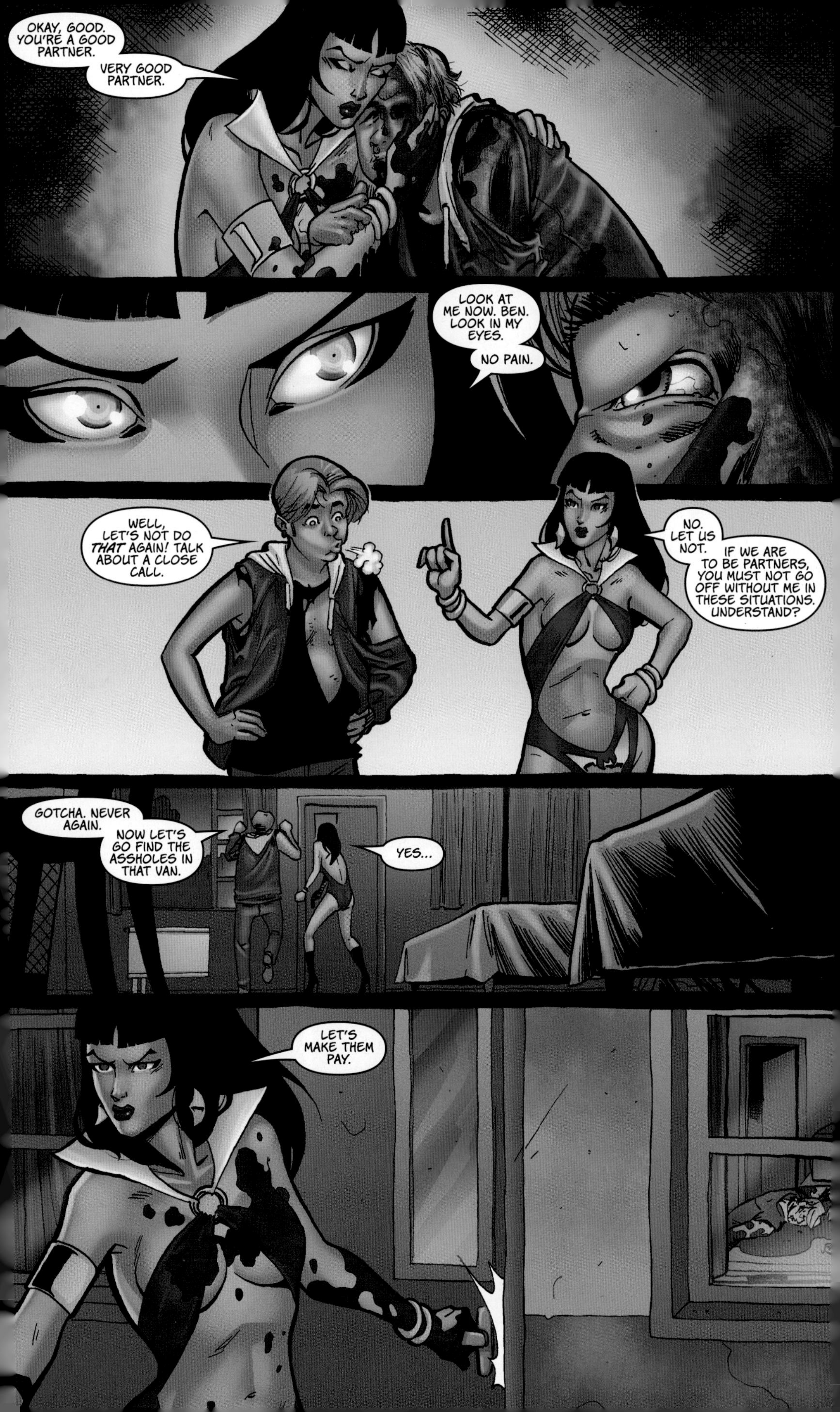
OKAY, GOOD. YOU'RE A GOOD PARTNER.
VERY GOOD PARTNER.
LOOK AT ME NOW. BEN. LOOK IN MY EYES.
NO PAIN.
WELL, LET'S NOT DO *THAT* AGAIN! TALK ABOUT A CLOSE CALL.
NO. LET US NOT.
IF WE ARE TO BE PARTNERS, YOU MUST NOT GO OFF WITHOUT ME IN THESE SITUATIONS. UNDERSTAND?
GOTCHA. NEVER AGAIN.
NOW LET'S GO FIND THE ASSHOLES IN THAT VAN.
YES...
LET'S MAKE THEM PAY.

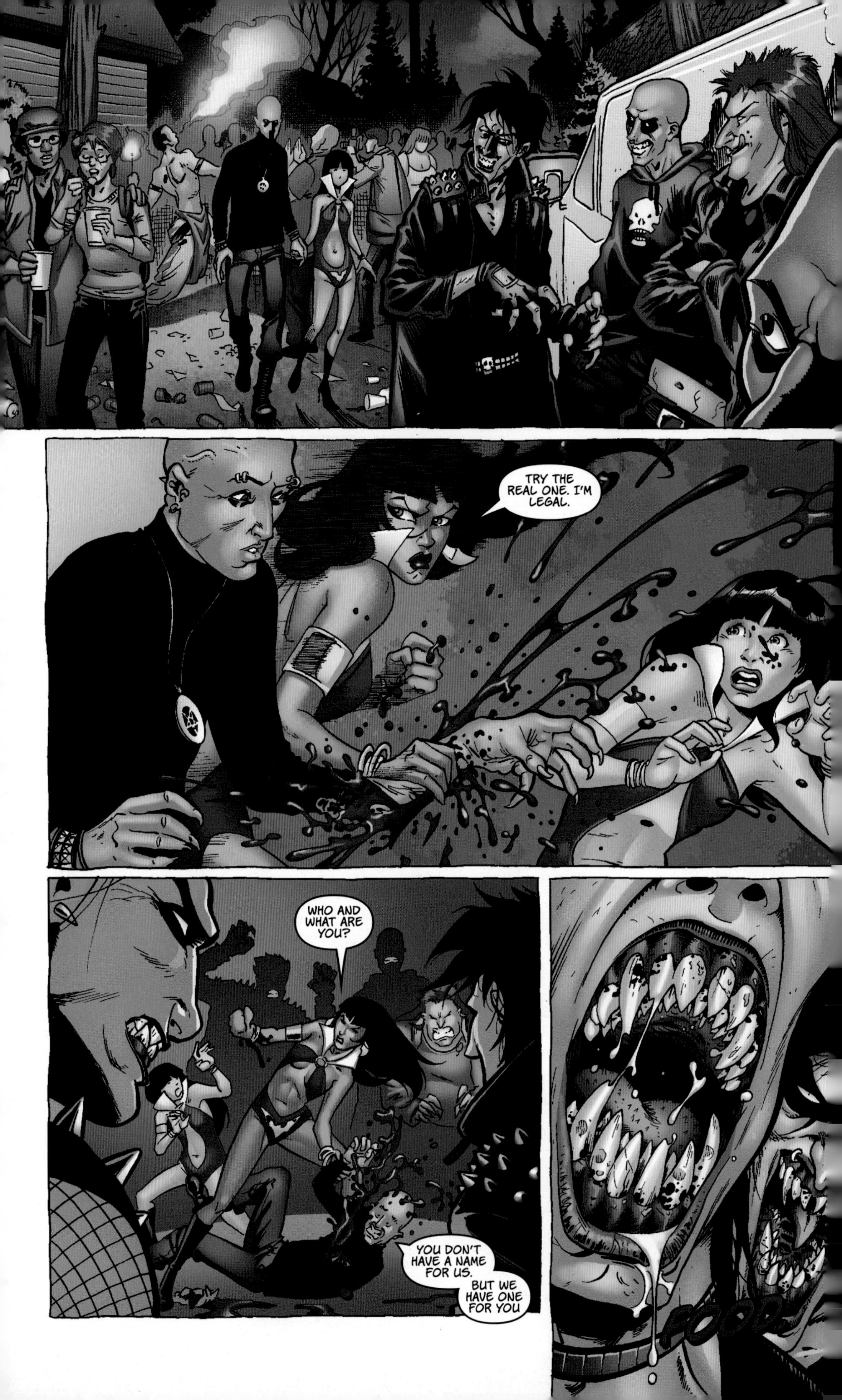
TRY THE REAL ONE. I'M LEGAL.
WHO AND WHAT ARE YOU?
YOU DON'T HAVE A NAME FOR US.
BUT WE HAVE ONE FOR YOU
FOOD

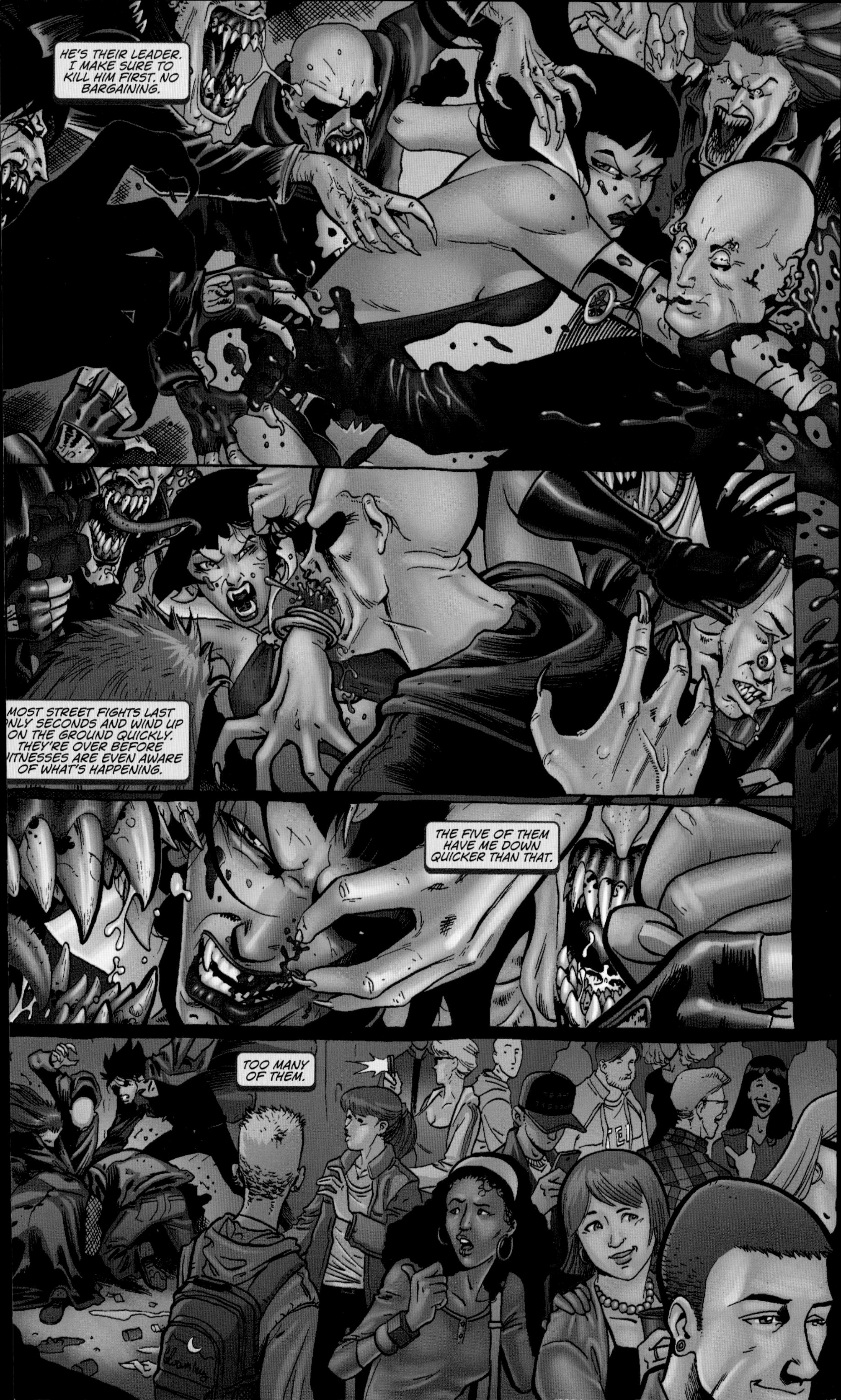
HE'S THEIR LEADER. I MAKE SURE TO KILL HIM FIRST. NO BARGAINING.
MOST STREET FIGHTS LAST ONLY SECONDS AND WIND UP ON THE GROUND QUICKLY. THEY'RE OVER BEFORE WITNESSES ARE EVEN AWARE OF WHAT'S HAPPENING.
THE FIVE OF THEM HAVE ME DOWN QUICKER THAN THAT.
TOO MANY OF THEM.

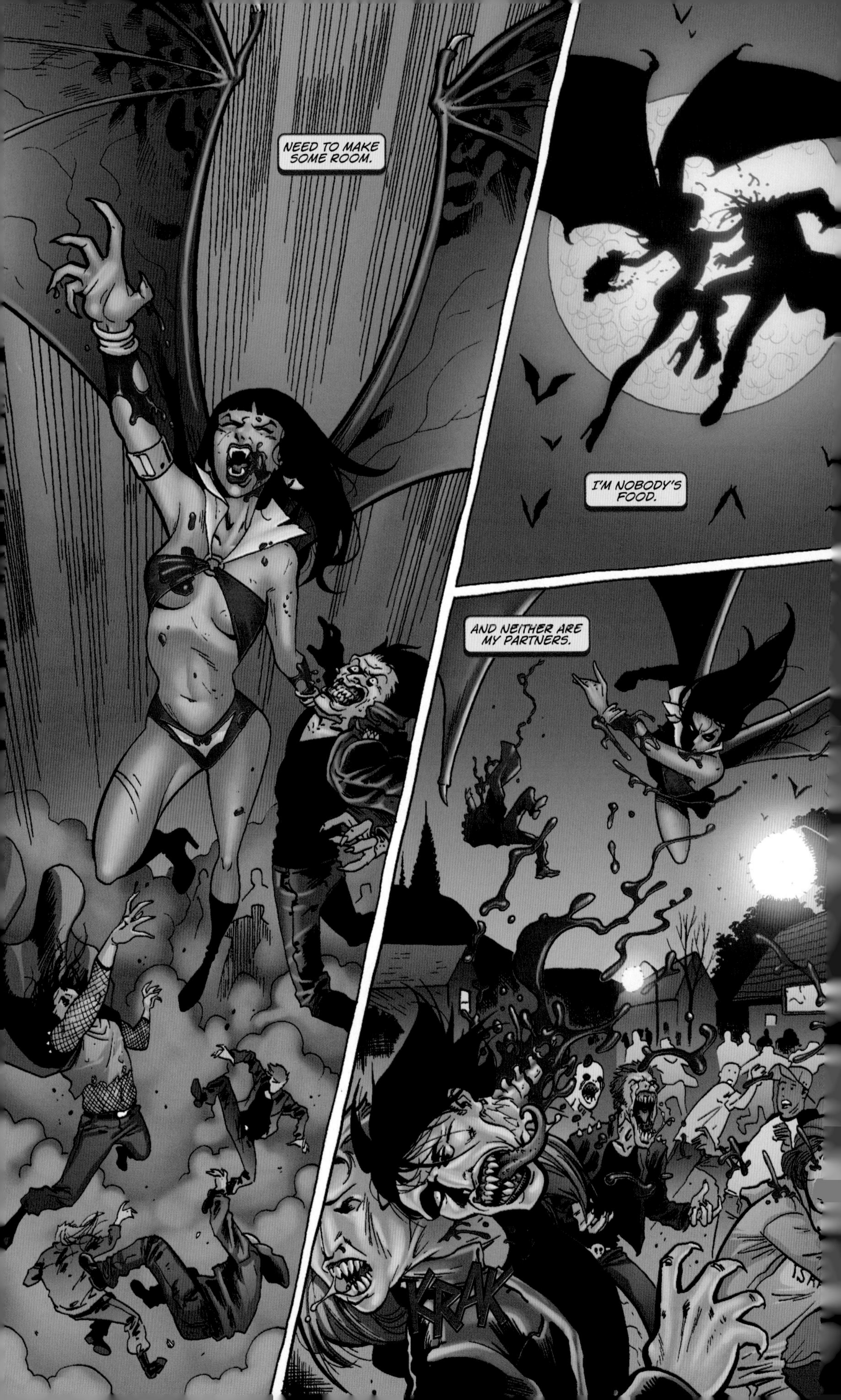
NEED TO MAKE SOME ROOM.
I'M NOBODY'S FOOD.
AND NEITHER ARE MY PARTNERS.
KRAK

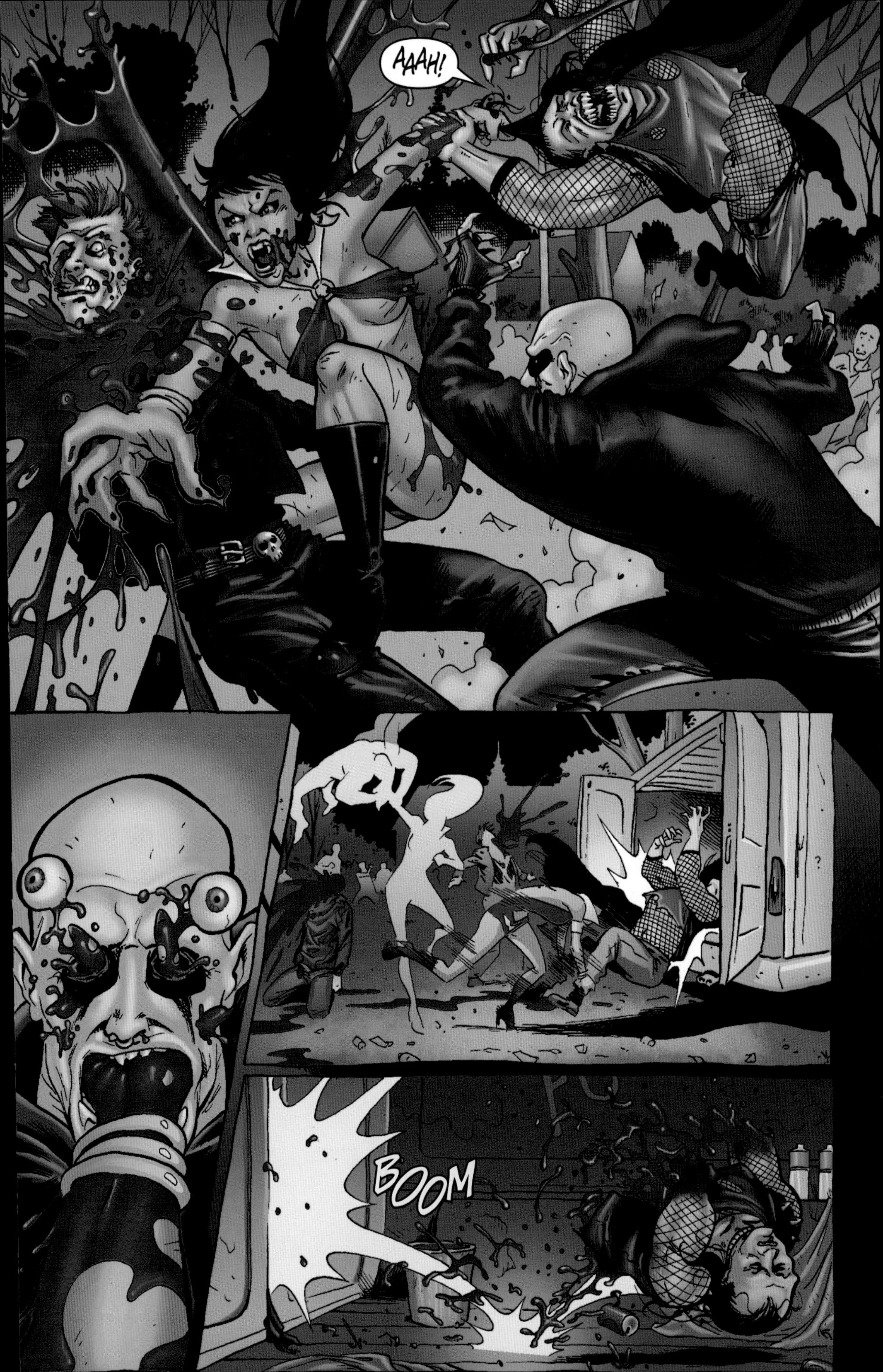
AAAH!
BOOM

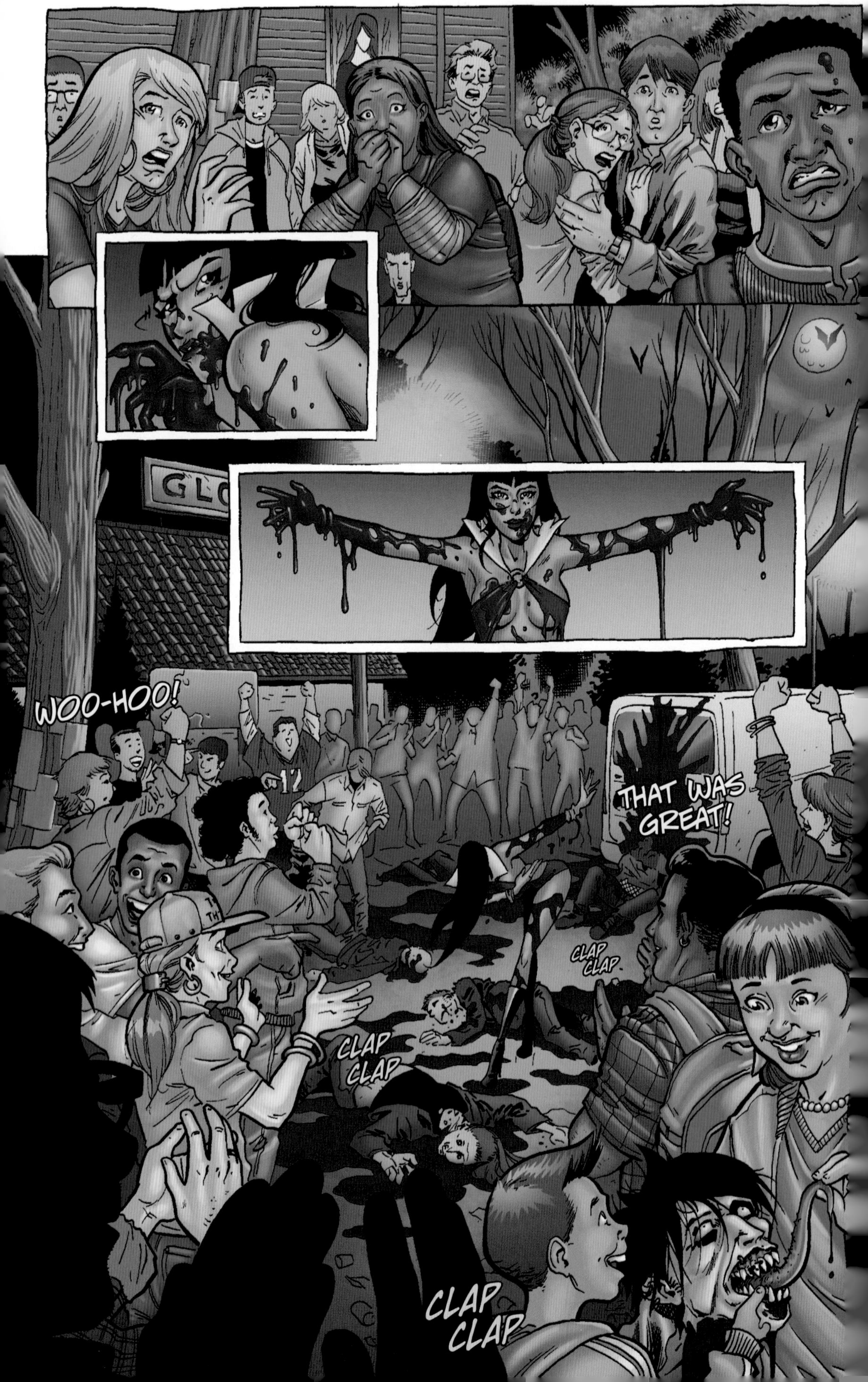
WOO-HOO!
THAT WAS GREAT!
CLAP CLAP
CLAP CLAP
CLAP CLAP

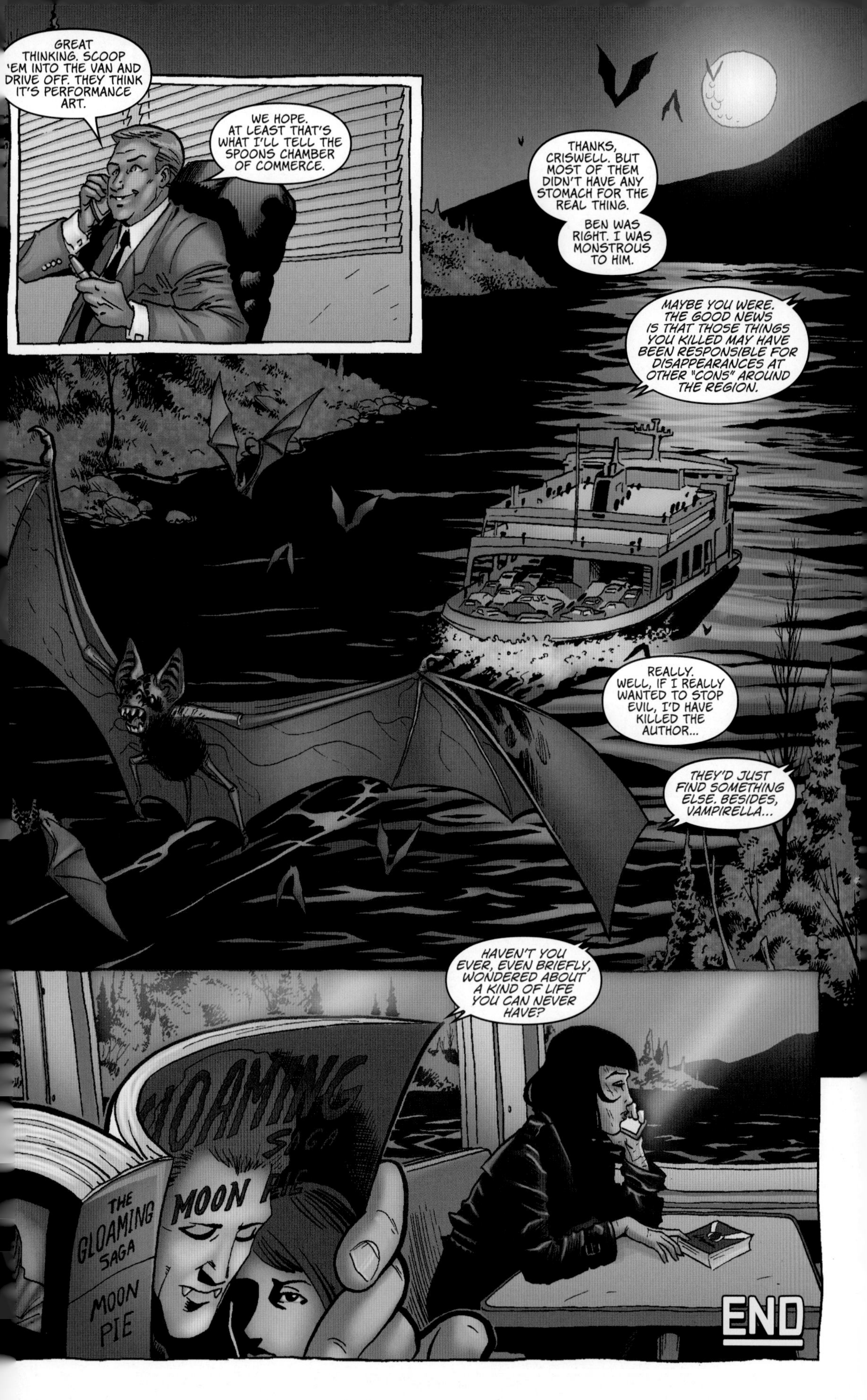
GREAT THINKING. SCOOP 'EM INTO THE VAN AND DRIVE OFF. THEY THINK IT'S PERFORMANCE ART.
WE HOPE. AT LEAST THAT'S WHAT I'LL TELL THE SPOONS CHAMBER OF COMMERCE.
THANKS, CRISWELL. BUT MOST OF THEM DIDN'T HAVE ANY STOMACH FOR THE REAL THING.
BEN WAS RIGHT. I WAS MONSTROUS TO HIM.
MAYBE YOU WERE. THE GOOD NEWS IS THAT THOSE THINGS YOU KILLED MAY HAVE BEEN RESPONSIBLE FOR DISAPPEARANCES AT OTHER "CONS" AROUND THE REGION.
REALLY. WELL, IF I REALLY WANTED TO STOP EVIL, I'D HAVE KILLED THE AUTHOR...
THEY'D JUST FIND SOMETHING ELSE. BESIDES, VAMPIRELLA...
HAVEN'T YOU EVER, EVEN BRIEFLY, WONDERED ABOUT A KIND OF LIFE YOU CAN NEVER HAVE?
THE GLOAMING SAGA
MOON PIE
END

VAMPIRELLA VS. FLUFFY THE VAMPIRE KILLER

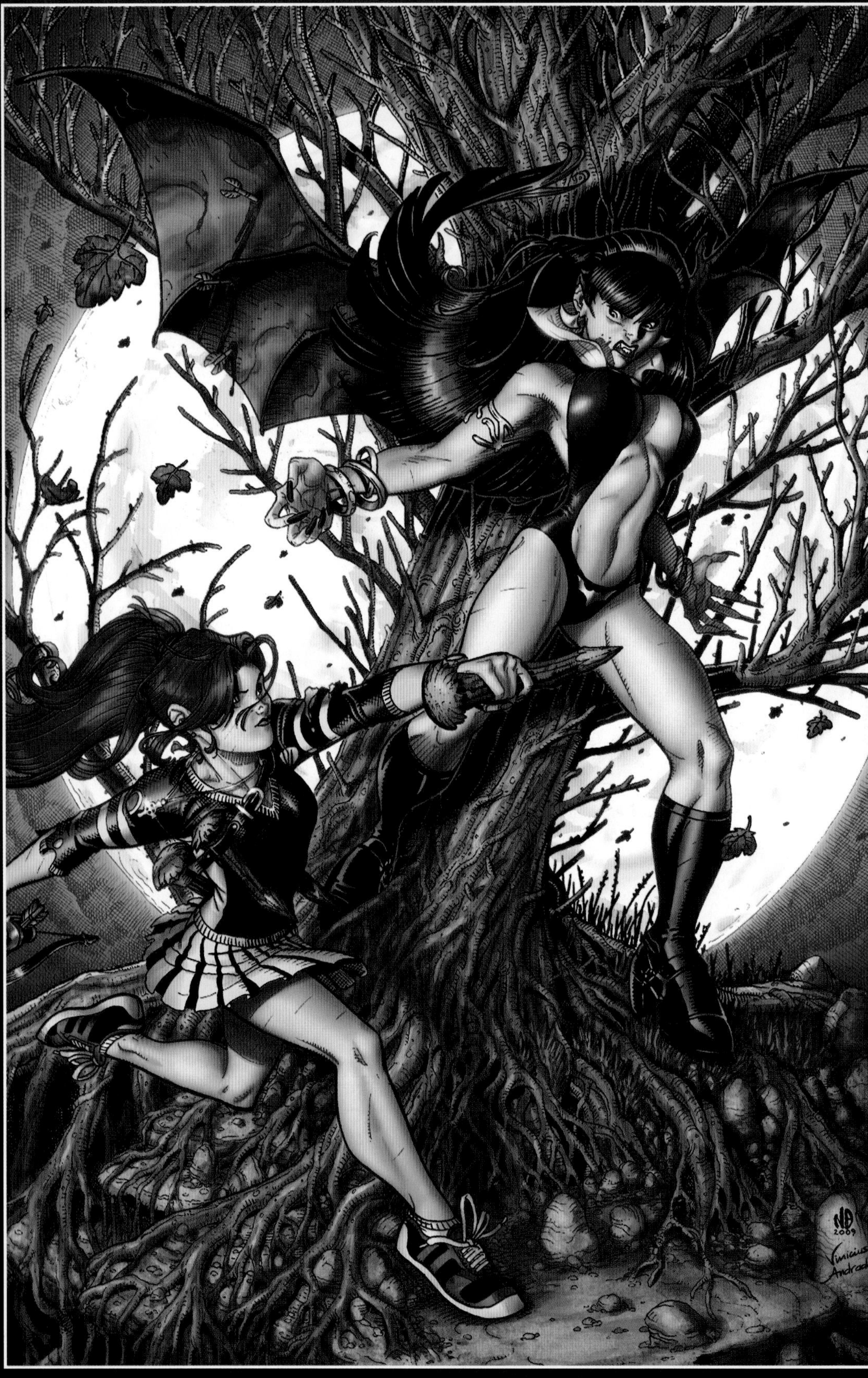

cover art by NICK BRADSHAW colors by VINICIUS ANDRADE

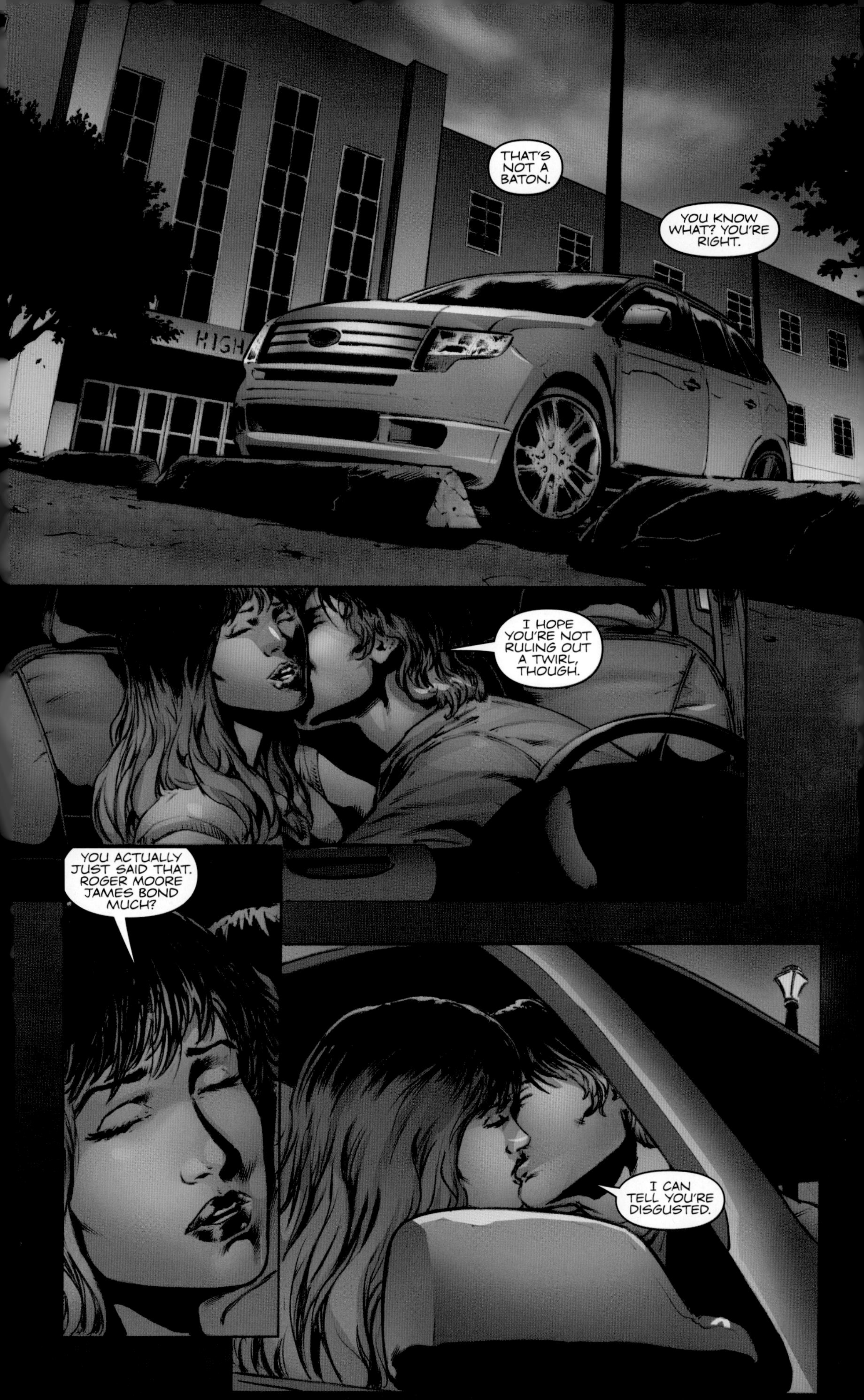
THAT'S NOT A BATON.
YOU KNOW WHAT? YOU'RE RIGHT.
HIGH
I HOPE YOU'RE NOT RULING OUT A TWIRL, THOUGH.
YOU ACTUALLY JUST SAID THAT. ROGER MOORE JAMES BOND MUCH?
I CAN TELL YOU'RE DISGUSTED.

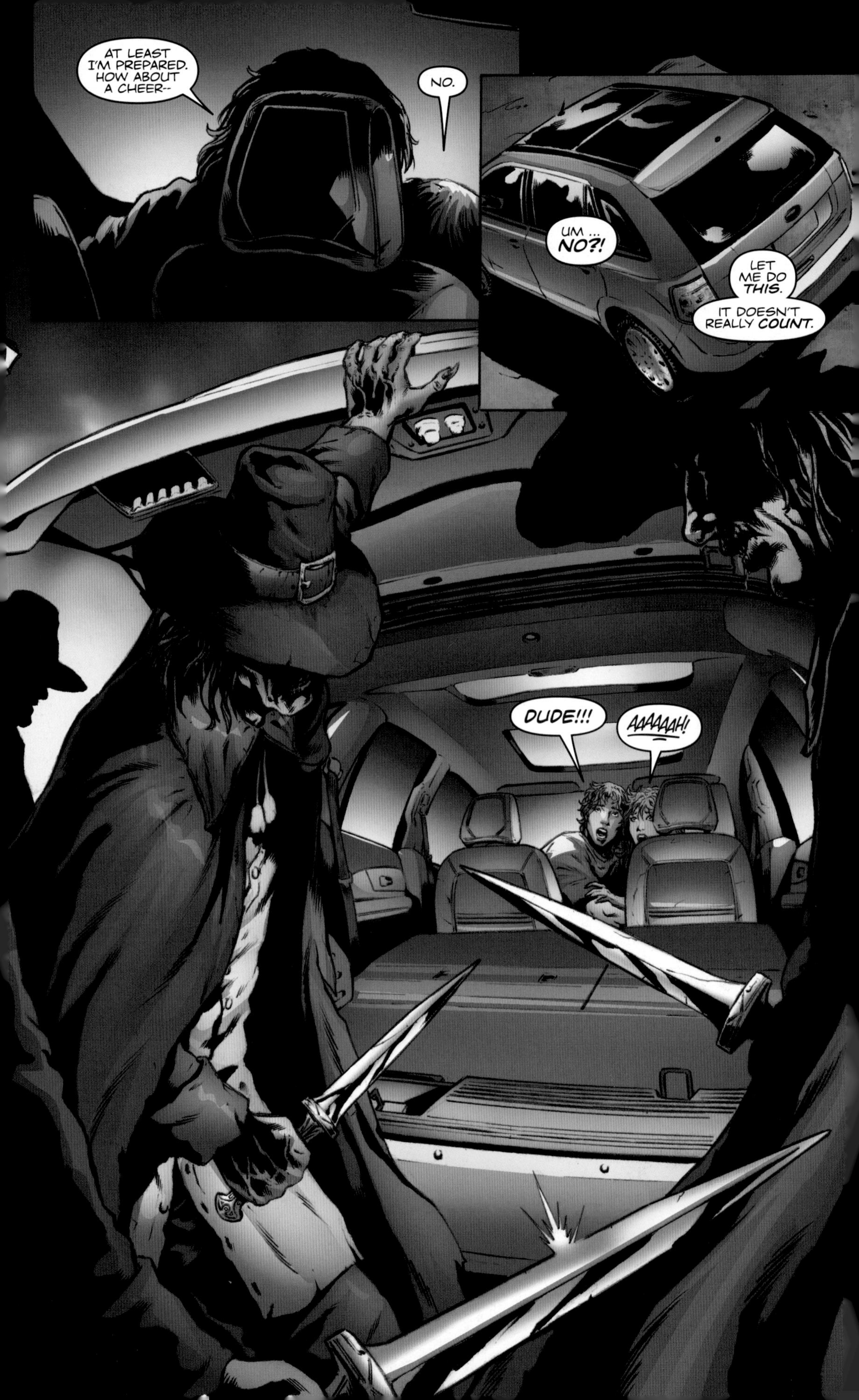
AT LEAST I'M PREPARED. HOW ABOUT A CHEER--
NO.
UM ... NO?!
LET ME DO THIS.
IT DOESN'T REALLY COUNT.
DUDE!!!
AAAAAAH!

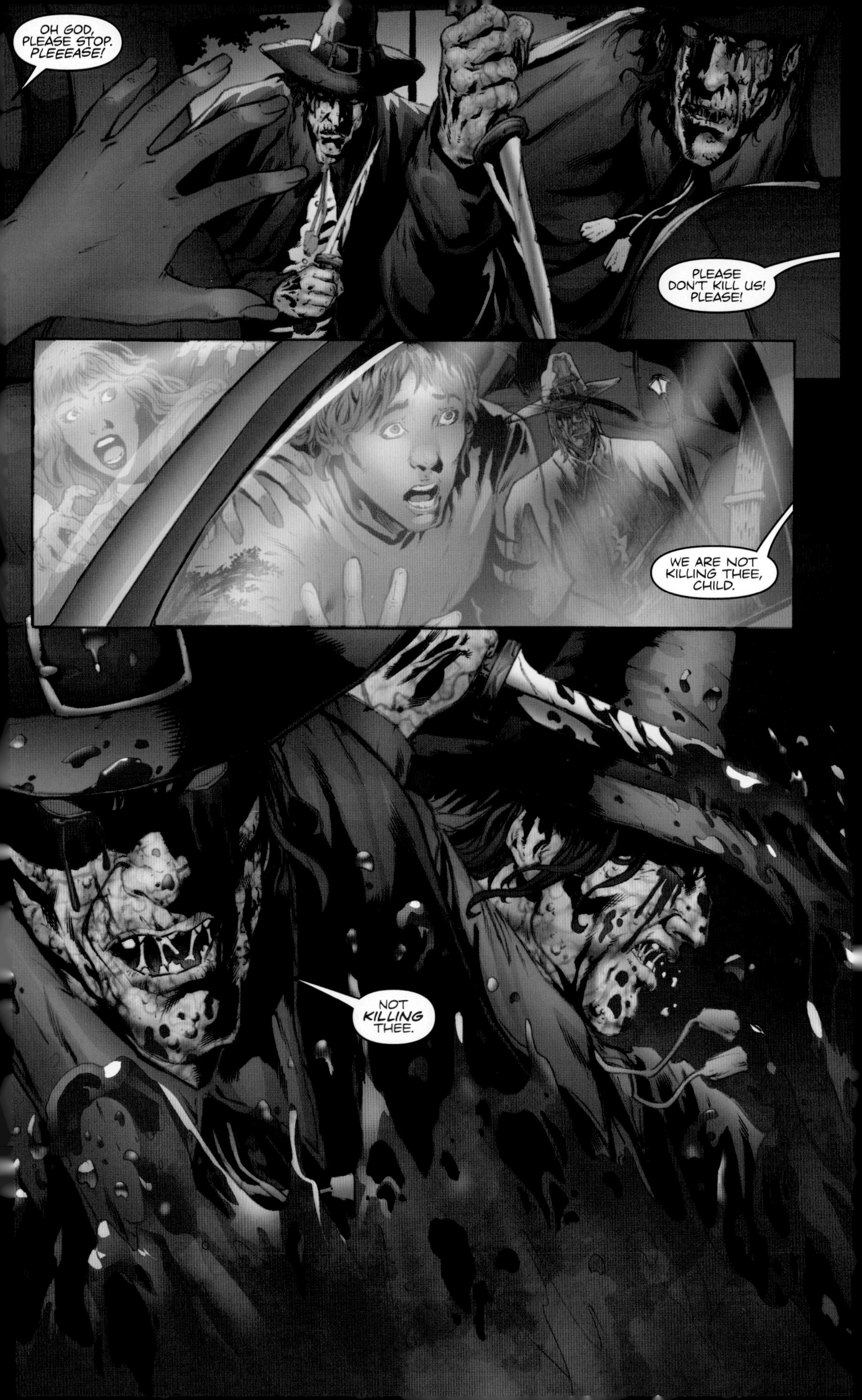
OH GOD, PLEASE STOP. PLEEEASE!
PLEASE DON'T KILL US! PLEASE!
WE ARE NOT KILLING THEE, CHILD.
NOT *KILLING* THEE.

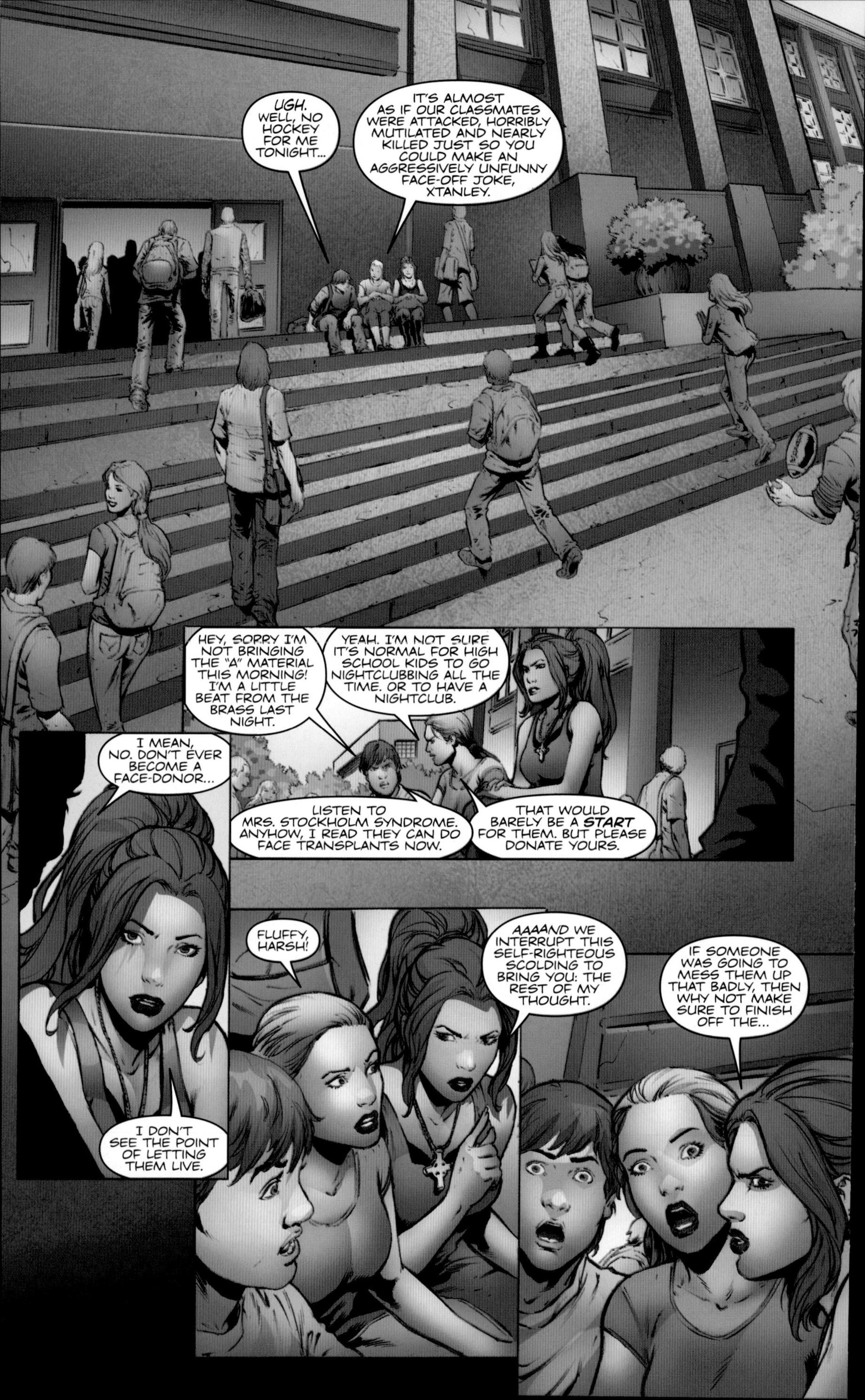
UGH. WELL, NO HOCKEY FOR ME TONIGHT...
IT'S ALMOST AS IF OUR CLASSMATES WERE ATTACKED, HORRIBLY MUTILATED AND NEARLY KILLED JUST SO YOU COULD MAKE AN AGGRESSIVELY UNFUNNY FACE-OFF JOKE, XTANLEY.
HEY, SORRY I'M NOT BRINGING THE "A" MATERIAL THIS MORNING! I'M A LITTLE BEAT FROM THE BRASS LAST NIGHT.
YEAH. I'M NOT SURE IT'S NORMAL FOR HIGH SCHOOL KIDS TO GO NIGHTCLUBBING ALL THE TIME. OR TO HAVE A NIGHTCLUB.
LISTEN TO MRS. STOCKHOLM SYNDROME. ANYHOW, I READ THEY CAN DO FACE TRANSPLANTS NOW.
THAT WOULD BARELY BE A START FOR THEM. BUT PLEASE DONATE YOURS.
I MEAN, NO. DON'T EVER BECOME A FACE-DONOR...
I DON'T SEE THE POINT OF LETTING THEM LIVE.
FLUFFY, HARSH!
AAAAND WE INTERRUPT THIS SELF-RIGHTEOUS SCOLDING TO BRING YOU: THE REST OF MY THOUGHT.
IF SOMEONE WAS GOING TO MESS THEM UP THAT BADLY, THEN WHY NOT MAKE SURE TO FINISH OFF THE...

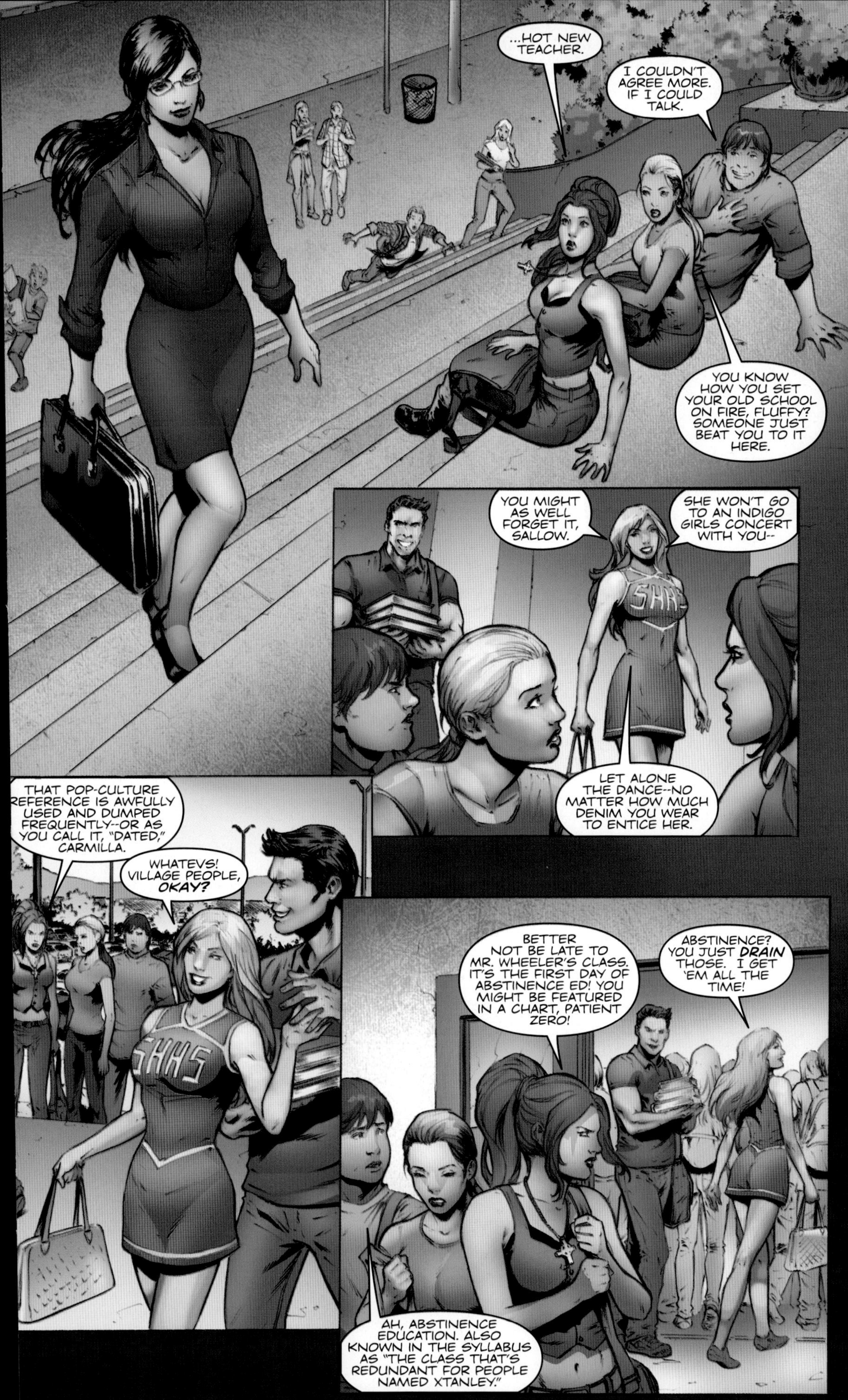
...HOT NEW TEACHER.
I COULDN'T AGREE MORE. IF I COULD TALK.
YOU KNOW HOW YOU SET YOUR OLD SCHOOL ON FIRE, FLUFFY? SOMEONE JUST BEAT YOU TO IT HERE.
YOU MIGHT AS WELL FORGET IT, SALLOW.
SHE WON'T GO TO AN INDIGO GIRLS CONCERT WITH YOU--
SHHS
LET ALONE THE DANCE--NO MATTER HOW MUCH DENIM YOU WEAR TO ENTICE HER.
THAT POP-CULTURE REFERENCE IS AWFULLY USED AND DUMPED FREQUENTLY--OR AS YOU CALL IT, "DATED," CARMILLA.
WHATEVS! VILLAGE PEOPLE, **OKAY?**
SHHS
BETTER NOT BE LATE TO MR. WHEELER'S CLASS. IT'S THE FIRST DAY OF ABSTINENCE ED! YOU MIGHT BE FEATURED IN A CHART, PATIENT ZERO!
ABSTINENCE? YOU JUST **DRAIN** THOSE. I GET 'EM ALL THE TIME!
AH, ABSTINENCE EDUCATION. ALSO KNOWN IN THE SYLLABUS AS "THE CLASS THAT'S REDUNDANT FOR PEOPLE NAMED XTANLEY."

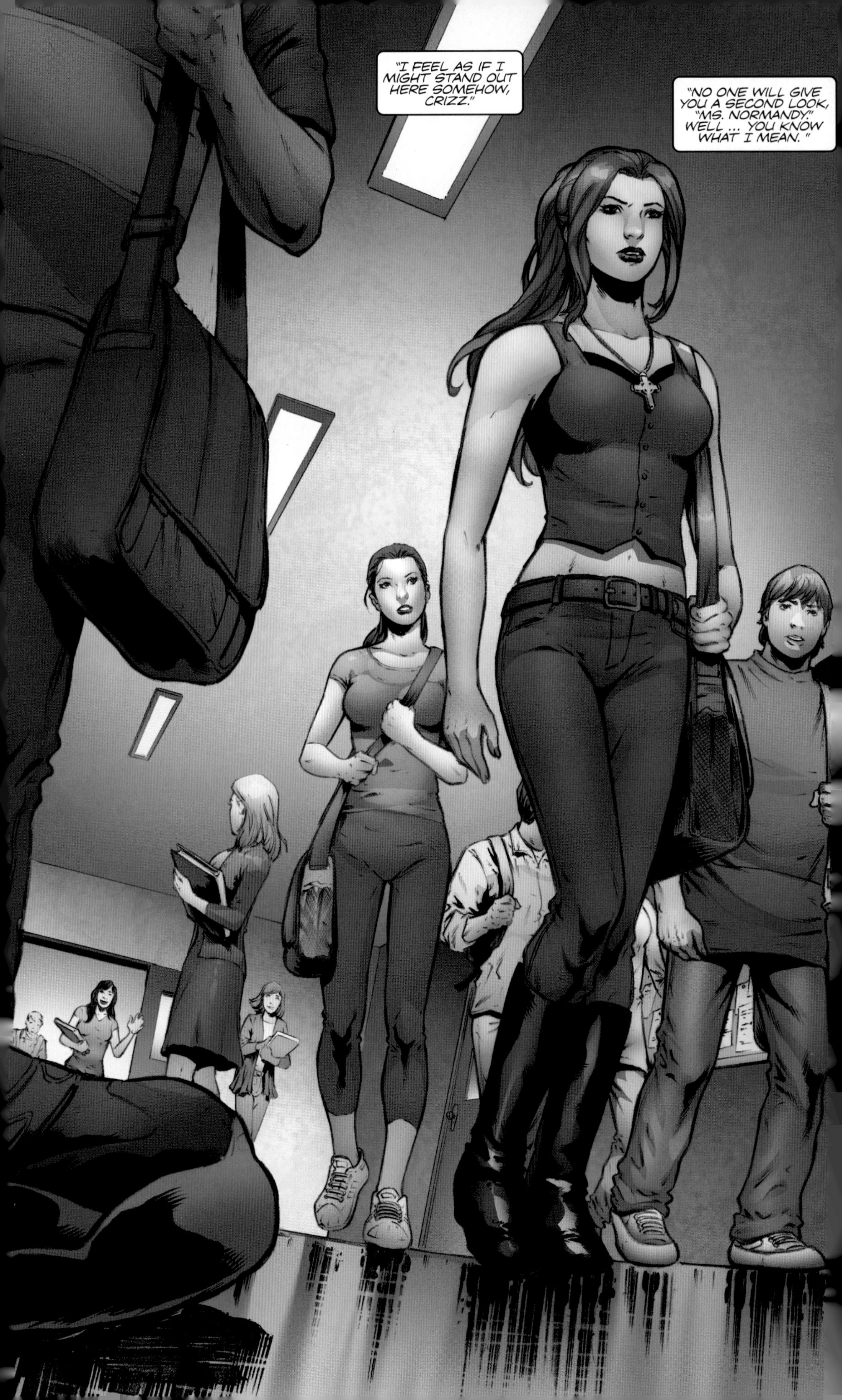
"I FEEL AS IF I MIGHT STAND OUT HERE SOMEHOW, CRIZZ."
"NO ONE WILL GIVE YOU A SECOND LOOK, "MS. NORMANDY." WELL ... YOU KNOW WHAT I MEAN."

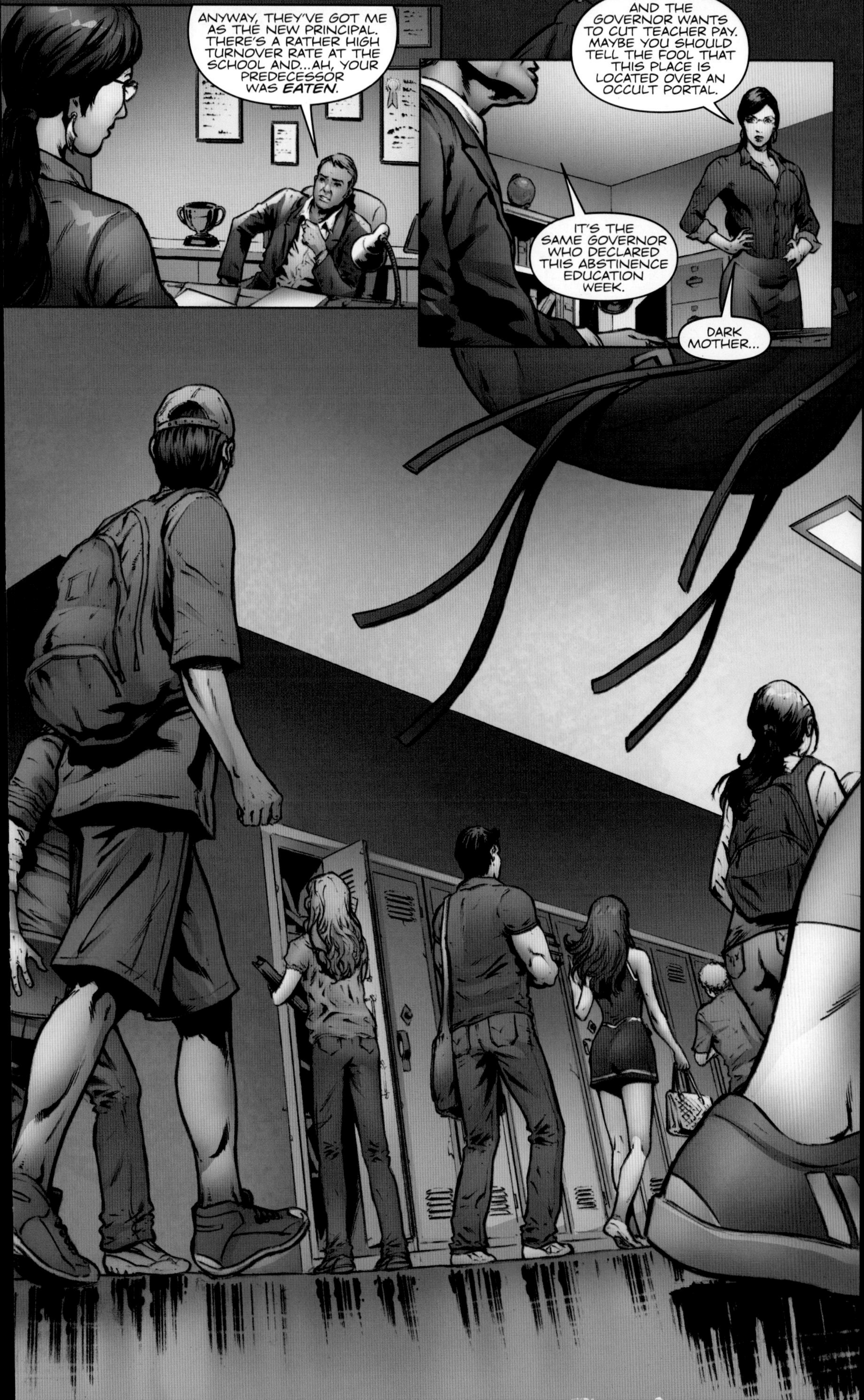
ANYWAY, THEY'VE GOT ME AS THE NEW PRINCIPAL. THERE'S A RATHER HIGH TURNOVER RATE AT THE SCHOOL AND...AH, YOUR PREDECESSOR WAS EATEN.
AND THE GOVERNOR WANTS TO CUT TEACHER PAY. MAYBE YOU SHOULD TELL THE FOOL THAT THIS PLACE IS LOCATED OVER AN OCCULT PORTAL.
IT'S THE SAME GOVERNOR WHO DECLARED THIS ABSTINENCE EDUCATION WEEK.
DARK MOTHER...

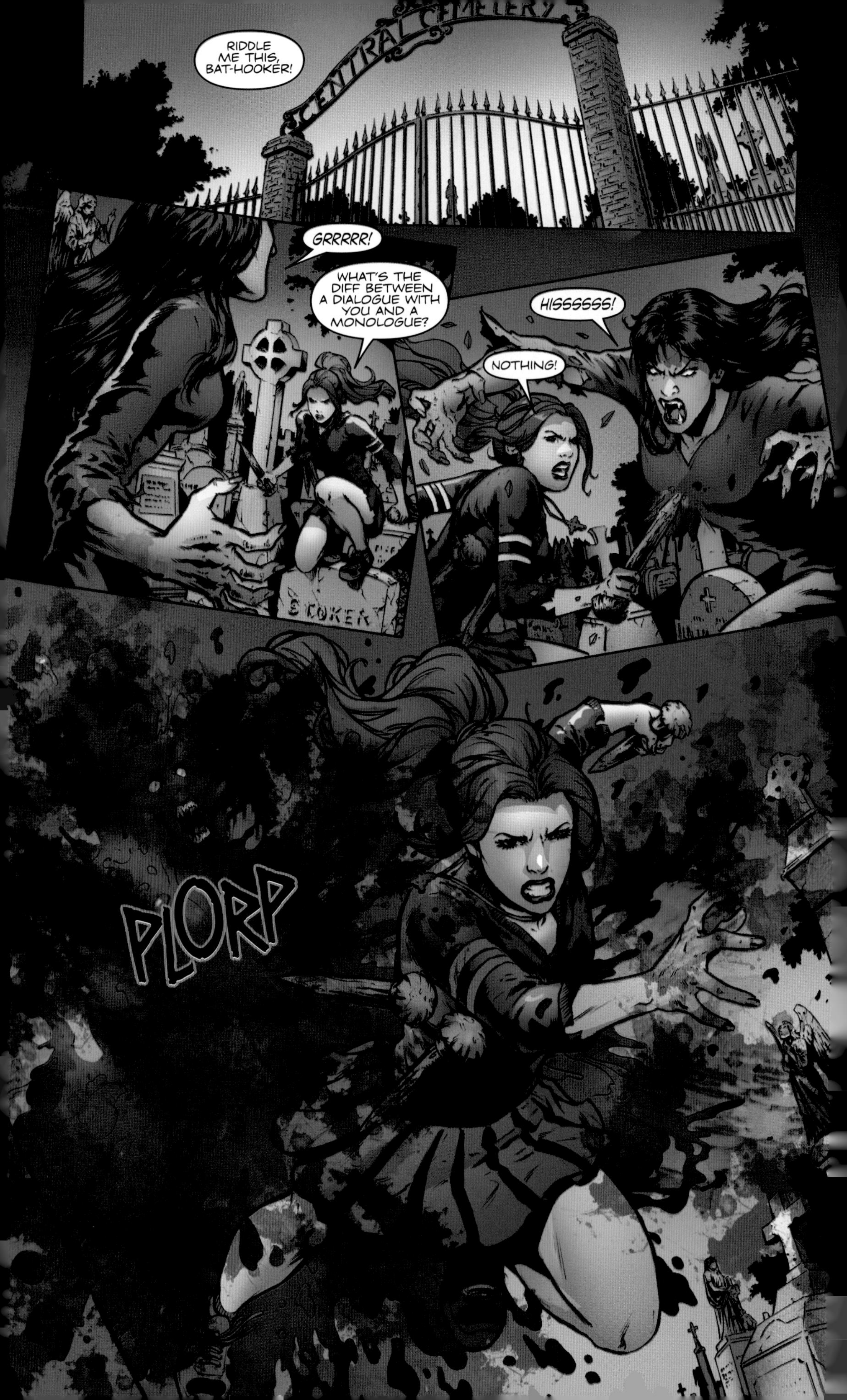
CENTRAL CEMETERY
RIDDLE ME THIS, BAT-HOOKER!
GRRRRR!
WHAT'S THE DIFF BETWEEN A DIALOGUE WITH YOU AND A MONOLOGUE?
HISSSSSS!
NOTHING!
PLORP

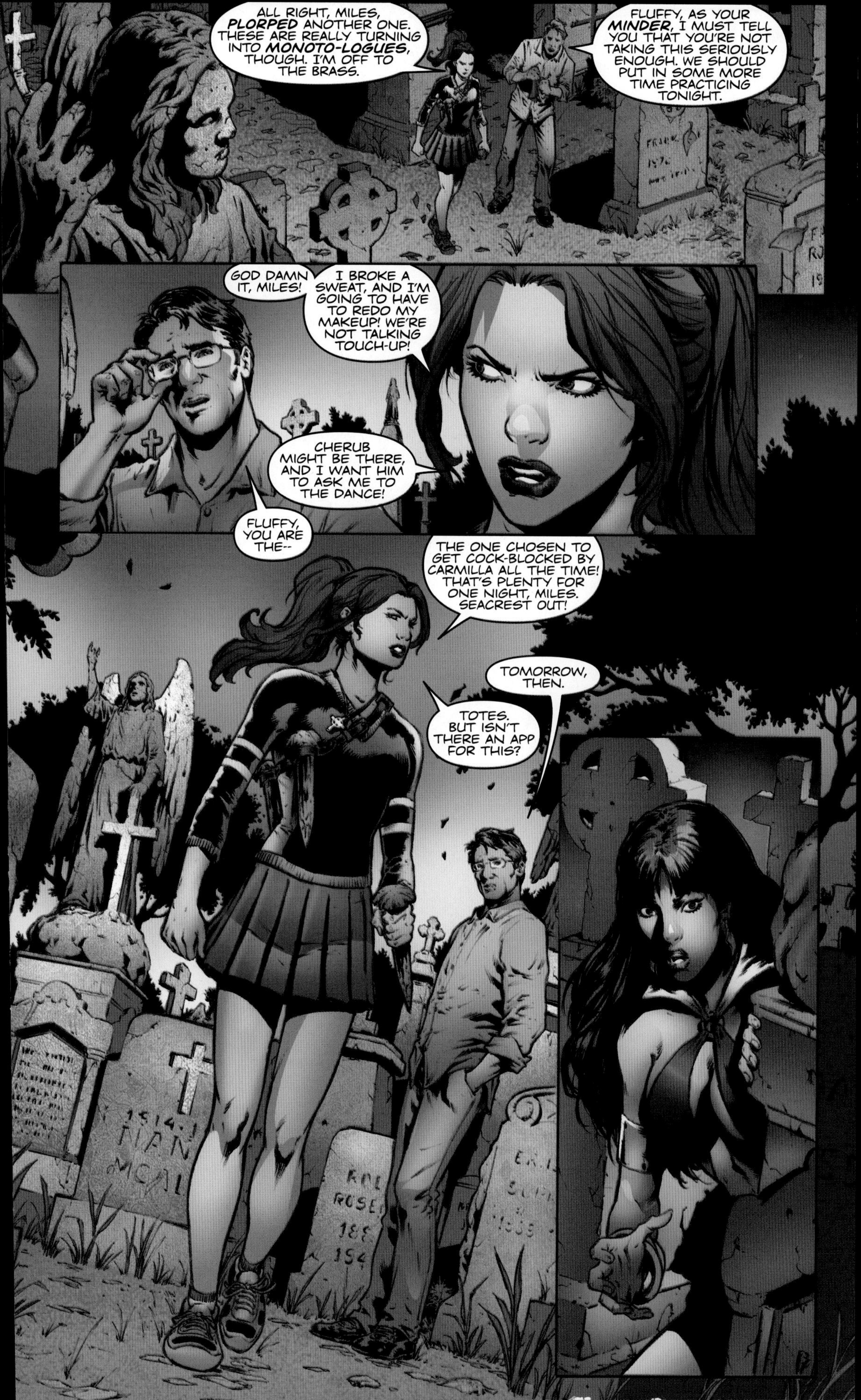
ALL RIGHT, MILES, PLORPED ANOTHER ONE. THESE ARE REALLY TURNING INTO MONOTO-LOGUES, THOUGH. I'M OFF TO THE BRASS.
FLUFFY, AS YOUR MINDER, I MUST TELL YOU THAT YOU'RE NOT TAKING THIS SERIOUSLY ENOUGH. WE SHOULD PUT IN SOME MORE TIME PRACTICING TONIGHT.
GOD DAMN IT, MILES!
I BROKE A SWEAT, AND I'M GOING TO HAVE TO REDO MY MAKEUP! WE'RE NOT TALKING TOUCH-UP!
CHERUB MIGHT BE THERE, AND I WANT HIM TO ASK ME TO THE DANCE!
FLUFFY, YOU ARE THE--
THE ONE CHOSEN TO GET COCK-BLOCKED BY CARMILLA ALL THE TIME! THAT'S PLENTY FOR ONE NIGHT, MILES. SEACREST OUT!
TOMORROW, THEN.
TOTES. BUT ISN'T THERE AN APP FOR THIS?

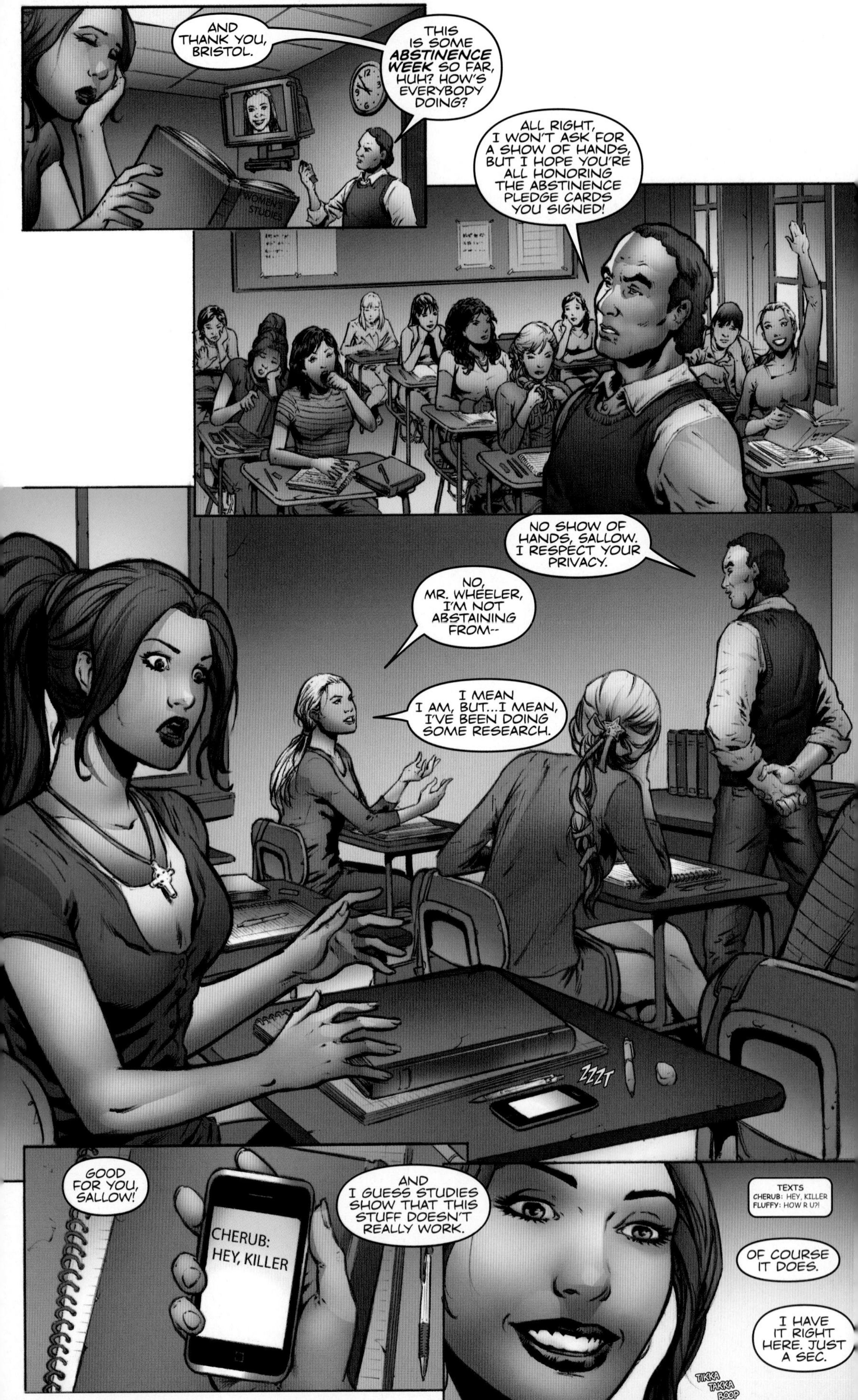
AND THANK YOU, BRISTOL.
THIS IS SOME ABSTINENCE WEEK SO FAR, HUH? HOW'S EVERYBODY DOING?
WOMEN'S STUDIES
ALL RIGHT, I WON'T ASK FOR A SHOW OF HANDS, BUT I HOPE YOU'RE ALL HONORING THE ABSTINENCE PLEDGE CARDS YOU SIGNED!
NO SHOW OF HANDS, SALLOW. I RESPECT YOUR PRIVACY.
NO, MR. WHEELER, I'M NOT ABSTAINING FROM--
I MEAN I AM, BUT...I MEAN, I'VE BEEN DOING SOME RESEARCH.
ZZZT
GOOD FOR YOU, SALLOW!
CHERUB: HEY, KILLER
AND I GUESS STUDIES SHOW THAT THIS STUFF DOESN'T REALLY WORK.
TEXTS
CHERUB: HEY, KILLER
FLUFFY: HOW R U?!
OF COURSE IT DOES.
I HAVE IT RIGHT HERE. JUST A SEC.
TIKKA TAKKA BOOP

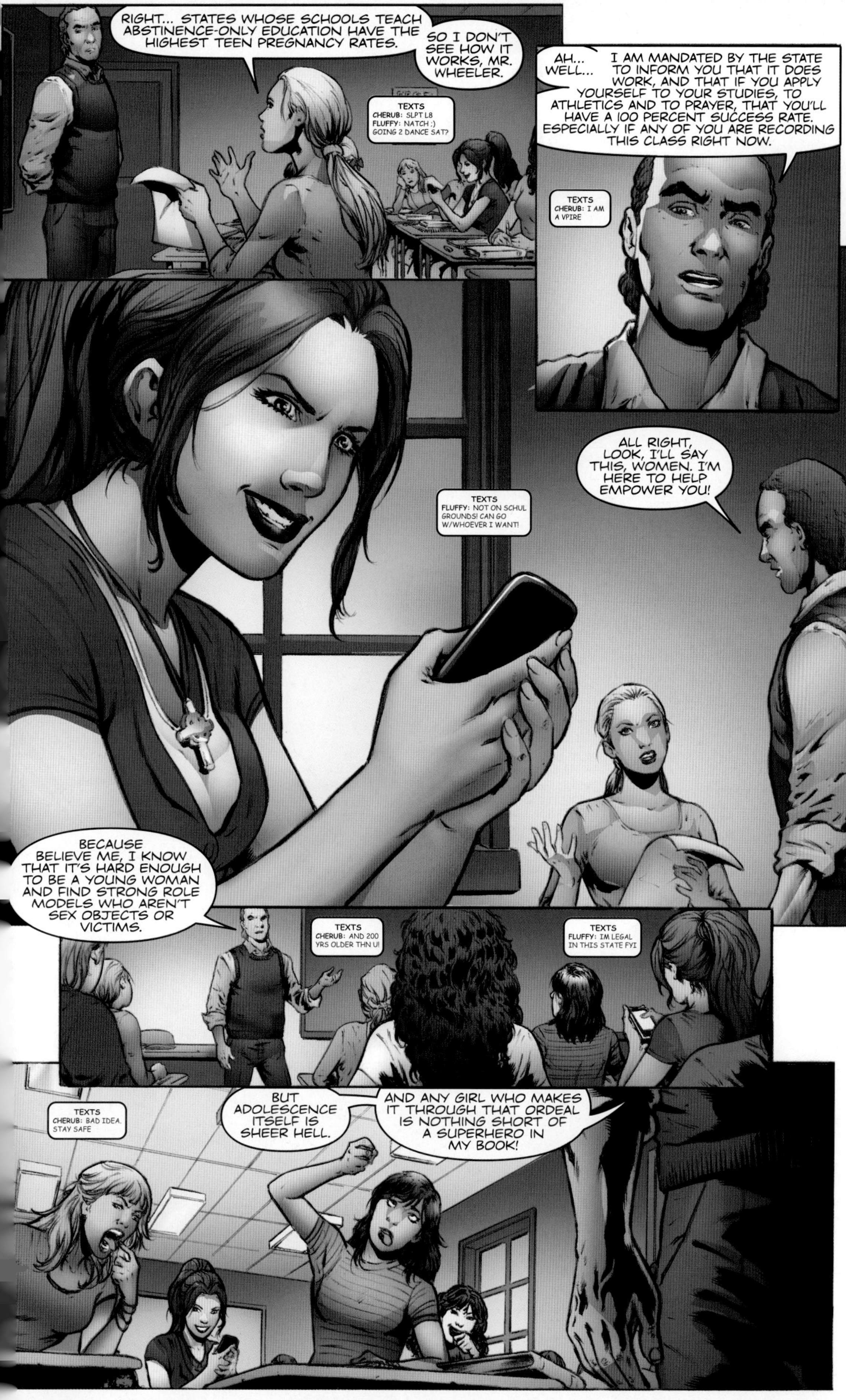
RIGHT... STATES WHOSE SCHOOLS TEACH ABSTINENCE-ONLY EDUCATION HAVE THE HIGHEST TEEN PREGNANCY RATES.
SO I DON'T SEE HOW IT WORKS, MR. WHEELER.
TEXTS
CHERUB: SLPT L8
FLUFFY: NATCH ;)
GOING 2 DANCE SAT?
AH... WELL...
I AM MANDATED BY THE STATE TO INFORM YOU THAT IT DOES WORK, AND THAT IF YOU APPLY YOURSELF TO YOUR STUDIES, TO ATHLETICS AND TO PRAYER, THAT YOU'LL HAVE A 100 PERCENT SUCCESS RATE. ESPECIALLY IF ANY OF YOU ARE RECORDING THIS CLASS RIGHT NOW.
TEXTS
CHERUB: I AM A VPIRE
TEXTS
FLUFFY: NOT ON SCHUL GROUNDS! CAN GO W/WHOEVER I WANT!
ALL RIGHT, LOOK, I'LL SAY THIS, WOMEN. I'M HERE TO HELP EMPOWER YOU!
BECAUSE BELIEVE ME, I KNOW THAT IT'S HARD ENOUGH TO BE A YOUNG WOMAN AND FIND STRONG ROLE MODELS WHO AREN'T SEX OBJECTS OR VICTIMS.
TEXTS
CHERUB: AND 200 YRS OLDER THN U!
TEXTS
FLUFFY: IM LEGAL IN THIS STATE FYI
TEXTS
CHERUB: BAD IDEA. STAY SAFE
BUT ADOLESCENCE ITSELF IS SHEER HELL.
AND ANY GIRL WHO MAKES IT THROUGH THAT ORDEAL IS NOTHING SHORT OF A SUPERHERO IN MY BOOK!

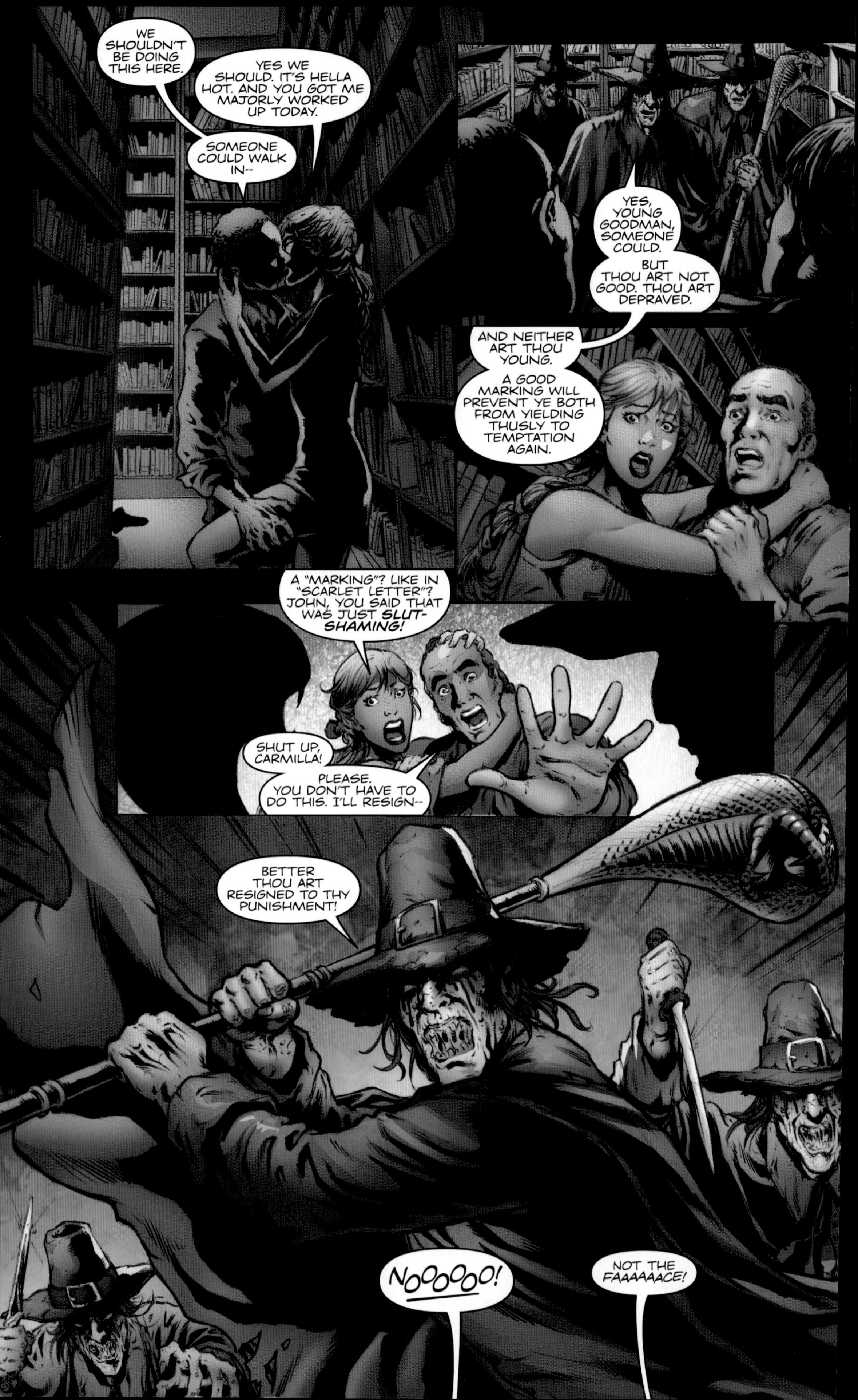
WE SHOULDN'T BE DOING THIS HERE.
YES WE SHOULD. IT'S HELLA HOT. AND YOU GOT ME MAJORLY WORKED UP TODAY.
SOMEONE COULD WALK IN--
YES, YOUNG GOODMAN, SOMEONE COULD.
BUT THOU ART NOT GOOD. THOU ART DEPRAVED.
AND NEITHER ART THOU YOUNG.
A GOOD MARKING WILL PREVENT YE BOTH FROM YIELDING THUSLY TO TEMPTATION AGAIN.
A "MARKING"? LIKE IN "SCARLET LETTER"? JOHN, YOU SAID THAT WAS JUST SLUT-SHAMING!
SHUT UP, CARMILLA!
PLEASE. YOU DON'T HAVE TO DO THIS. I'LL RESIGN--
BETTER THOU ART RESIGNED TO THY PUNISHMENT!
NOOOOOO!
NOT THE FAAAAAACE!

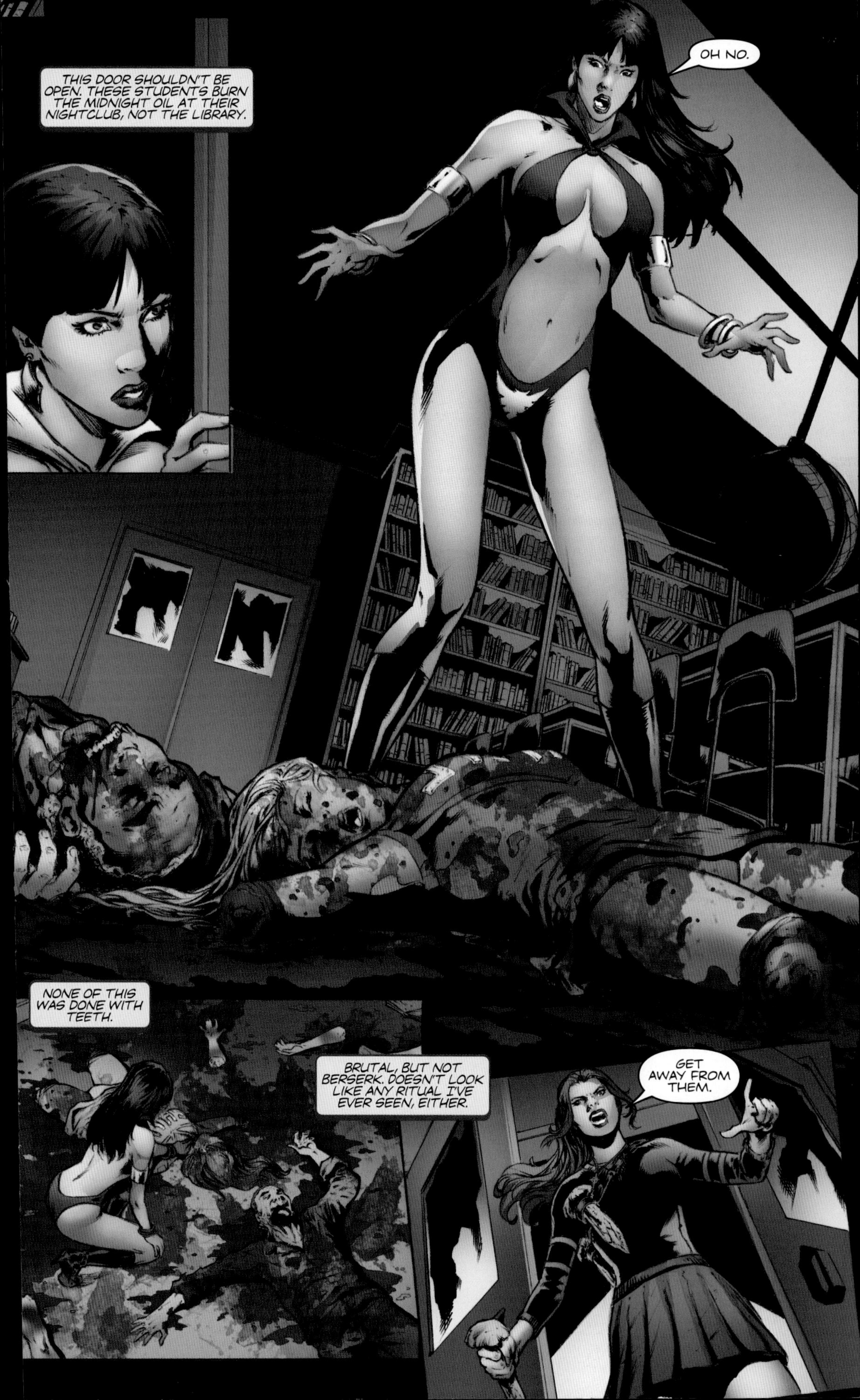
THIS DOOR SHOULDN'T BE OPEN. THESE STUDENTS BURN THE MIDNIGHT OIL AT THEIR NIGHTCLUB, NOT THE LIBRARY.
OH NO.
NONE OF THIS WAS DONE WITH TEETH.
BRUTAL, BUT NOT BERSERK. DOESN'T LOOK LIKE ANY RITUAL I'VE EVER SEEN, EITHER.
GET AWAY FROM THEM.

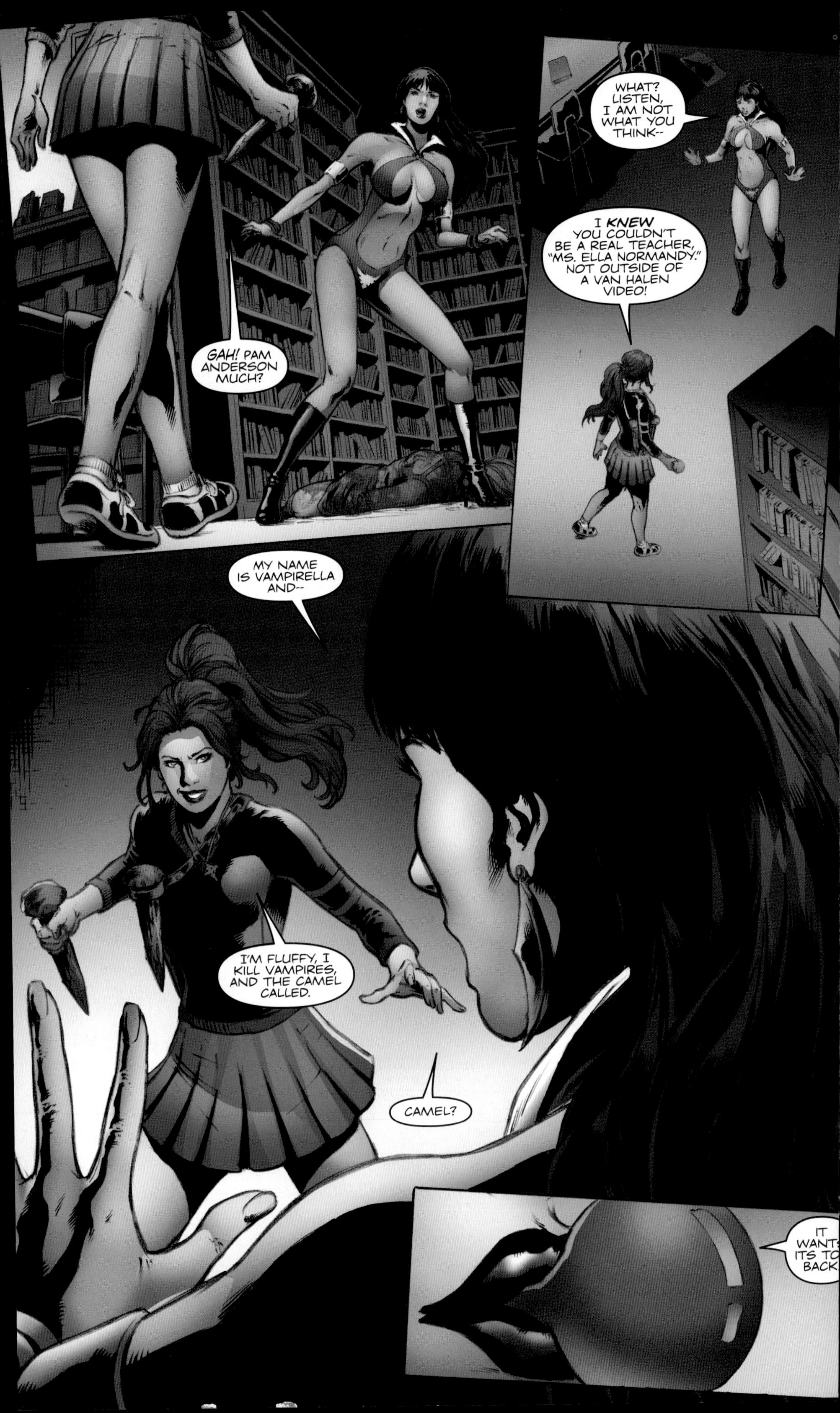
GAH! PAM ANDERSON MUCH?
WHAT? LISTEN, I AM NOT WHAT YOU THINK--
I KNEW YOU COULDN'T BE A REAL TEACHER, "MS. ELLA NORMANDY." NOT OUTSIDE OF A VAN HALEN VIDEO!
MY NAME IS VAMPIRELLA AND--
I'M FLUFFY, I KILL VAMPIRES, AND THE CAMEL CALLED.
CAMEL?
IT WANT ITS TO BACK

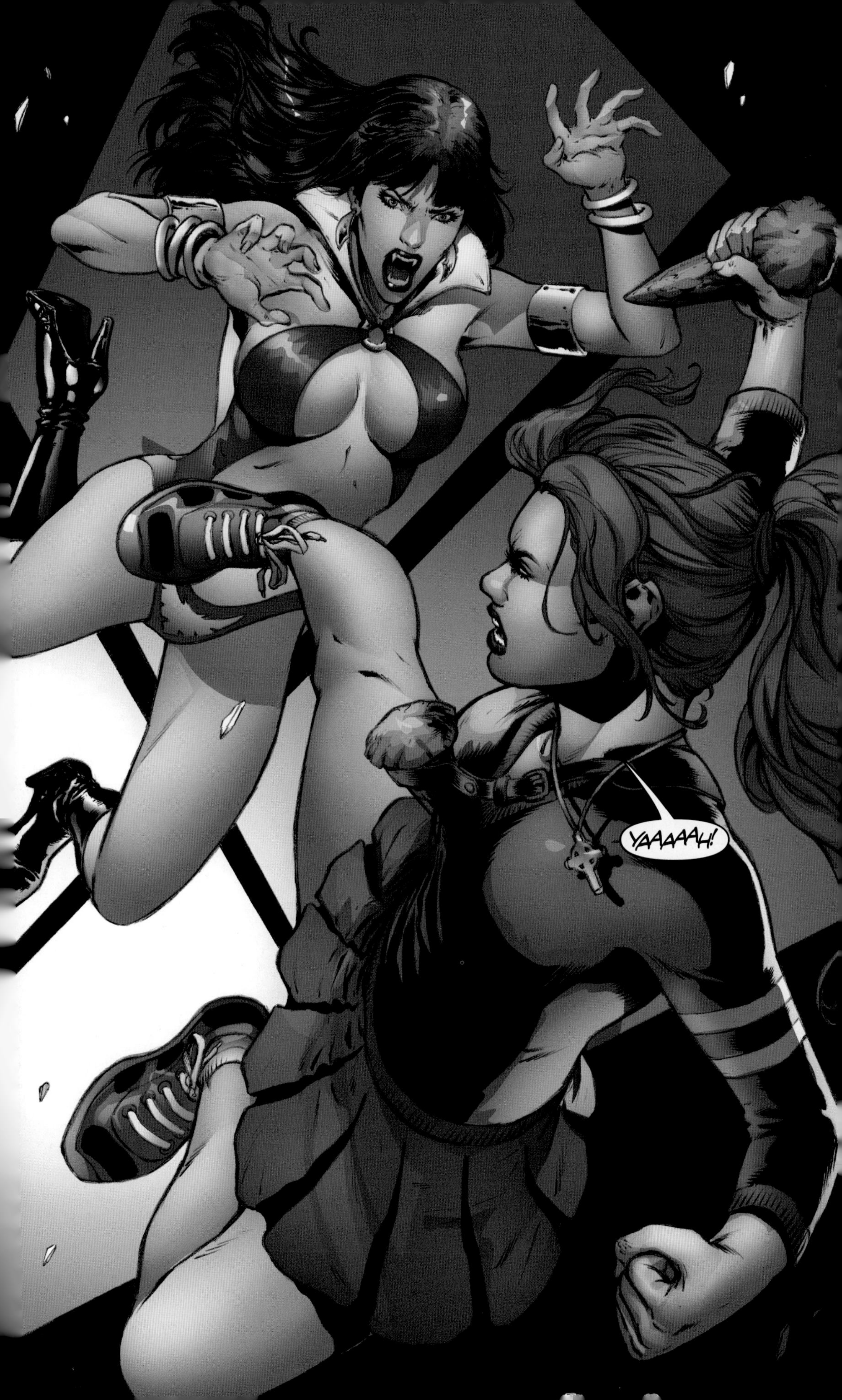
YAAAAAH!

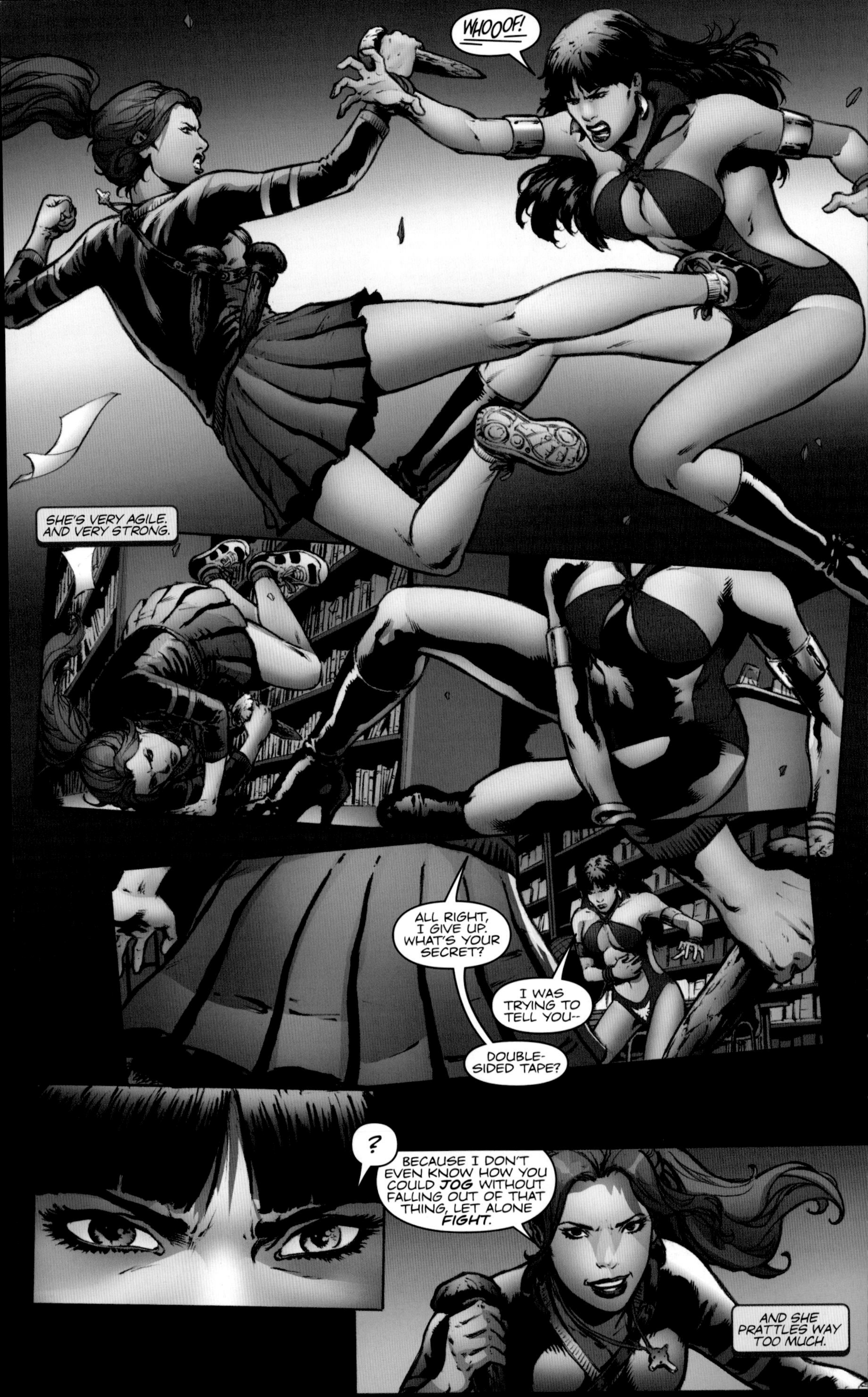
WHOOOF!
SHE'S VERY AGILE. AND VERY STRONG.
ALL RIGHT, I GIVE UP. WHAT'S YOUR SECRET?
I WAS TRYING TO TELL YOU--
DOUBLE-SIDED TAPE?
?
BECAUSE I DON'T EVEN KNOW HOW YOU COULD JOG WITHOUT FALLING OUT OF THAT THING, LET ALONE FIGHT.
AND SHE PRATTLES WAY TOO MUCH.

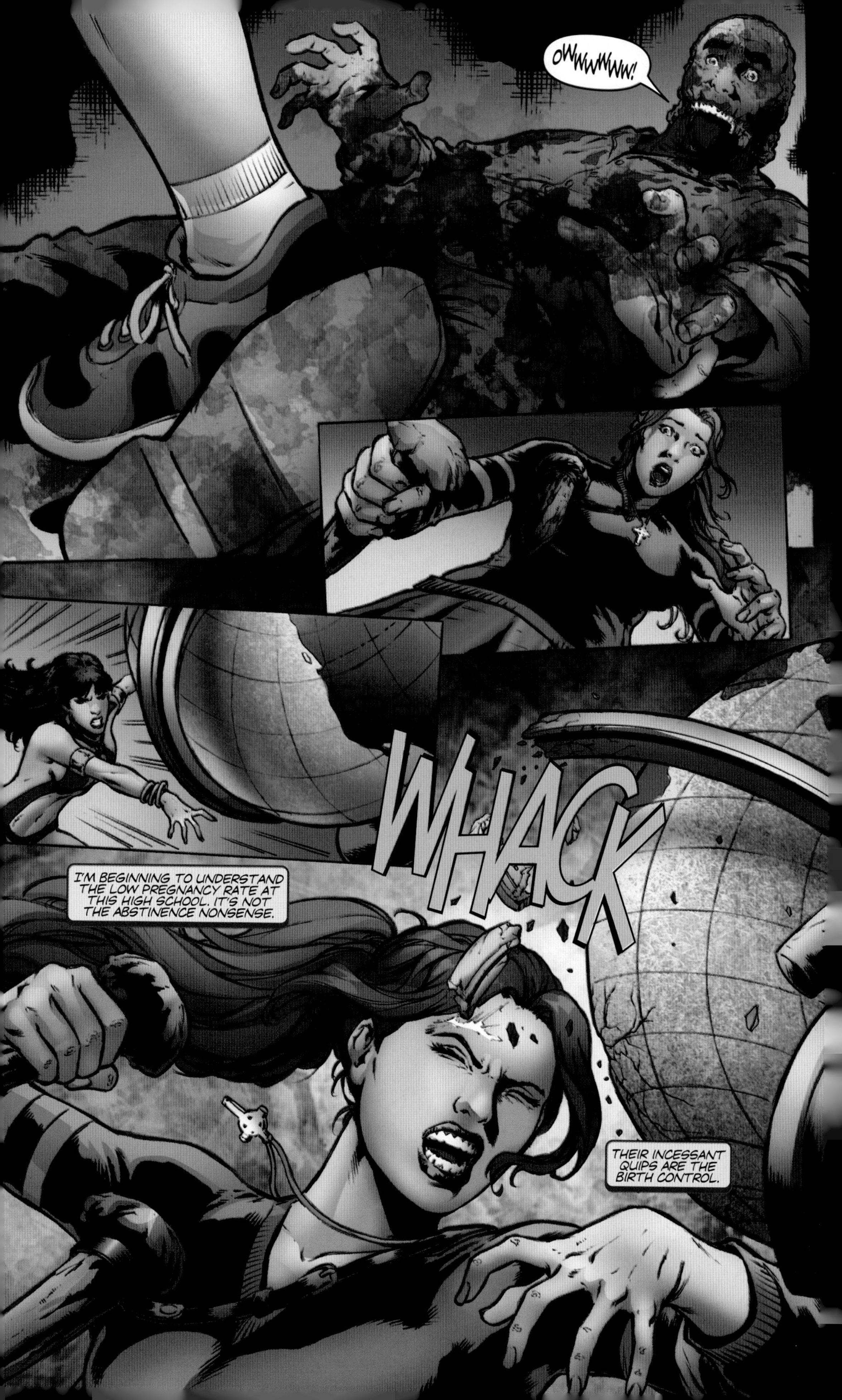
OWWWWWW!
WHACK
I'M BEGINNING TO UNDERSTAND THE LOW PREGNANCY RATE AT THIS HIGH SCHOOL. IT'S NOT THE ABSTINENCE NONSENSE.
THEIR INCESSANT QUIPS ARE THE BIRTH CONTROL.

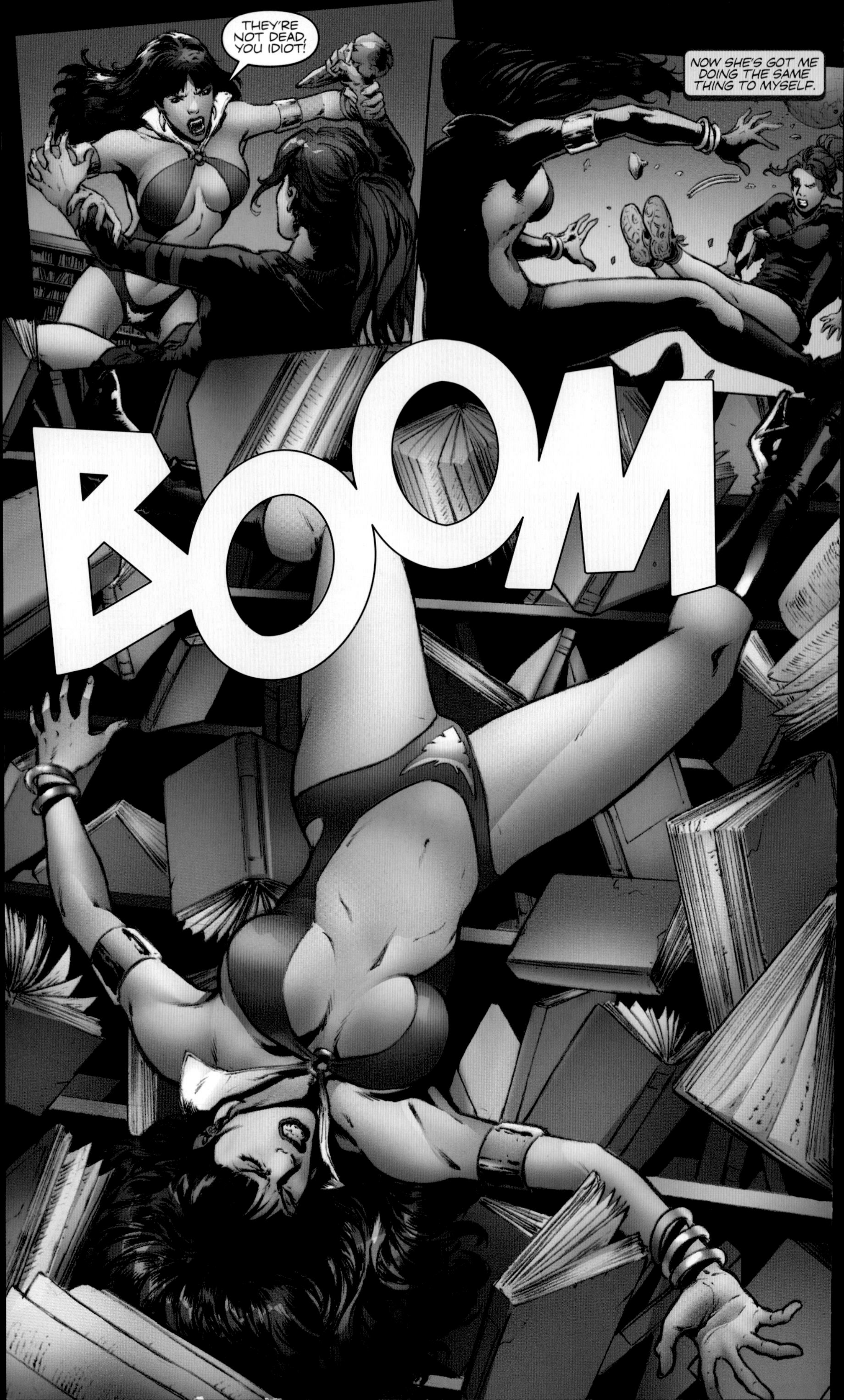
THEY'RE NOT DEAD, YOU IDIOT!
NOW SHE'S GOT ME DOING THE SAME THING TO MYSELF.
BOOM

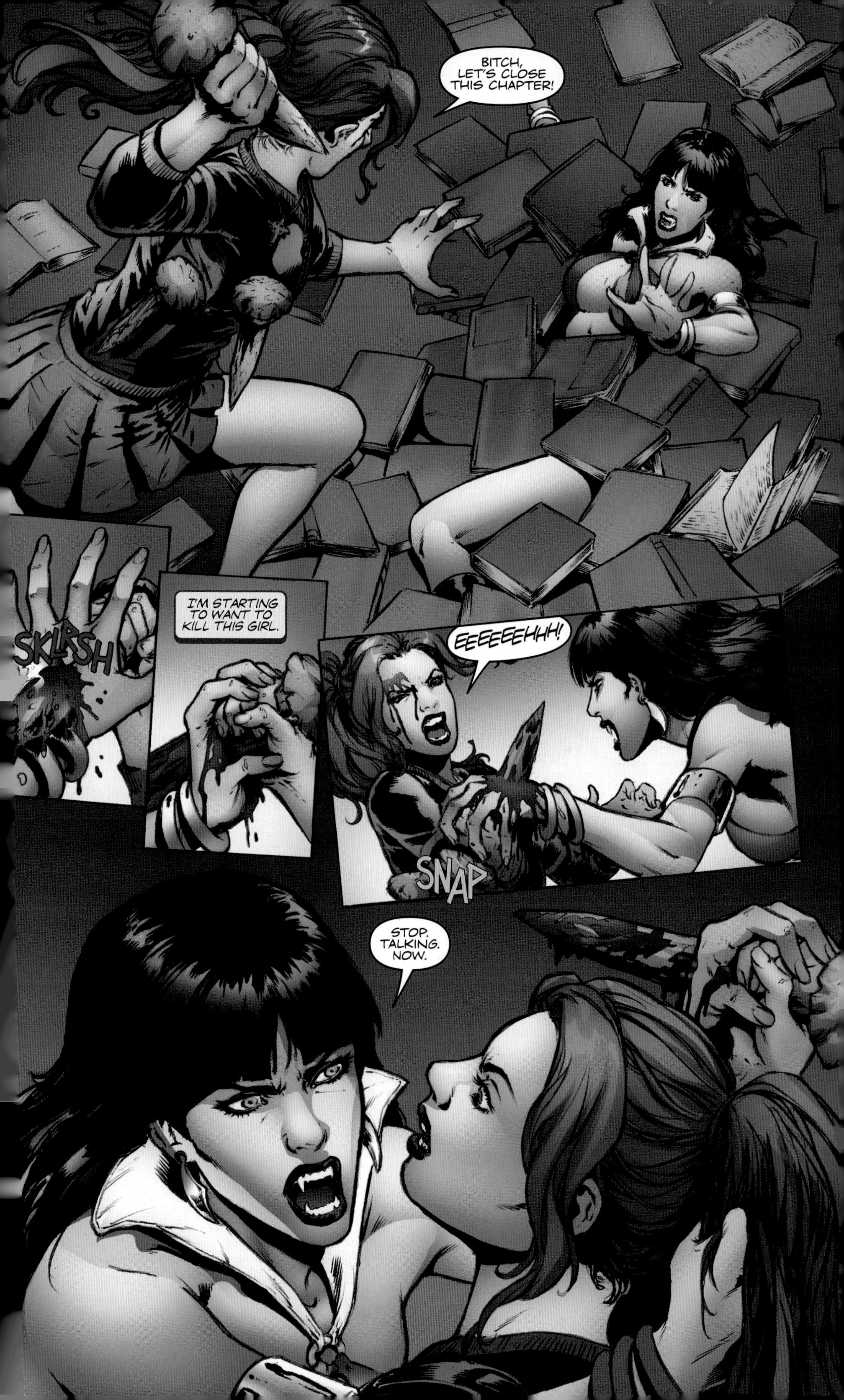
BITCH, LET'S CLOSE THIS CHAPTER!
SKLRSH
I'M STARTING TO WANT TO KILL THIS GIRL.
EEEEEEEHHH!
SNAP
STOP. TALKING. NOW.

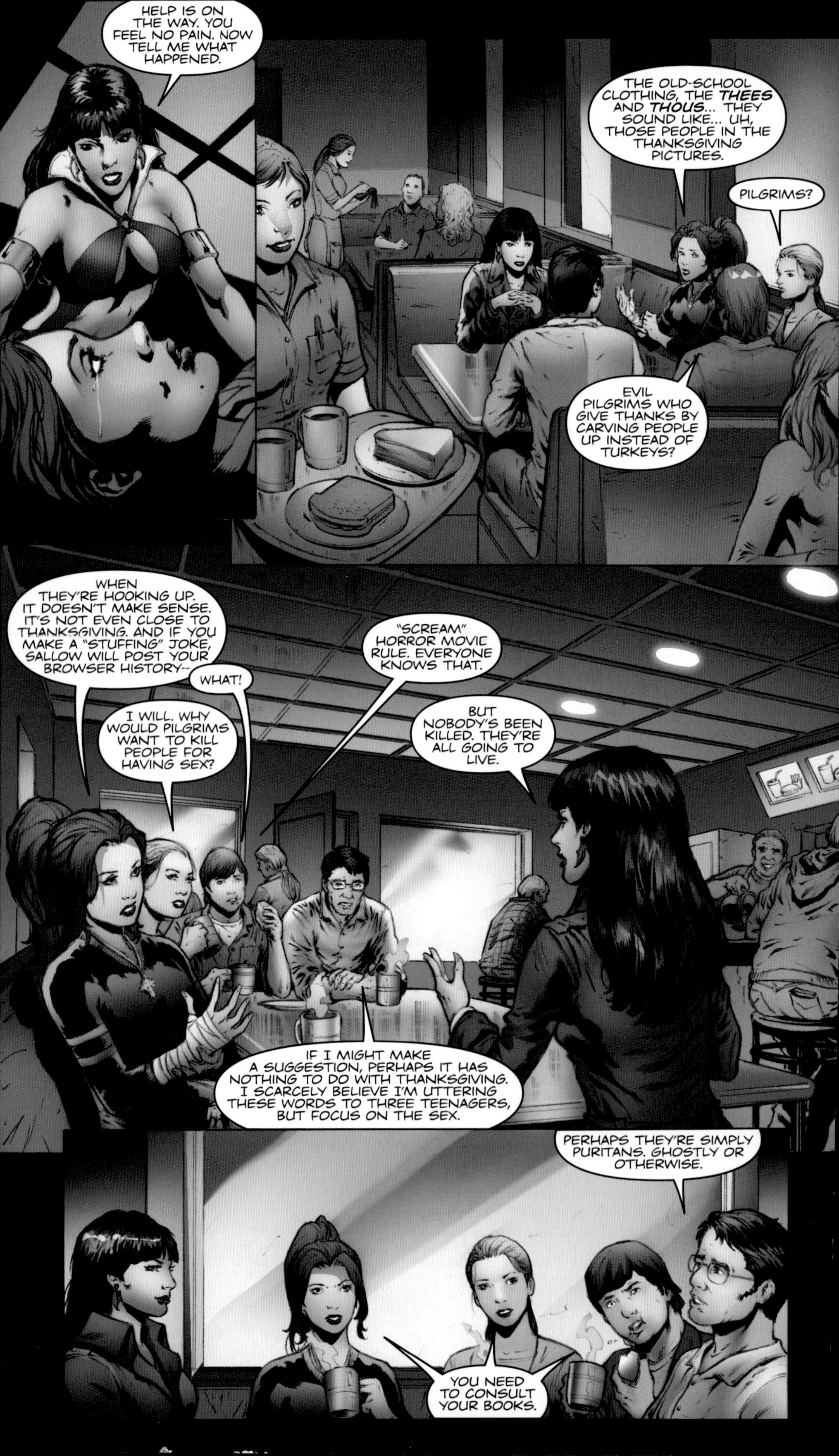
HELP IS ON THE WAY. YOU FEEL NO PAIN. NOW TELL ME WHAT HAPPENED.
THE OLD-SCHOOL CLOTHING, THE **THEES** AND **THOUS**... THEY SOUND LIKE... UH, THOSE PEOPLE IN THE THANKSGIVING PICTURES.
PILGRIMS?
EVIL PILGRIMS WHO GIVE THANKS BY CARVING PEOPLE UP INSTEAD OF TURKEYS?
WHEN THEY'RE HOOKING UP. IT DOESN'T MAKE SENSE. IT'S NOT EVEN CLOSE TO THANKSGIVING. AND IF YOU MAKE A "STUFFING" JOKE, SALLOW WILL POST YOUR BROWSER HISTORY--
WHAT!
I WILL. WHY WOULD PILGRIMS WANT TO KILL PEOPLE FOR HAVING SEX?
"SCREAM" HORROR MOVIE RULE. EVERYONE KNOWS THAT.
BUT NOBODY'S BEEN KILLED. THEY'RE ALL GOING TO LIVE.
IF I MIGHT MAKE A SUGGESTION, PERHAPS IT HAS NOTHING TO DO WITH THANKSGIVING. I SCARCELY BELIEVE I'M UTTERING THESE WORDS TO THREE TEENAGERS, BUT FOCUS ON THE SEX.
PERHAPS THEY'RE SIMPLY PURITANS. GHOSTLY OR OTHERWISE.
YOU NEED TO CONSULT YOUR BOOKS.

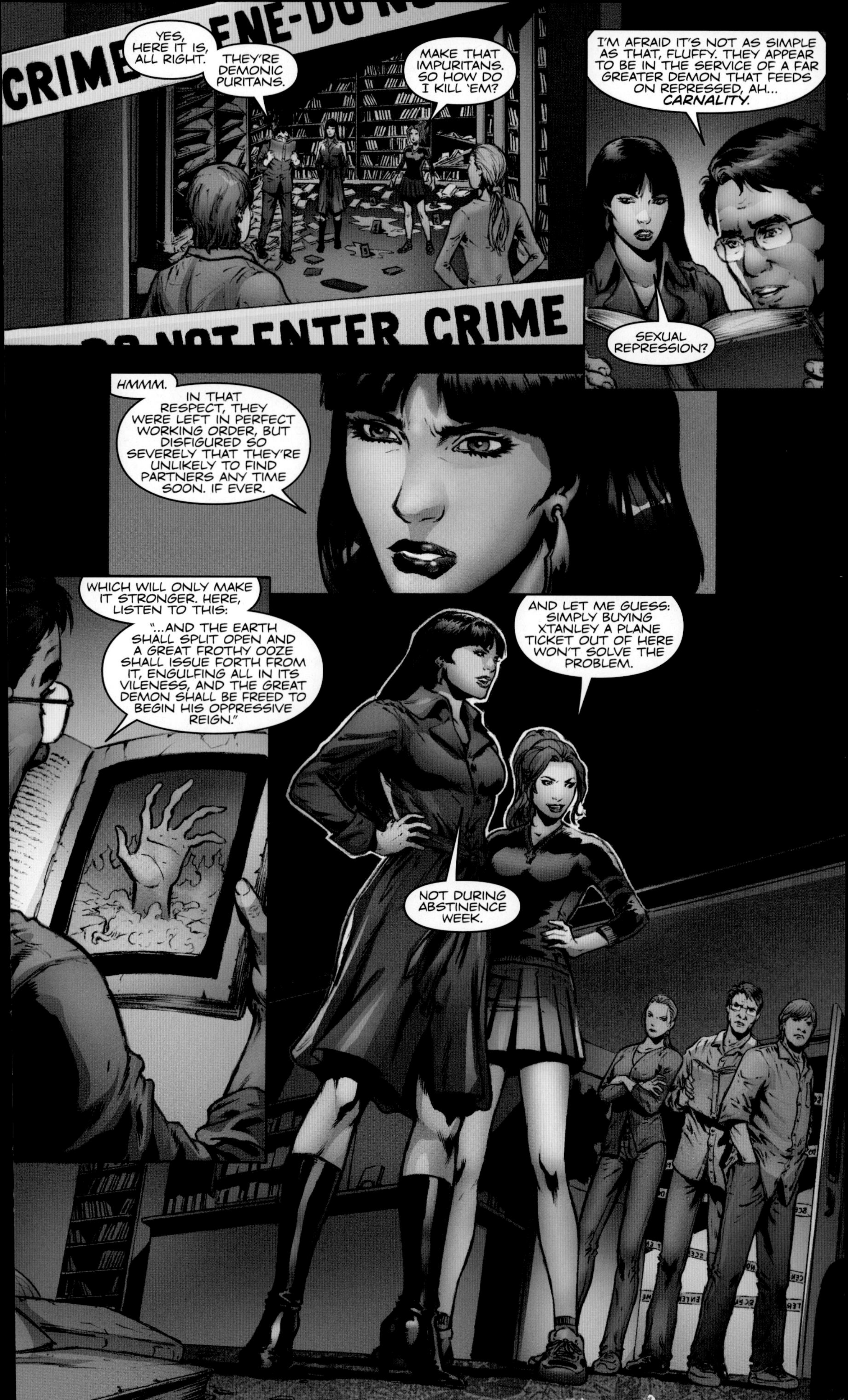
CRIME SCENE-DO NO
YES, HERE IT IS, ALL RIGHT.
THEY'RE DEMONIC PURITANS.
MAKE THAT IMPURITANS. SO HOW DO I KILL 'EM?
DO NOT ENTER CRIME
I'M AFRAID IT'S NOT AS SIMPLE AS THAT, FLUFFY. THEY APPEAR TO BE IN THE SERVICE OF A FAR GREATER DEMON THAT FEEDS ON REPRESSED, AH... CARNALITY.
SEXUAL REPRESSION?
HMMM.
IN THAT RESPECT, THEY WERE LEFT IN PERFECT WORKING ORDER, BUT DISFIGURED SO SEVERELY THAT THEY'RE UNLIKELY TO FIND PARTNERS ANY TIME SOON. IF EVER.
WHICH WILL ONLY MAKE IT STRONGER. HERE, LISTEN TO THIS:
"...AND THE EARTH SHALL SPLIT OPEN AND A GREAT FROTHY OOZE SHALL ISSUE FORTH FROM IT, ENGULFING ALL IN ITS VILENESS, AND THE GREAT DEMON SHALL BE FREED TO BEGIN HIS OPPRESSIVE REIGN."
AND LET ME GUESS: SIMPLY BUYING XTANLEY A PLANE TICKET OUT OF HERE WON'T SOLVE THE PROBLEM.
NOT DURING ABSTINENCE WEEK.

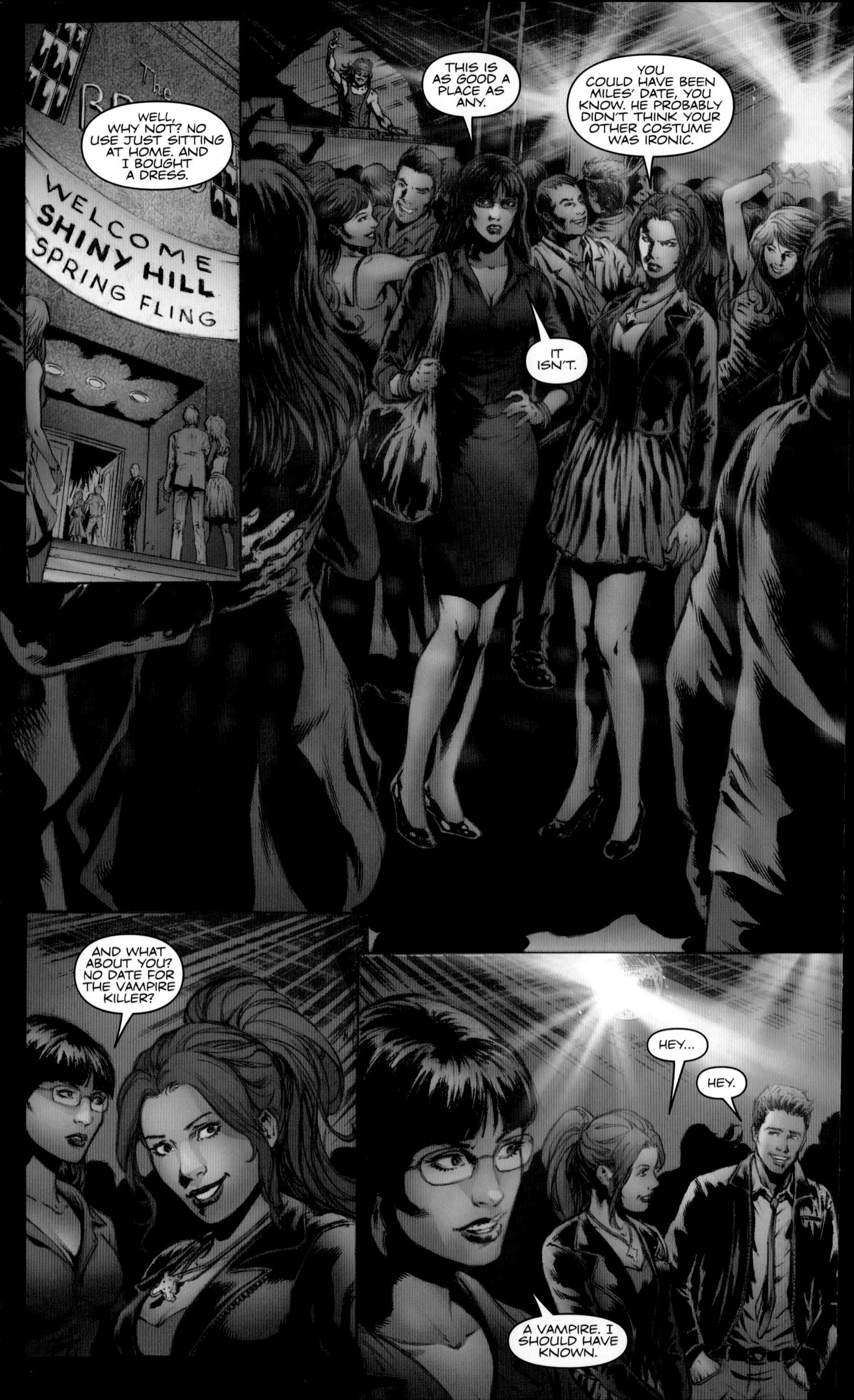

The
WELCOME SHINY HILL SPRING FLING
WELL, WHY NOT? NO USE JUST SITTING AT HOME. AND I BOUGHT A DRESS.
THIS IS AS GOOD A PLACE AS ANY.
YOU COULD HAVE BEEN MILES' DATE, YOU KNOW. HE PROBABLY DIDN'T THINK YOUR OTHER COSTUME WAS IRONIC.
IT ISN'T.
AND WHAT ABOUT YOU? NO DATE FOR THE VAMPIRE KILLER?
HEY...
HEY.
A VAMPIRE. I SHOULD HAVE KNOWN.

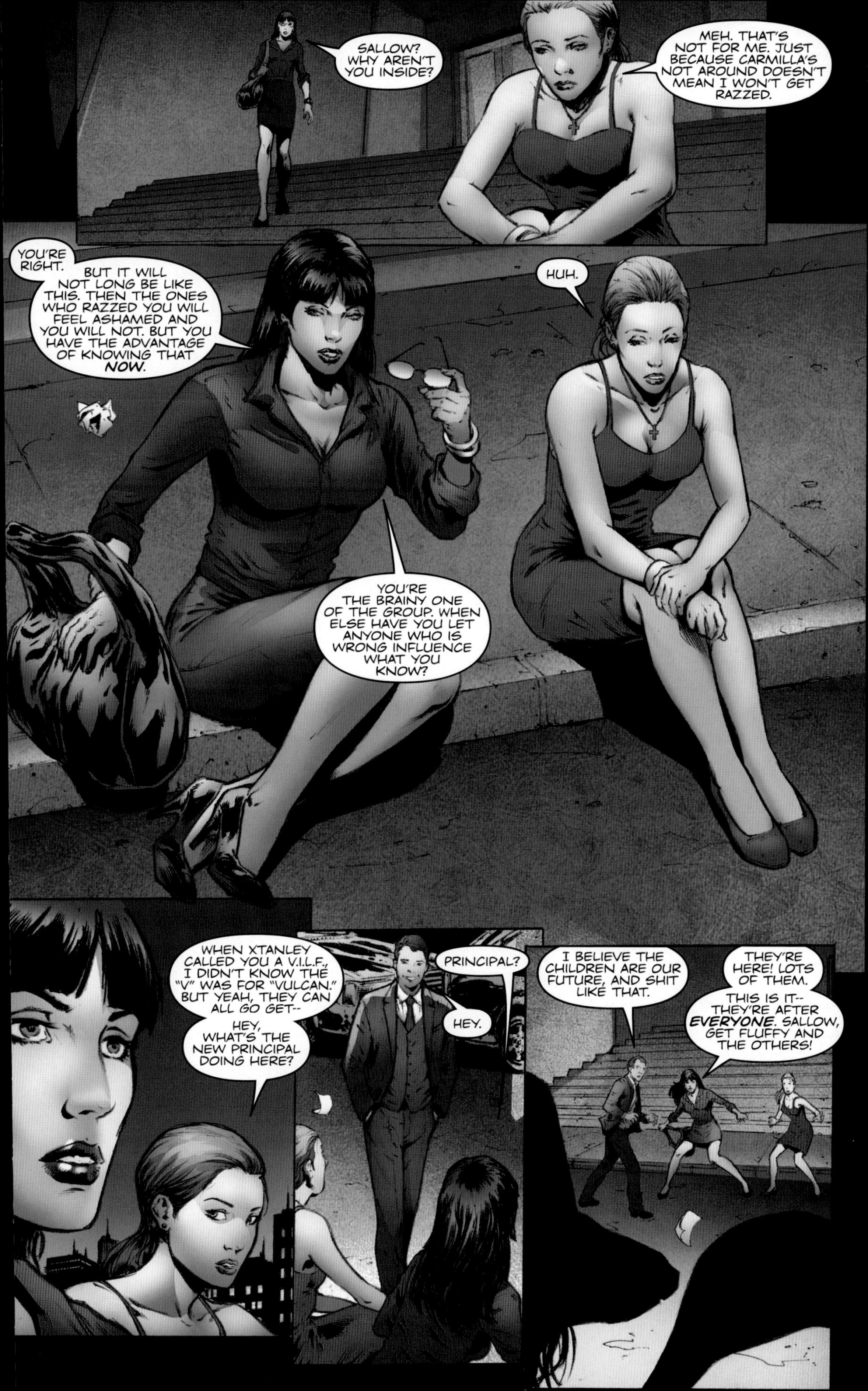
SALLOW? WHY AREN'T YOU INSIDE?
MEH. THAT'S NOT FOR ME. JUST BECAUSE CARMILLA'S NOT AROUND DOESN'T MEAN I WON'T GET RAZZED.
YOU'RE RIGHT.
BUT IT WILL NOT LONG BE LIKE THIS. THEN THE ONES WHO RAZZED YOU WILL FEEL ASHAMED AND YOU WILL NOT. BUT YOU HAVE THE ADVANTAGE OF KNOWING THAT NOW.
HUH.
YOU'RE THE BRAINY ONE OF THE GROUP. WHEN ELSE HAVE YOU LET ANYONE WHO IS WRONG INFLUENCE WHAT YOU KNOW?
WHEN XTANLEY CALLED YOU A V.I.L.F., I DIDN'T KNOW THE "V" WAS FOR "VULCAN." BUT YEAH, THEY CAN ALL GO GET--
HEY, WHAT'S THE NEW PRINCIPAL DOING HERE?
PRINCIPAL?
HEY.
I BELIEVE THE CHILDREN ARE OUR FUTURE, AND SHIT LIKE THAT.
THEY'RE HERE! LOTS OF THEM.
THIS IS IT-- THEY'RE AFTER EVERYONE. SALLOW, GET FLUFFY AND THE OTHERS!

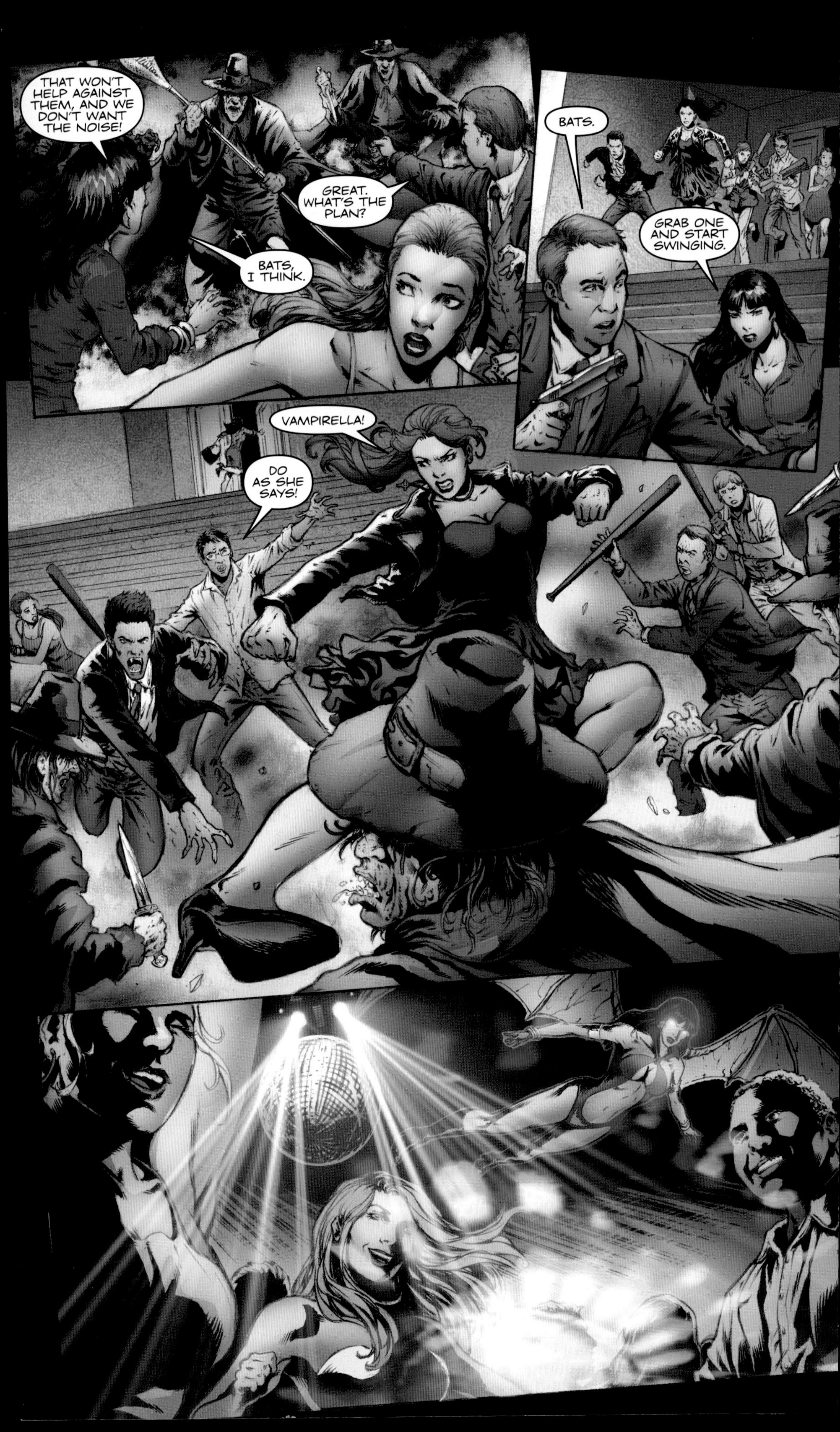
THAT WON'T HELP AGAINST THEM, AND WE DON'T WANT THE NOISE!
GREAT. WHAT'S THE PLAN?
BATS, I THINK.
BATS.
GRAB ONE AND START SWINGING.
VAMPIRELLA!
DO AS SHE SAYS!

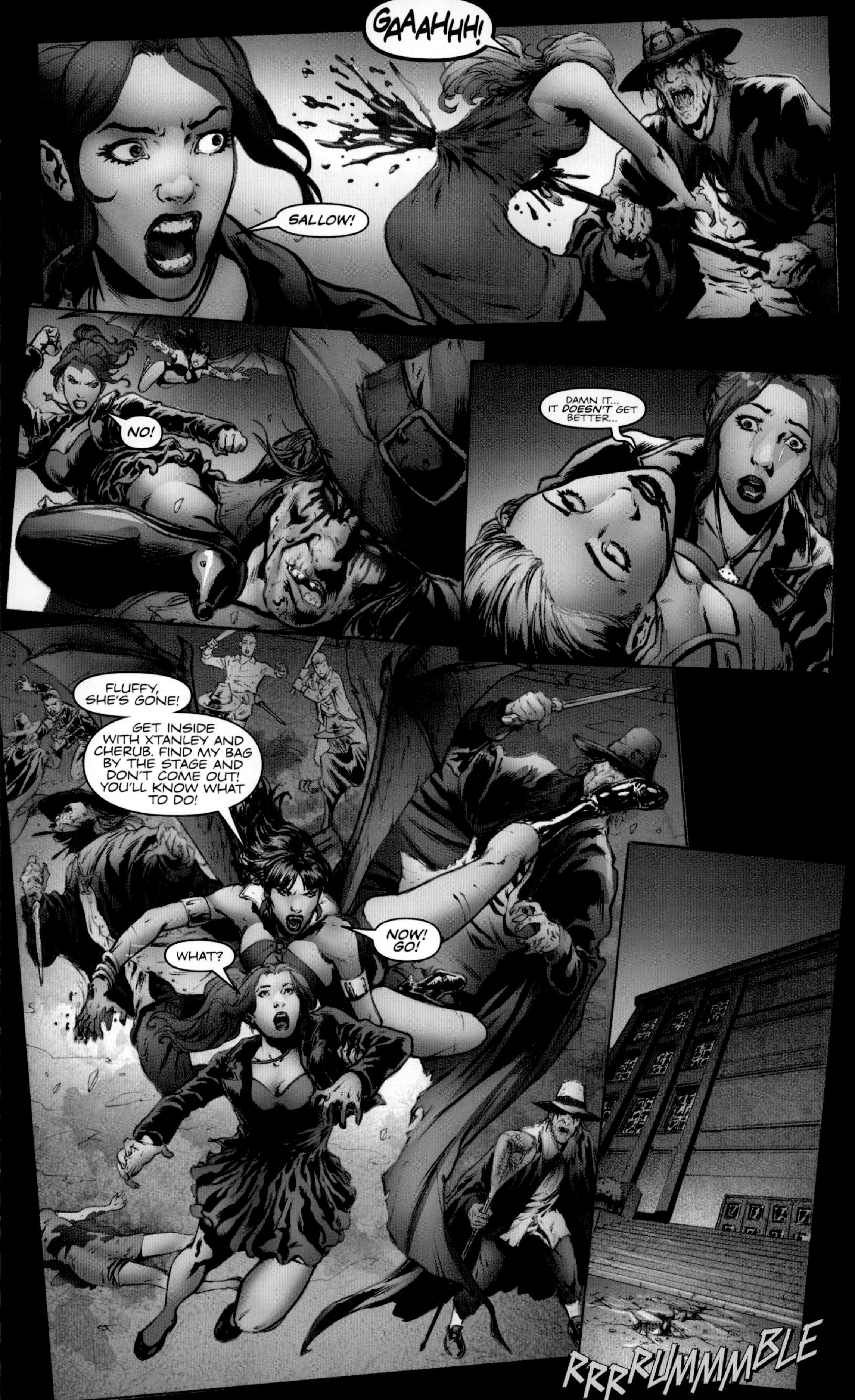
GAAAHHH!
SALLOW!
NO!
DAMN IT... IT DOESN'T GET BETTER...
FLUFFY, SHE'S GONE!
GET INSIDE WITH XTANLEY AND CHERUB. FIND MY BAG BY THE STAGE AND DON'T COME OUT! YOU'LL KNOW WHAT TO DO!
NOW! GO!
WHAT?
RRRRUMMMMBLE

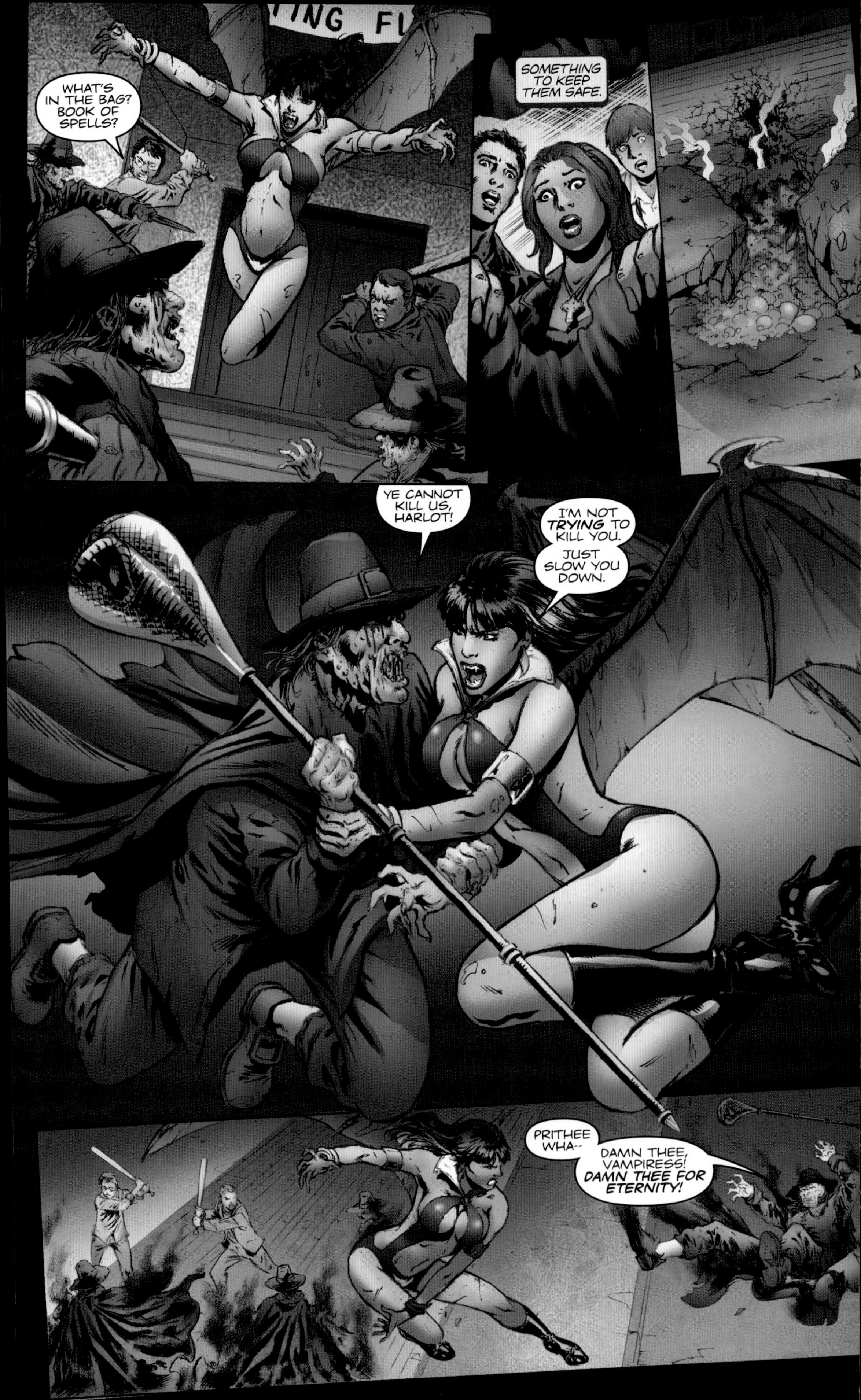

...ING FL...
WHAT'S IN THE BAG? BOOK OF SPELLS?
SOMETHING TO KEEP THEM SAFE.
YE CANNOT KILL US, HARLOT!
I'M NOT *TRYING* TO KILL YOU.
JUST SLOW YOU DOWN.
PRITHEE WHA--
DAMN THEE, VAMPIRESS! *DAMN THEE FOR ETERNITY!*

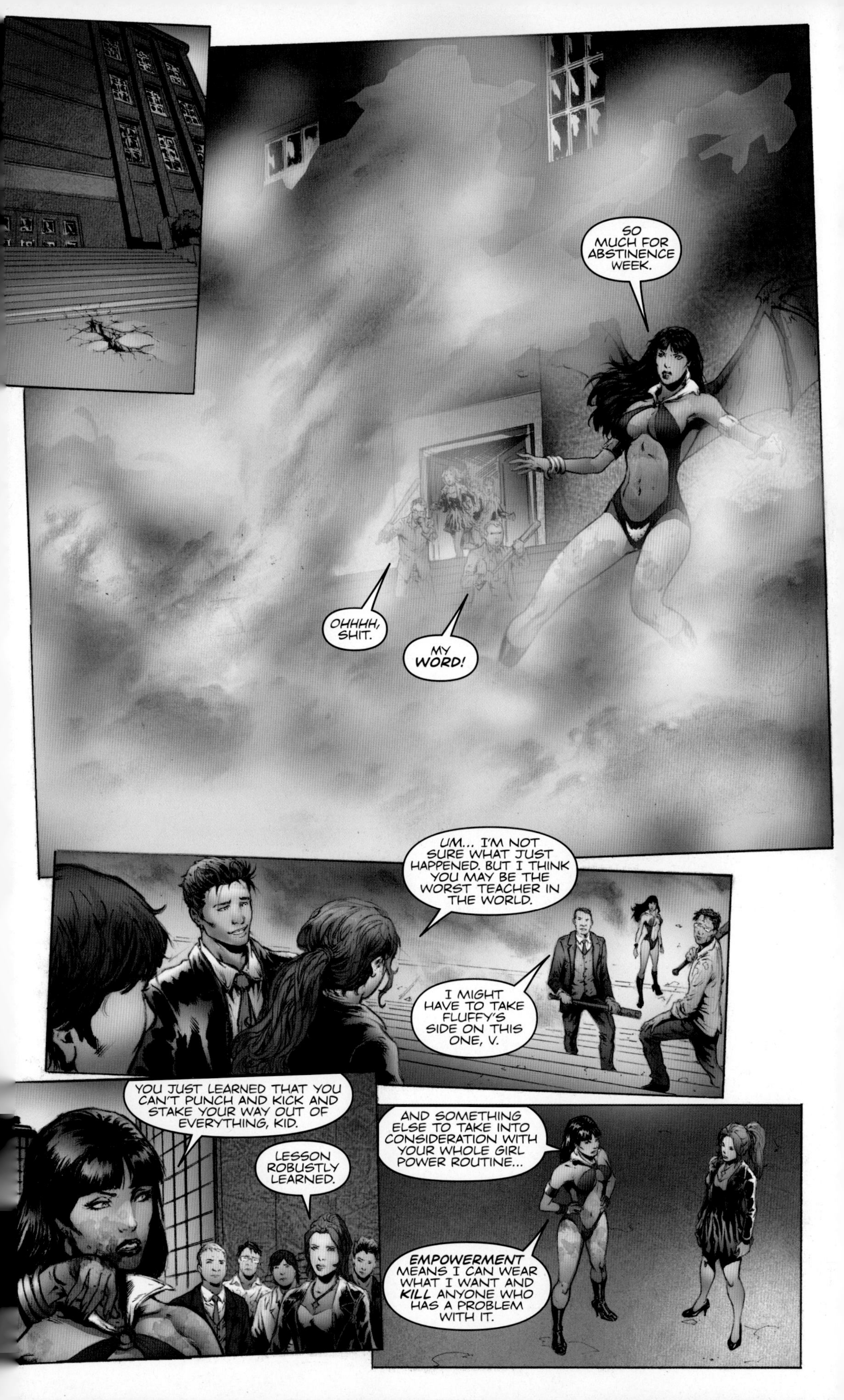
SO MUCH FOR ABSTINENCE WEEK.
OHHHH, SHIT.
MY WORD!
UM... I'M NOT SURE WHAT JUST HAPPENED. BUT I THINK YOU MAY BE THE WORST TEACHER IN THE WORLD.
I MIGHT HAVE TO TAKE FLUFFY'S SIDE ON THIS ONE, V.
YOU JUST LEARNED THAT YOU CAN'T PUNCH AND KICK AND STAKE YOUR WAY OUT OF EVERYTHING, KID.
LESSON ROBUSTLY LEARNED.
AND SOMETHING ELSE TO TAKE INTO CONSIDERATION WITH YOUR WHOLE GIRL POWER ROUTINE...
EMPOWERMENT MEANS I CAN WEAR WHAT I WANT AND KILL ANYONE WHO HAS A PROBLEM WITH IT.

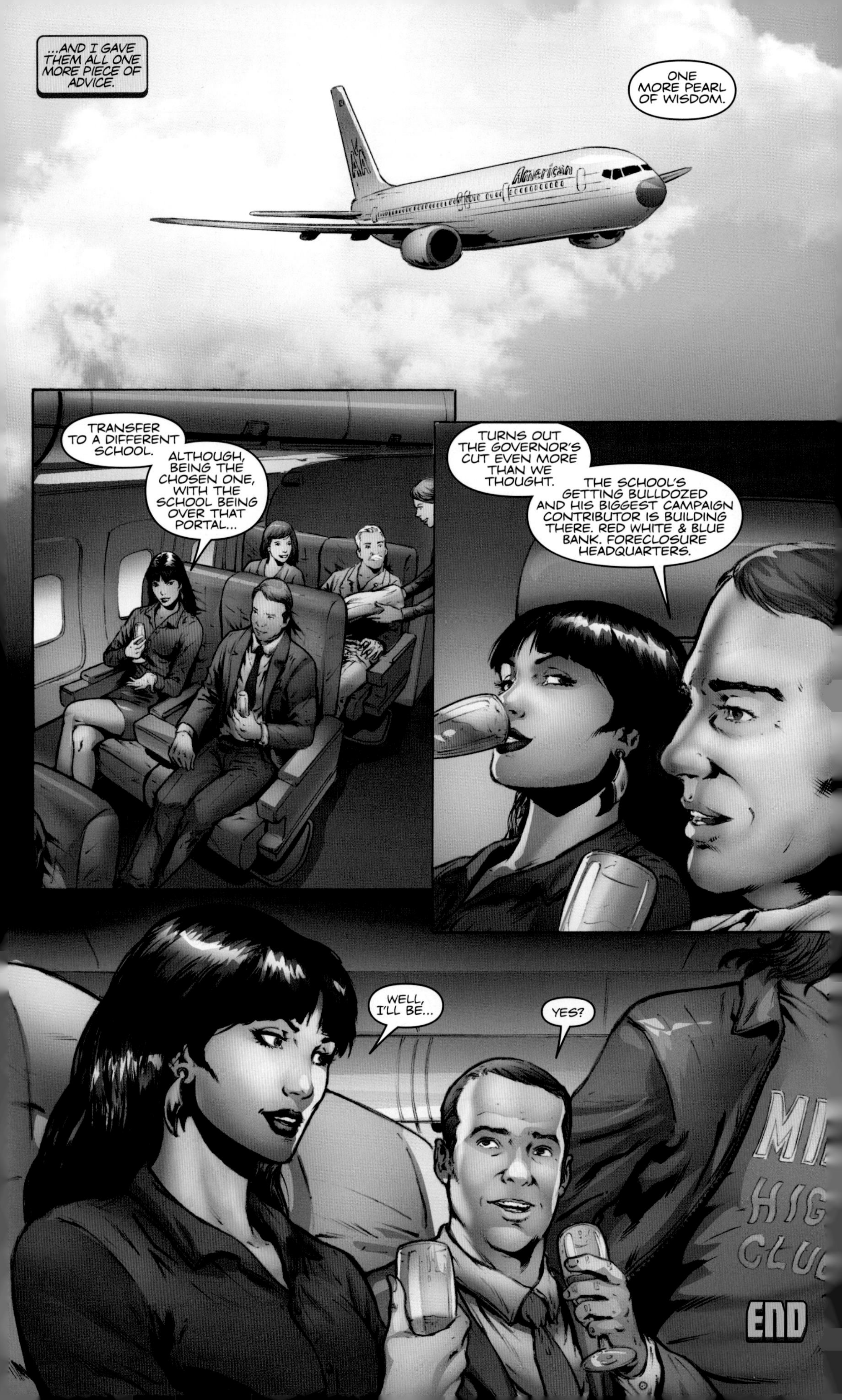
...AND I GAVE THEM ALL ONE MORE PIECE OF ADVICE.
ONE MORE PEARL OF WISDOM.
American
TRANSFER TO A DIFFERENT SCHOOL.
ALTHOUGH, BEING THE CHOSEN ONE, WITH THE SCHOOL BEING OVER THAT PORTAL...
TURNS OUT THE GOVERNOR'S CUT EVEN MORE THAN WE THOUGHT.
THE SCHOOL'S GETTING BULLDOZED AND HIS BIGGEST CAMPAIGN CONTRIBUTOR IS BUILDING THERE. RED WHITE & BLUE BANK. FORECLOSURE HEADQUARTERS.
WELL, I'LL BE...
YES?
END

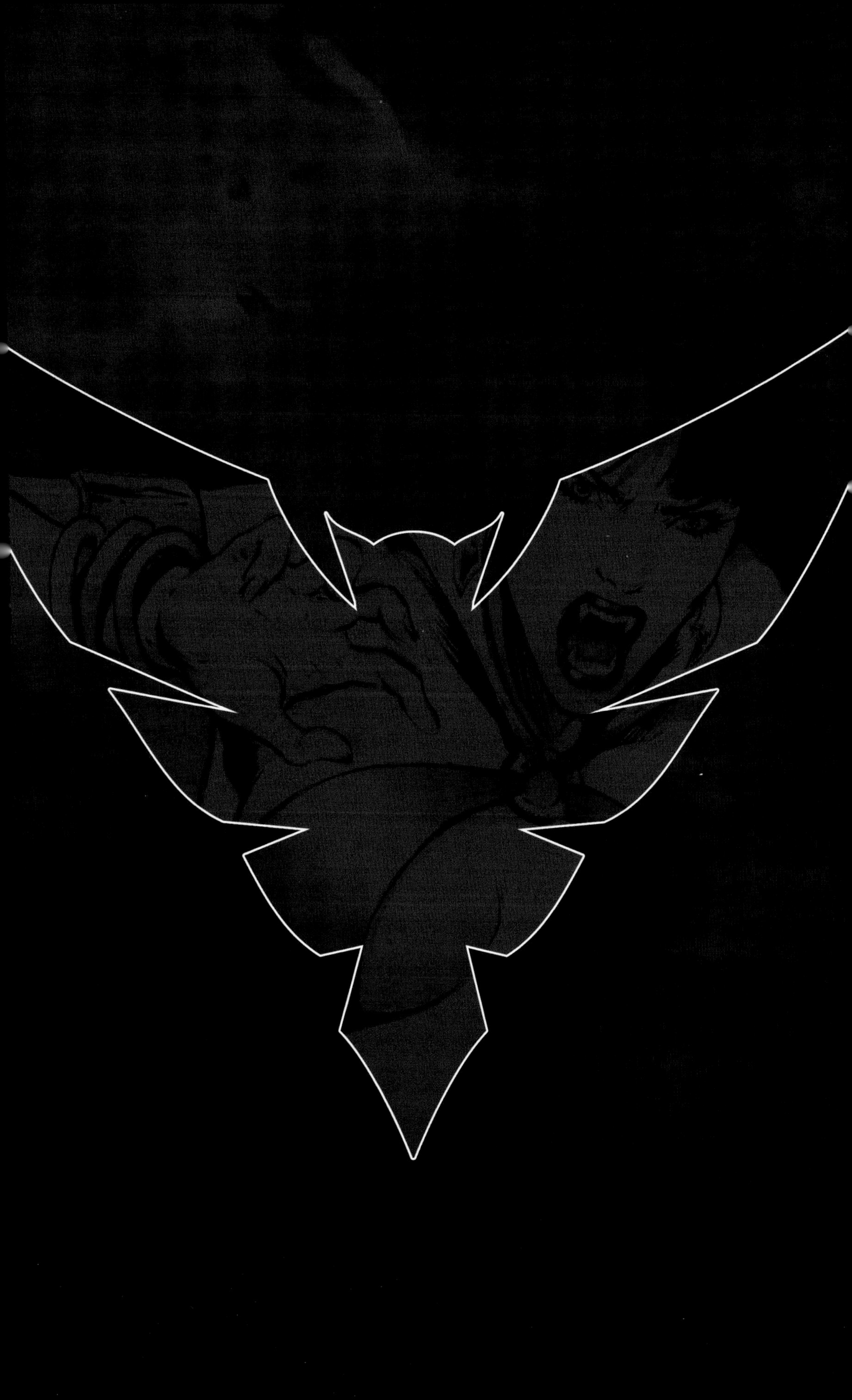

VAMPIRELLA: NUBLOOD

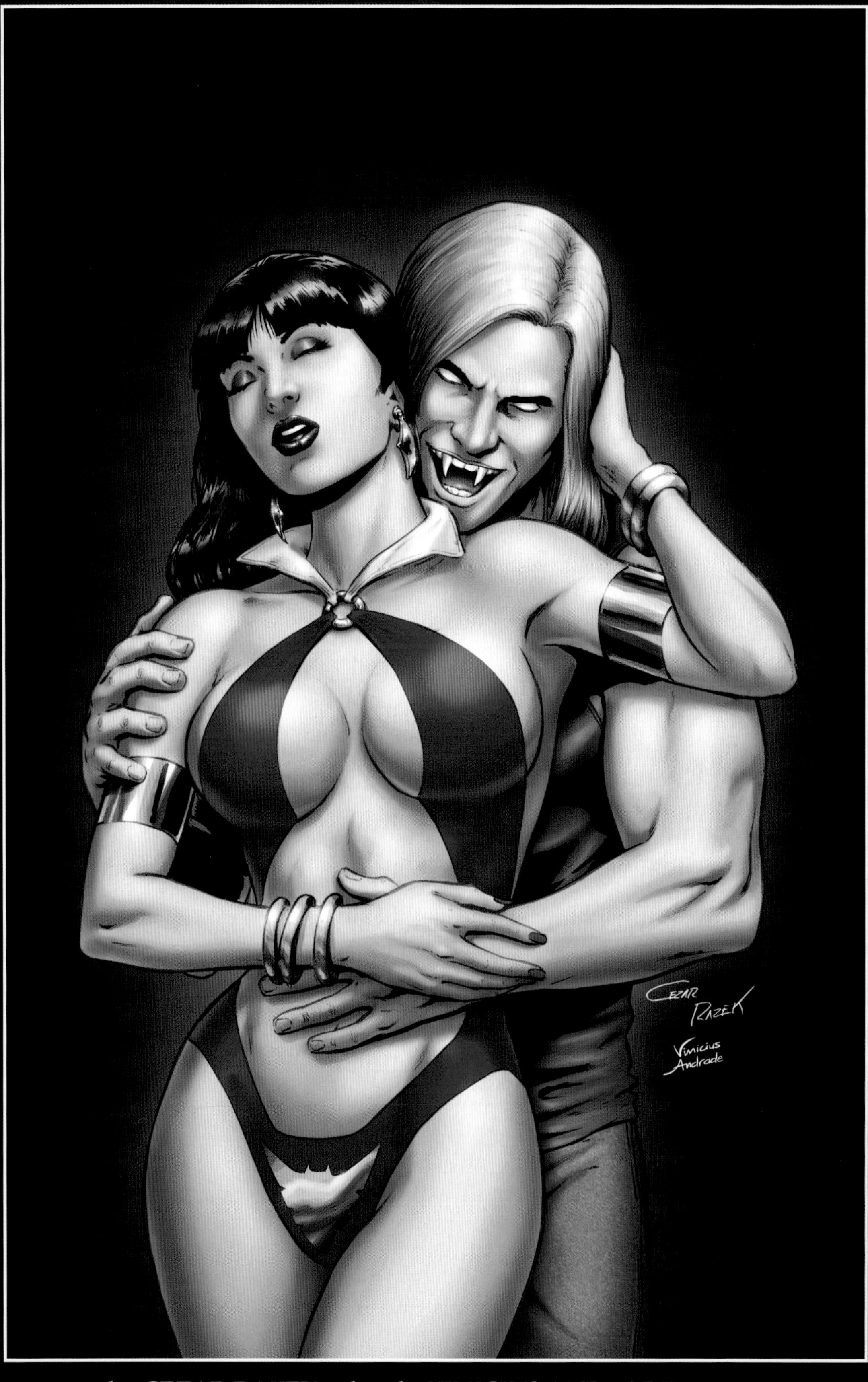
CEZAR RAZEK
Vinicius Andrade

cover art by CEZAR RAZEK colors byVINICIUS ANDRADE

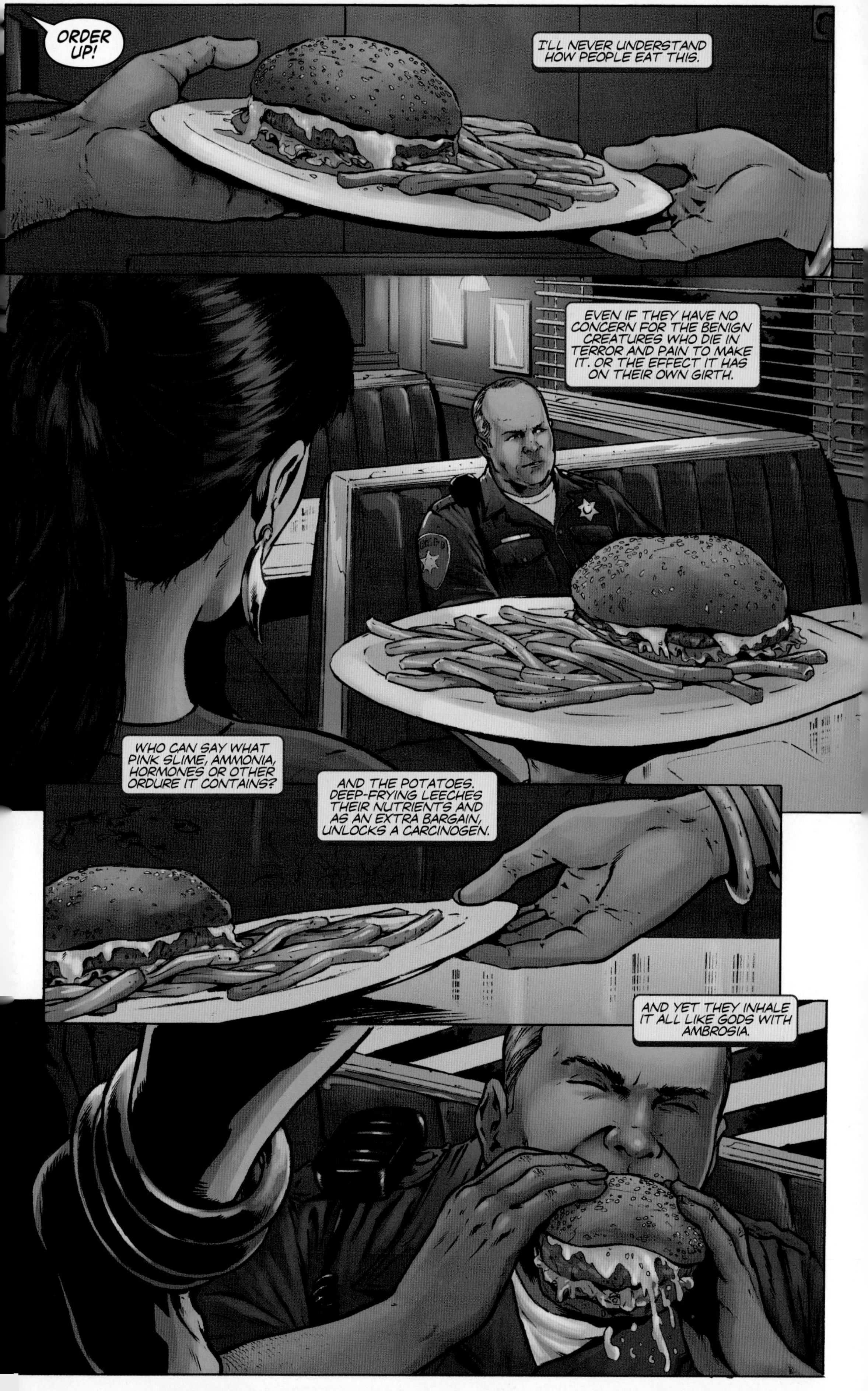
ORDER UP!
I'LL NEVER UNDERSTAND HOW PEOPLE EAT THIS.
EVEN IF THEY HAVE NO CONCERN FOR THE BENIGN CREATURES WHO DIE IN TERROR AND PAIN TO MAKE IT. OR THE EFFECT IT HAS ON THEIR OWN GIRTH.
WHO CAN SAY WHAT PINK SLIME, AMMONIA, HORMONES OR OTHER ORDURE IT CONTAINS?
AND THE POTATOES. DEEP-FRYING LEECHES THEIR NUTRIENTS AND AS AN EXTRA BARGAIN, UNLOCKS A CARCINOGEN.
AND YET THEY INHALE IT ALL LIKE GODS WITH AMBROSIA.

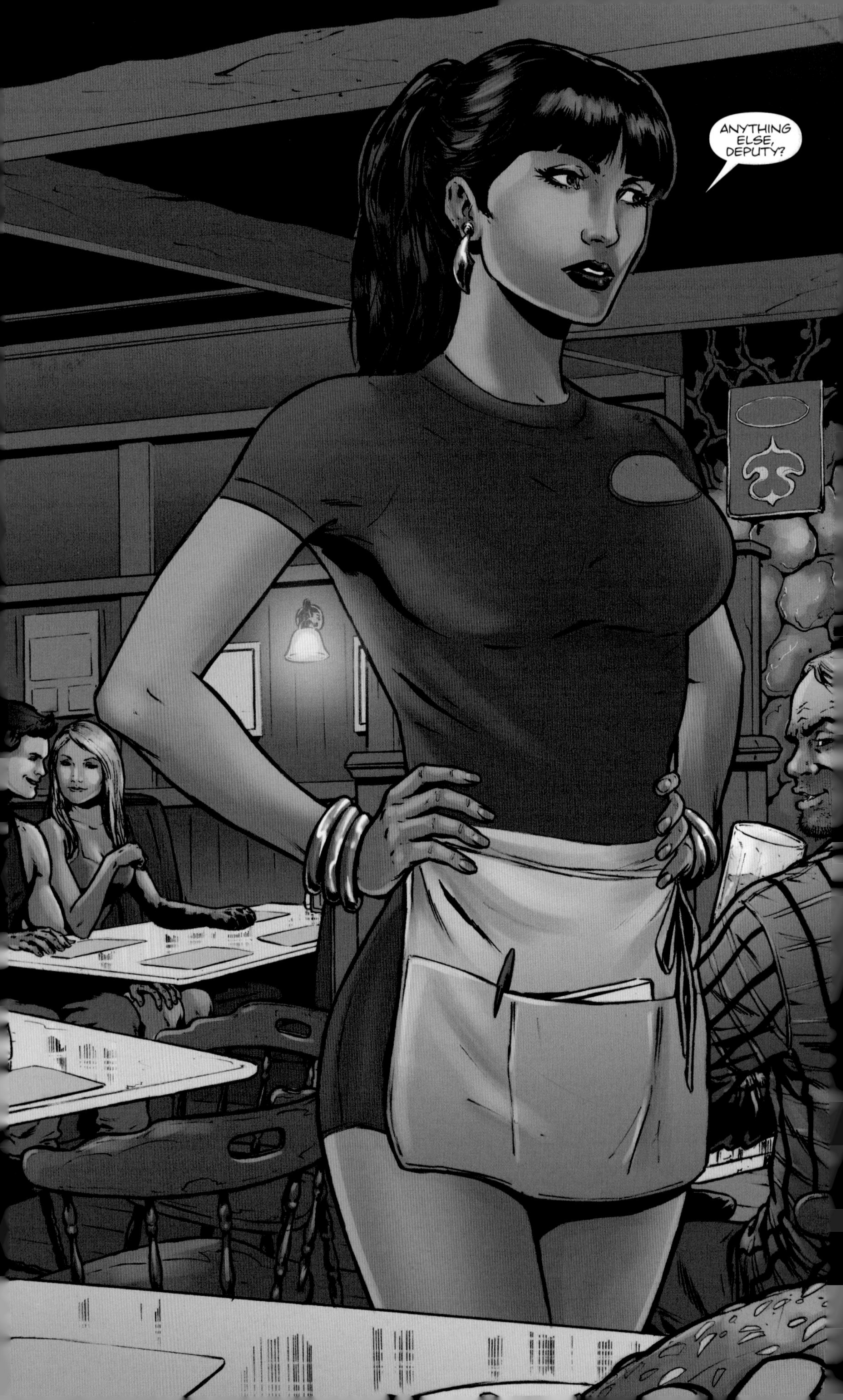
ANYTHING ELSE, DEPUTY?

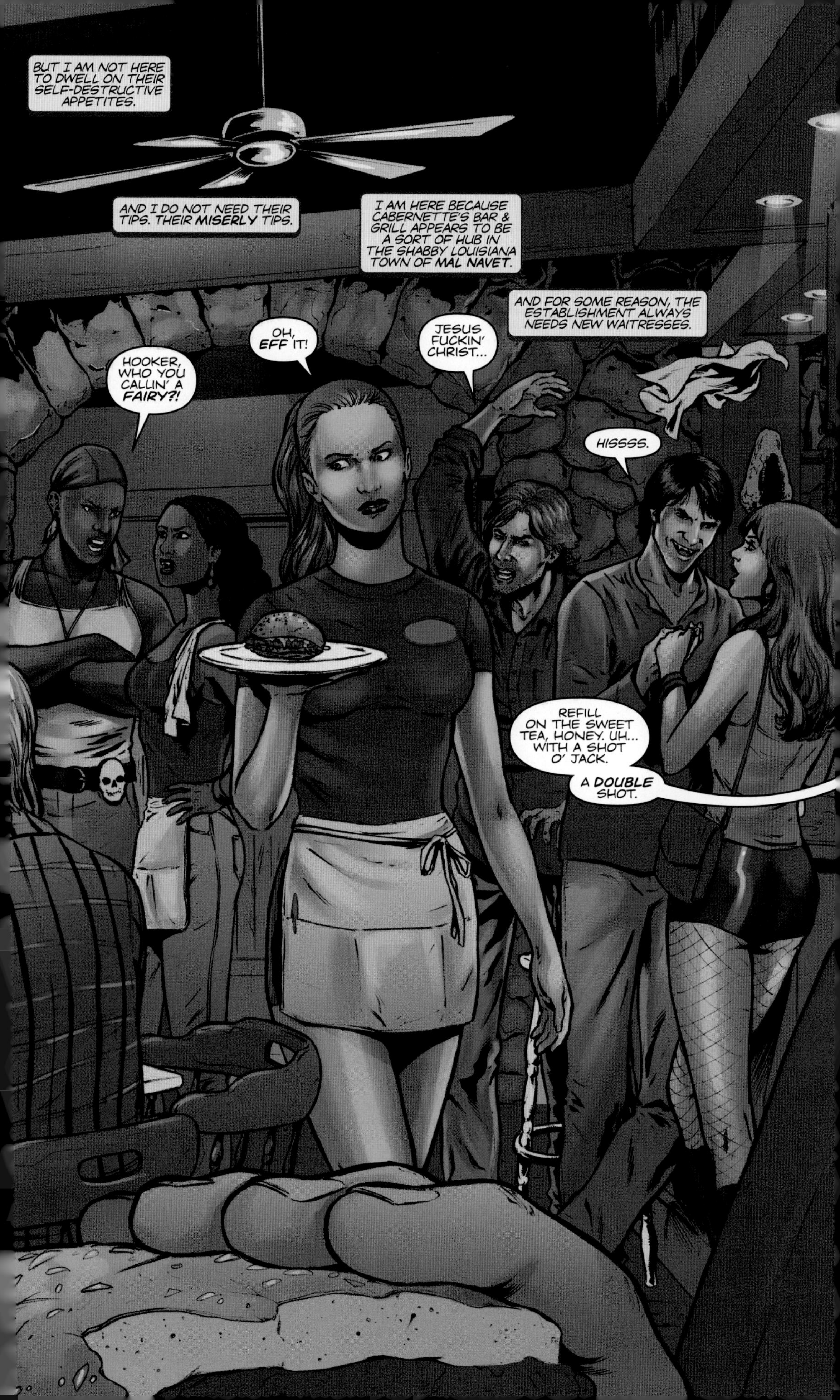
BUT I AM NOT HERE TO DWELL ON THEIR SELF-DESTRUCTIVE APPETITES.
AND I DO NOT NEED THEIR TIPS. THEIR **MISERLY** TIPS.
I AM HERE BECAUSE CABERNETTE'S BAR & GRILL APPEARS TO BE A SORT OF HUB IN THE SHABBY LOUISIANA TOWN OF **MAL NAVET**.
AND FOR SOME REASON, THE ESTABLISHMENT ALWAYS NEEDS NEW WAITRESSES.
HOOKER, WHO YOU CALLIN' A **FAIRY?!**
OH, **EFF** IT!
JESUS FUCKIN' CHRIST...
HISSSS.
REFILL ON THE SWEET TEA, HONEY. UH... WITH A SHOT O' JACK.
A **DOUBLE** SHOT.

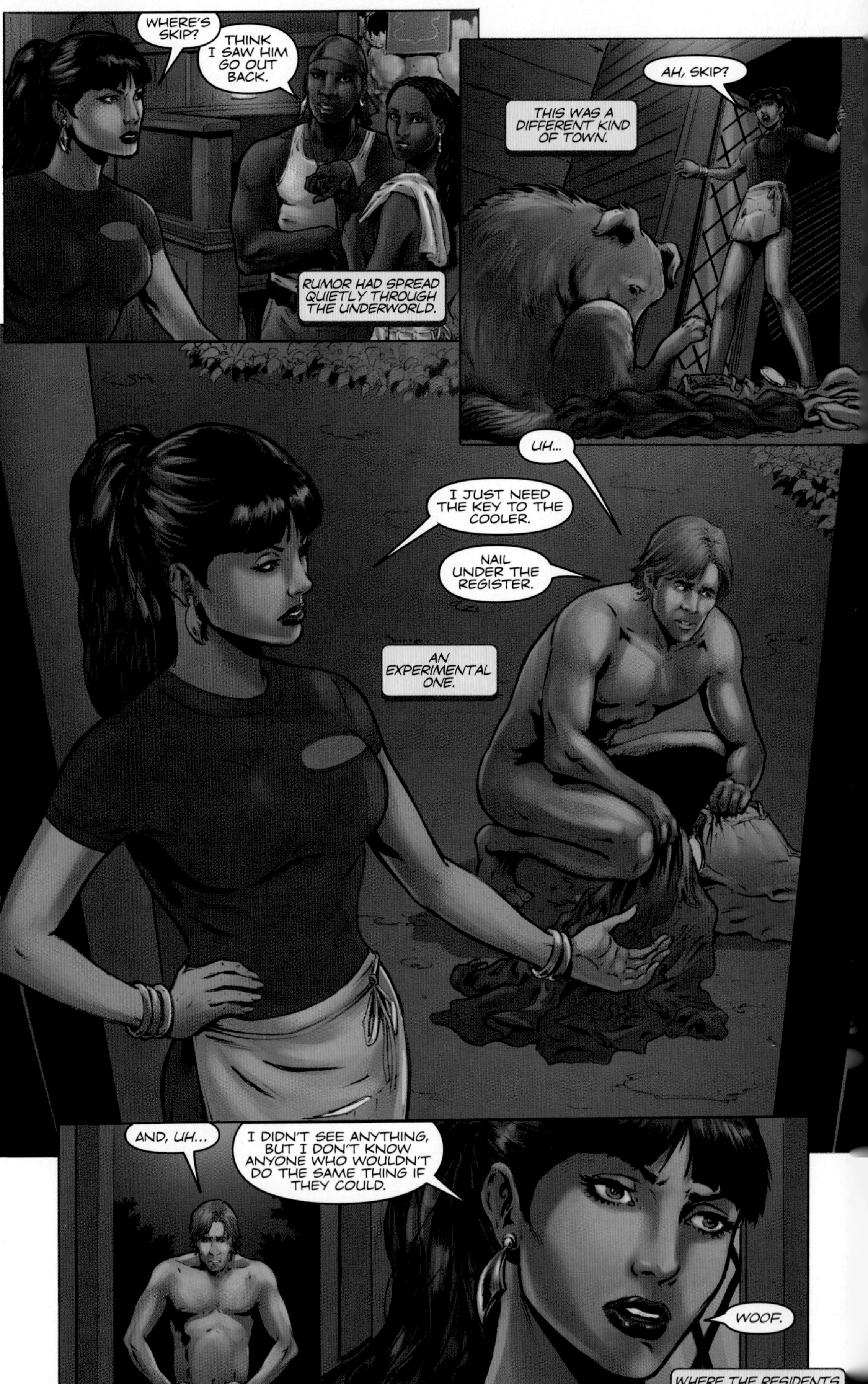
WHERE'S SKIP?
THINK I SAW HIM GO OUT BACK.
RUMOR HAD SPREAD QUIETLY THROUGH THE UNDERWORLD.
AH, SKIP?
THIS WAS A DIFFERENT KIND OF TOWN.
UH...
I JUST NEED THE KEY TO THE COOLER.
NAIL UNDER THE REGISTER.
AN EXPERIMENTAL ONE.
AND, UH...
I DIDN'T SEE ANYTHING, BUT I DON'T KNOW ANYONE WHO WOULDN'T DO THE SAME THING IF THEY COULD.
WOOF.
WHERE THE RESIDENTS AREN'T ASHAMED OF WHAT THEY ARE.

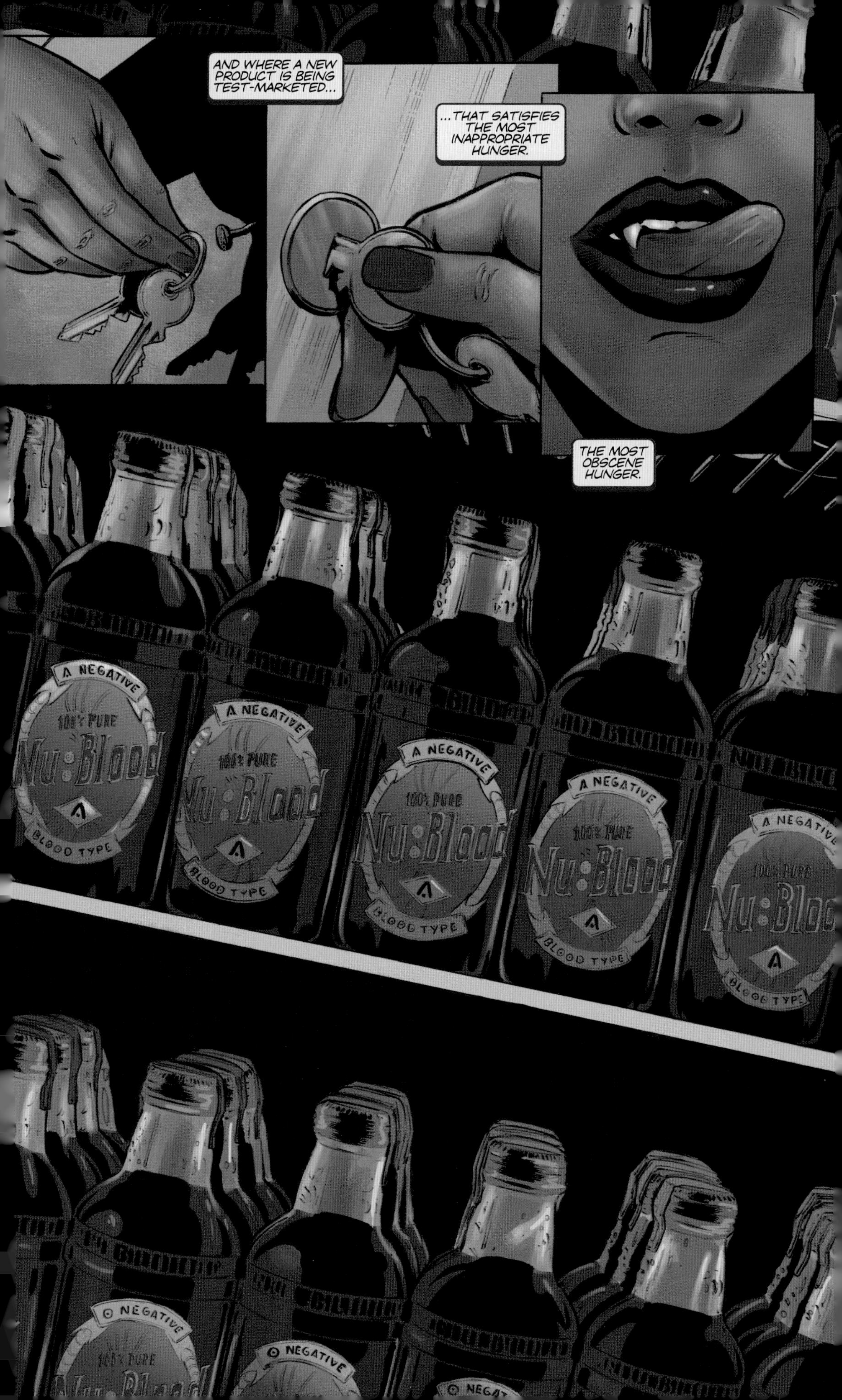
AND WHERE A NEW PRODUCT IS BEING TEST-MARKETED...
...THAT SATISFIES THE MOST INAPPROPRIATE HUNGER.
THE MOST OBSCENE HUNGER.
A NEGATIVE
100% PURE
Nu:Blood
BLOOD TYPE
O NEGATIVE

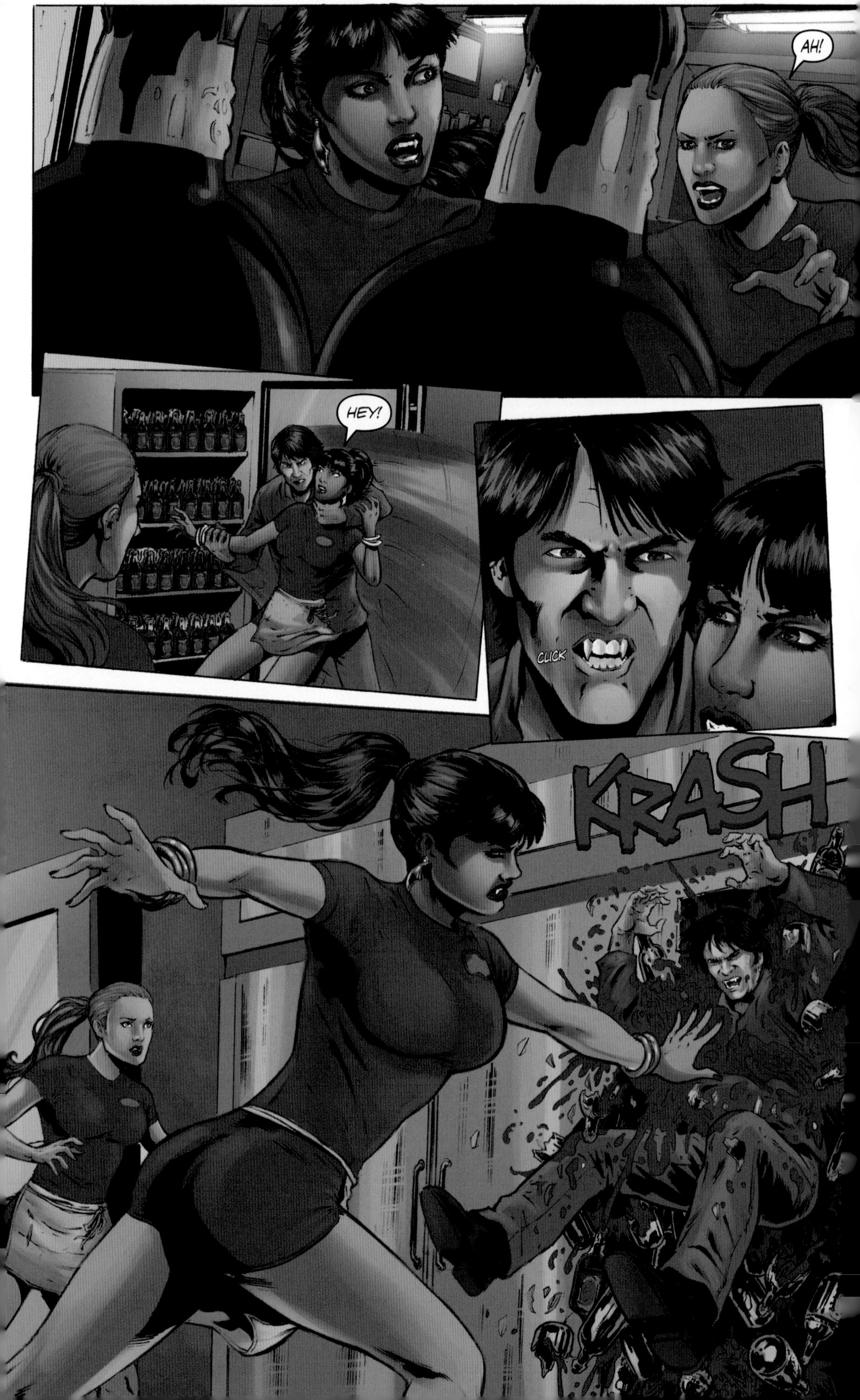
AH!
HEY!
CLICK
KRASH

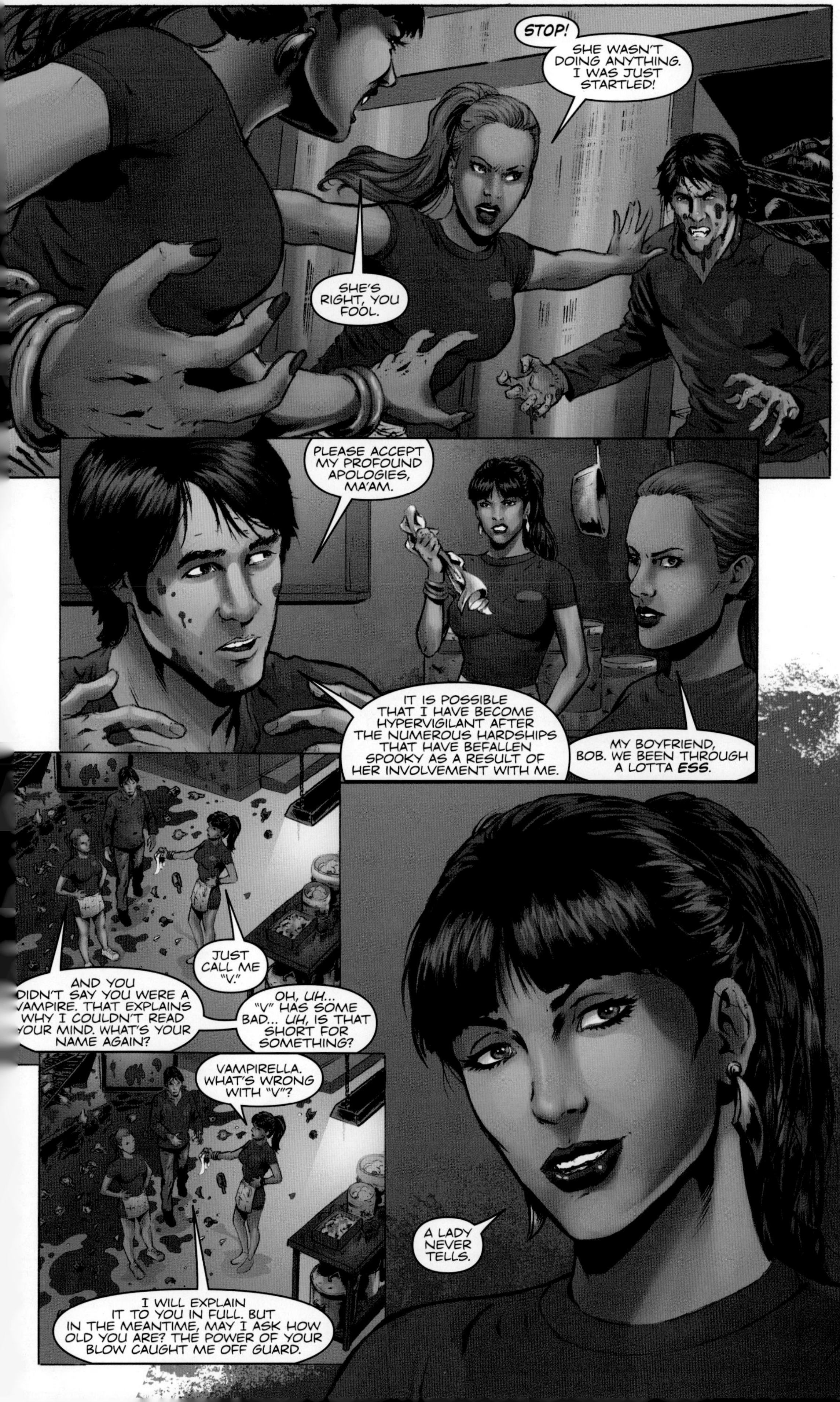
STOP!
SHE WASN'T DOING ANYTHING. I WAS JUST STARTLED!
SHE'S RIGHT, YOU FOOL.
PLEASE ACCEPT MY PROFOUND APOLOGIES, MA'AM.
IT IS POSSIBLE THAT I HAVE BECOME HYPERVIGILANT AFTER THE NUMEROUS HARDSHIPS THAT HAVE BEFALLEN SPOOKY AS A RESULT OF HER INVOLVEMENT WITH ME.
MY BOYFRIEND, BOB. WE BEEN THROUGH A LOTTA ESS.
AND YOU DIDN'T SAY YOU WERE A VAMPIRE. THAT EXPLAINS WHY I COULDN'T READ YOUR MIND. WHAT'S YOUR NAME AGAIN?
JUST CALL ME "V."
OH, UH... "V" HAS SOME BAD... UH, IS THAT SHORT FOR SOMETHING?
VAMPIRELLA. WHAT'S WRONG WITH "V"?
I WILL EXPLAIN IT TO YOU IN FULL. BUT IN THE MEANTIME, MAY I ASK HOW OLD YOU ARE? THE POWER OF YOUR BLOW CAUGHT ME OFF GUARD.
A LADY NEVER TELLS.

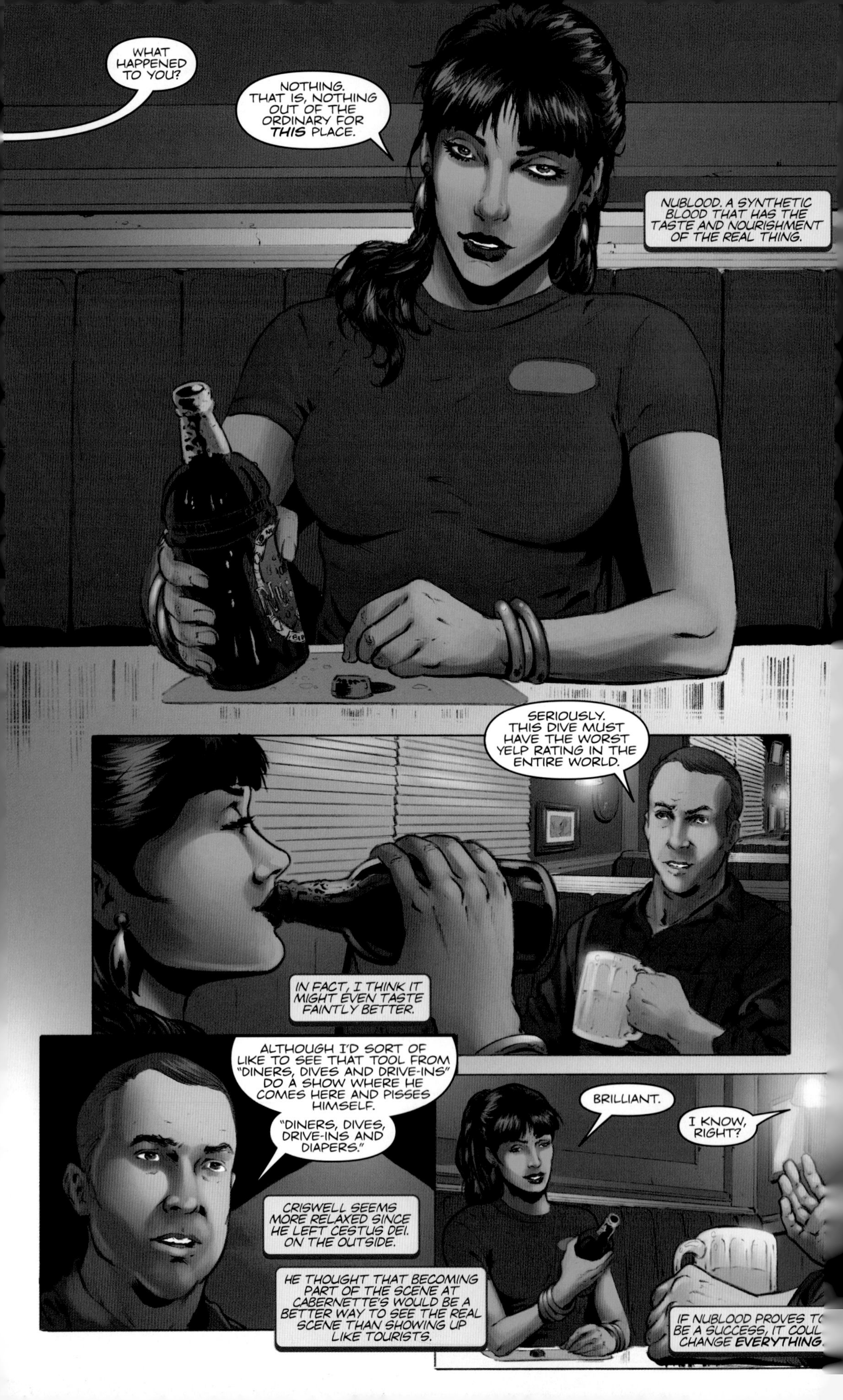
WHAT HAPPENED TO YOU?
NOTHING. THAT IS, NOTHING OUT OF THE ORDINARY FOR THIS PLACE.
NUBLOOD. A SYNTHETIC BLOOD THAT HAS THE TASTE AND NOURISHMENT OF THE REAL THING.
SERIOUSLY. THIS DIVE MUST HAVE THE WORST YELP RATING IN THE ENTIRE WORLD.
IN FACT, I THINK IT MIGHT EVEN TASTE FAINTLY BETTER.
ALTHOUGH I'D SORT OF LIKE TO SEE THAT TOOL FROM "DINERS, DIVES AND DRIVE-INS" DO A SHOW WHERE HE COMES HERE AND PISSES HIMSELF.
"DINERS, DIVES, DRIVE-INS AND DIAPERS."
BRILLIANT.
I KNOW, RIGHT?
CRISWELL SEEMS MORE RELAXED SINCE HE LEFT CESTUS DEI. ON THE OUTSIDE.
HE THOUGHT THAT BECOMING PART OF THE SCENE AT CABERNETTE'S WOULD BE A BETTER WAY TO SEE THE REAL SCENE THAN SHOWING UP LIKE TOURISTS.
IF NUBLOOD PROVES TO BE A SUCCESS, IT COULD CHANGE EVERYTHING.

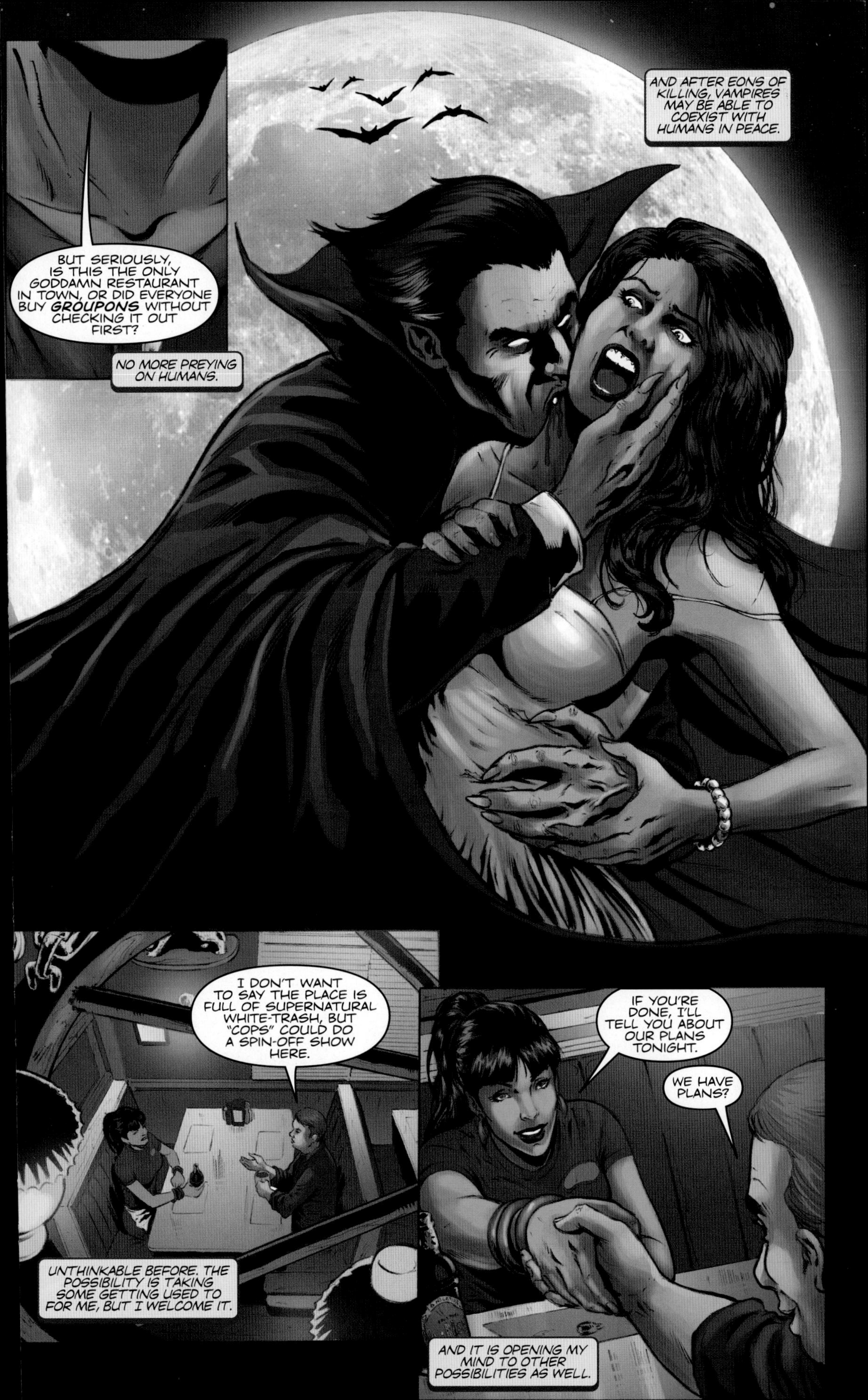

BUT SERIOUSLY, IS THIS THE ONLY GODDAMN RESTAURANT IN TOWN, OR DID EVERYONE BUY **GROUPONS** WITHOUT CHECKING IT OUT FIRST?
NO MORE PREYING ON HUMANS.
AND AFTER EONS OF KILLING, VAMPIRES MAY BE ABLE TO COEXIST WITH HUMANS IN PEACE.
I DON'T WANT TO SAY THE PLACE IS FULL OF SUPERNATURAL WHITE-TRASH, BUT "COPS" COULD DO A SPIN-OFF SHOW HERE.
UNTHINKABLE BEFORE. THE POSSIBILITY IS TAKING SOME GETTING USED TO FOR ME, BUT I WELCOME IT.
IF YOU'RE DONE, I'LL TELL YOU ABOUT OUR PLANS TONIGHT.
WE HAVE PLANS?
AND IT IS OPENING MY MIND TO OTHER POSSIBILITIES AS WELL.

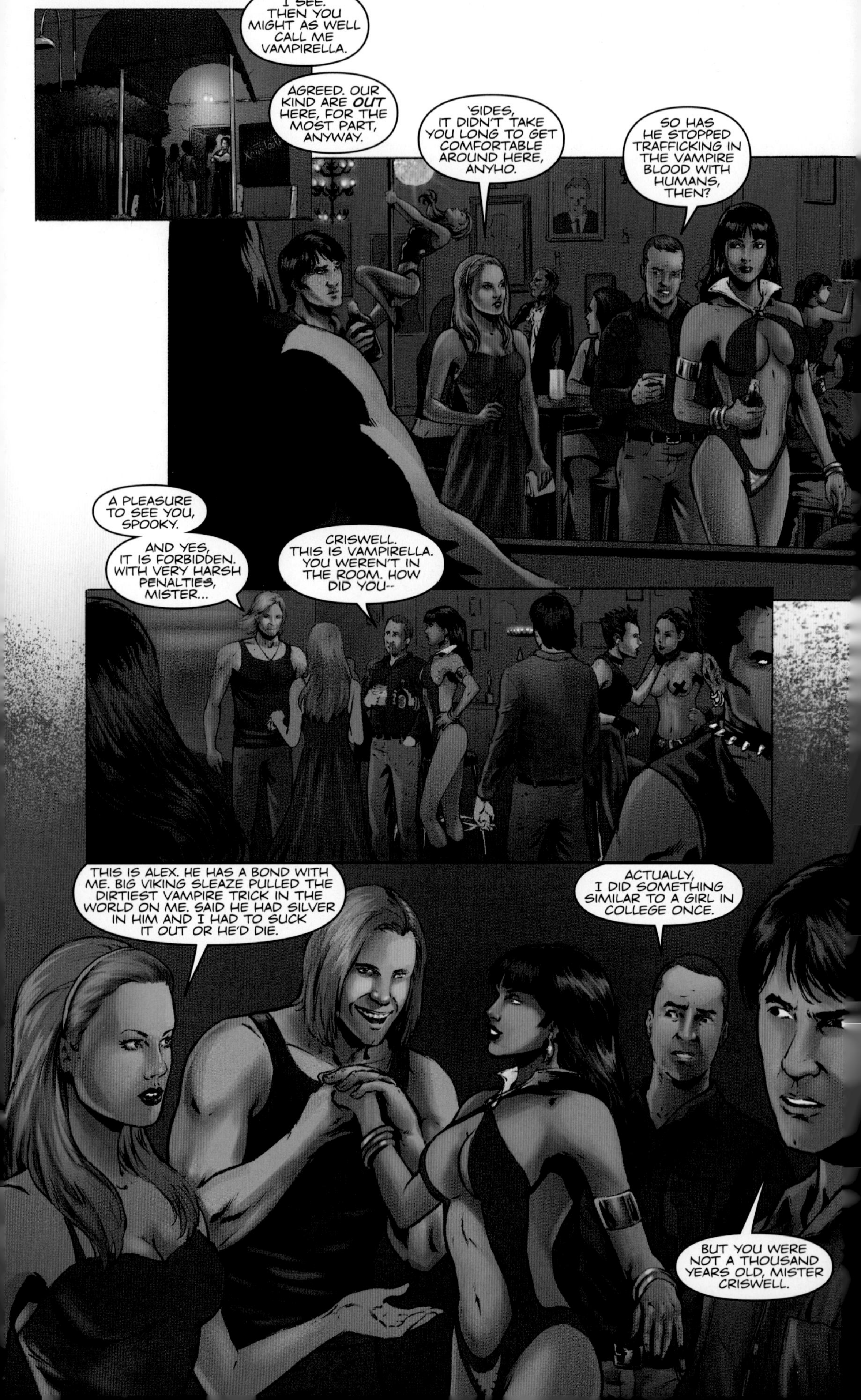
I SEE. THEN YOU MIGHT AS WELL CALL ME VAMPIRELLA.
AGREED. OUR KIND ARE ***OUT*** HERE, FOR THE MOST PART, ANYWAY.
'SIDES, IT DIDN'T TAKE YOU LONG TO GET COMFORTABLE AROUND HERE, ANYHO.
SO HAS HE STOPPED TRAFFICKING IN THE VAMPIRE BLOOD WITH HUMANS, THEN?
A PLEASURE TO SEE YOU, SPOOKY.
AND YES, IT IS FORBIDDEN. WITH VERY HARSH PENALTIES, MISTER...
CRISWELL. THIS IS VAMPIRELLA. YOU WEREN'T IN THE ROOM. HOW DID YOU--
THIS IS ALEX. HE HAS A BOND WITH ME. BIG VIKING SLEAZE PULLED THE DIRTIEST VAMPIRE TRICK IN THE WORLD ON ME. SAID HE HAD SILVER IN HIM AND I HAD TO SUCK IT OUT OR HE'D DIE.
ACTUALLY, I DID SOMETHING SIMILAR TO A GIRL IN COLLEGE ONCE.
BUT YOU WERE NOT A THOUSAND YEARS OLD, MISTER CRISWELL.

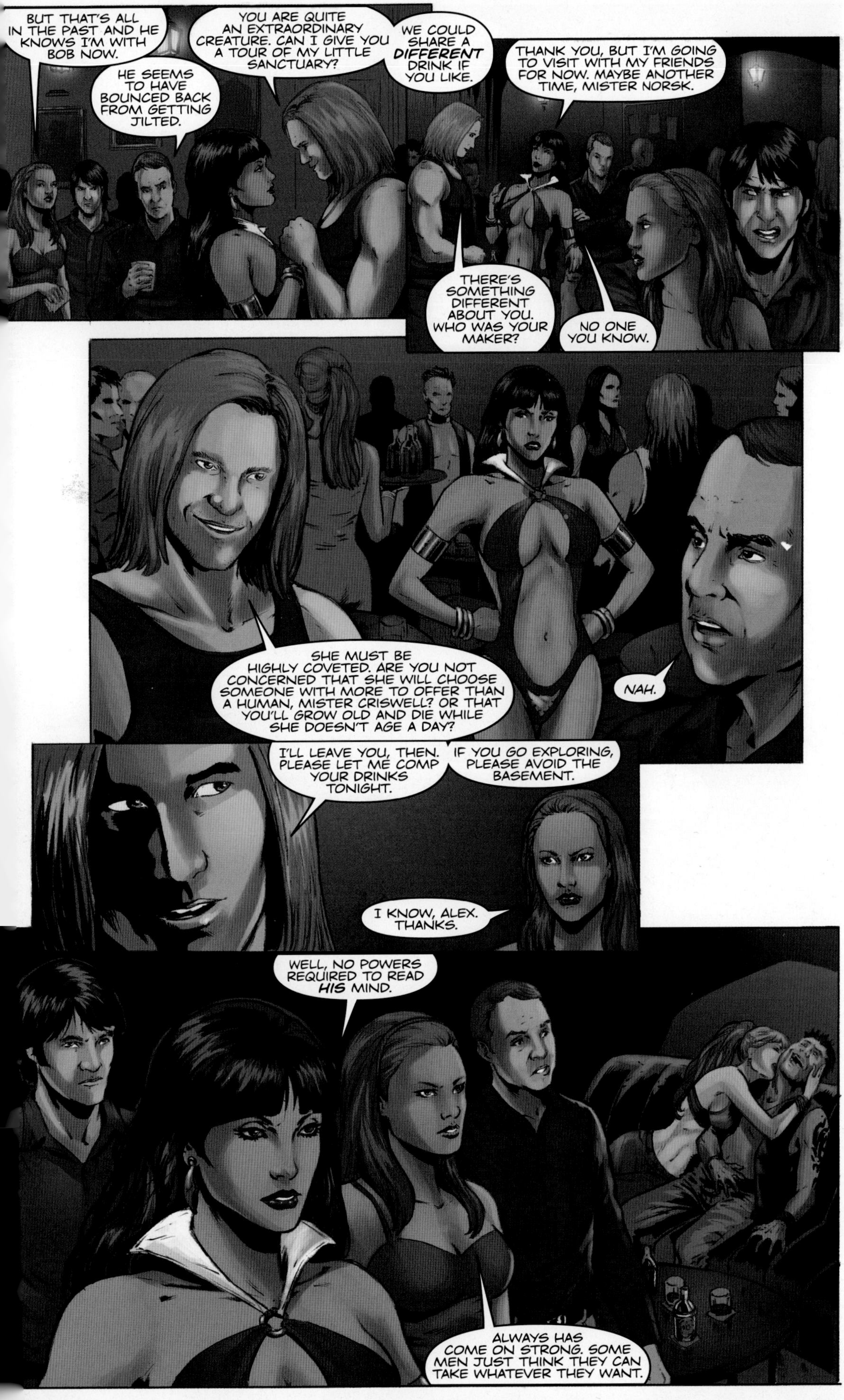
BUT THAT'S ALL IN THE PAST AND HE KNOWS I'M WITH BOB NOW.
HE SEEMS TO HAVE BOUNCED BACK FROM GETTING JILTED.
YOU ARE QUITE AN EXTRAORDINARY CREATURE. CAN I GIVE YOU A TOUR OF MY LITTLE SANCTUARY?
WE COULD SHARE A DIFFERENT DRINK IF YOU LIKE.
THANK YOU, BUT I'M GOING TO VISIT WITH MY FRIENDS FOR NOW. MAYBE ANOTHER TIME, MISTER NORSK.
THERE'S SOMETHING DIFFERENT ABOUT YOU. WHO WAS YOUR MAKER?
NO ONE YOU KNOW.
SHE MUST BE HIGHLY COVETED. ARE YOU NOT CONCERNED THAT SHE WILL CHOOSE SOMEONE WITH MORE TO OFFER THAN A HUMAN, MISTER CRISWELL? OR THAT YOU'LL GROW OLD AND DIE WHILE SHE DOESN'T AGE A DAY?
NAH.
I'LL LEAVE YOU, THEN. PLEASE LET ME COMP YOUR DRINKS TONIGHT.
IF YOU GO EXPLORING, PLEASE AVOID THE BASEMENT.
I KNOW, ALEX. THANKS.
WELL, NO POWERS REQUIRED TO READ HIS MIND.
ALWAYS HAS COME ON STRONG. SOME MEN JUST THINK THEY CAN TAKE WHATEVER THEY WANT.

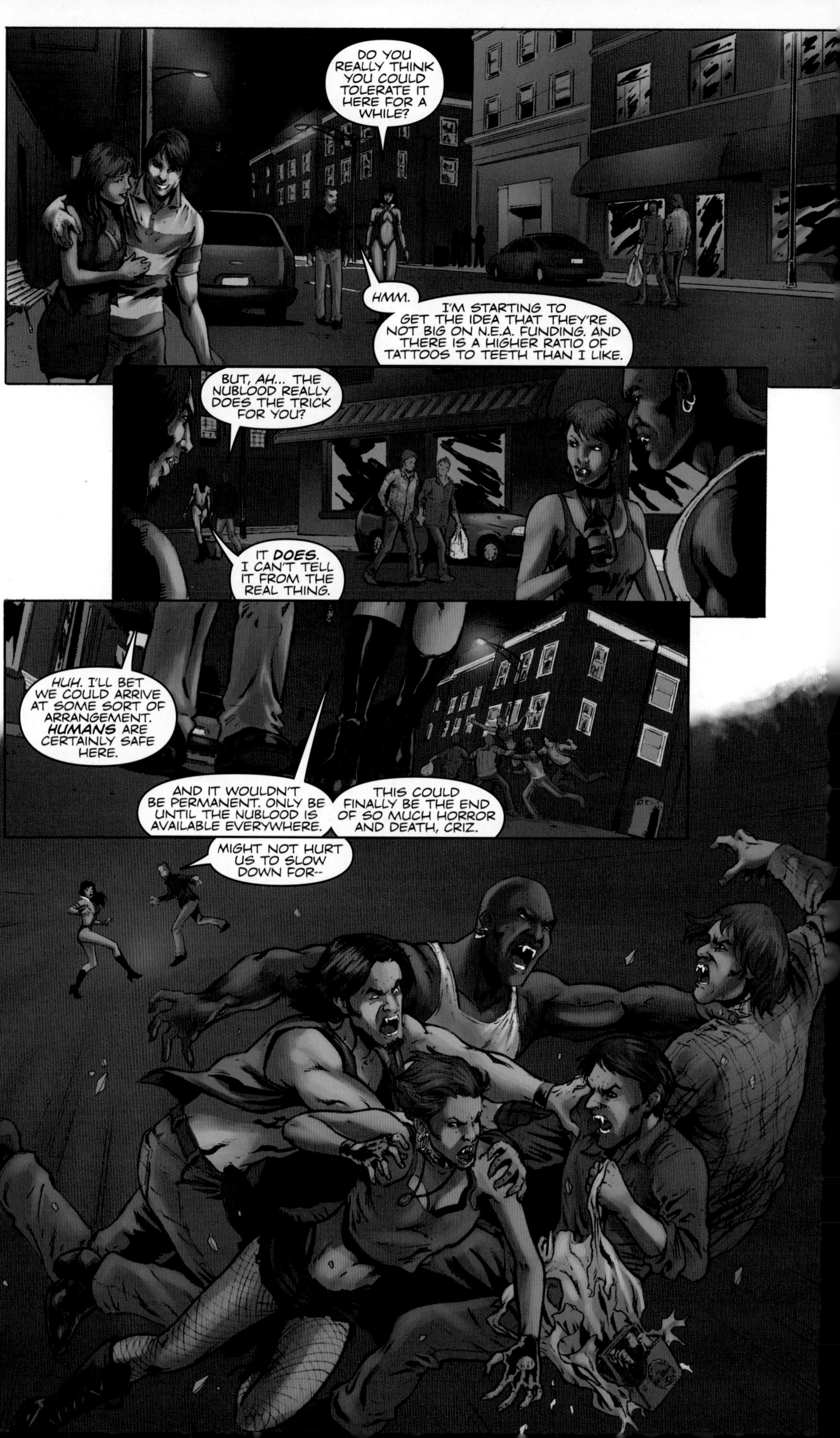
DO YOU REALLY THINK YOU COULD TOLERATE IT HERE FOR A WHILE?
HMM.
I'M STARTING TO GET THE IDEA THAT THEY'RE NOT BIG ON N.E.A. FUNDING. AND THERE IS A HIGHER RATIO OF TATTOOS TO TEETH THAN I LIKE.
BUT, AH... THE NUBLOOD REALLY DOES THE TRICK FOR YOU?
IT DOES. I CAN'T TELL IT FROM THE REAL THING.
HUH. I'LL BET WE COULD ARRIVE AT SOME SORT OF ARRANGEMENT. HUMANS ARE CERTAINLY SAFE HERE.
AND IT WOULDN'T BE PERMANENT. ONLY BE UNTIL THE NUBLOOD IS AVAILABLE EVERYWHERE.
THIS COULD FINALLY BE THE END OF SO MUCH HORROR AND DEATH, CRIZ.
MIGHT NOT HURT US TO SLOW DOWN FOR--

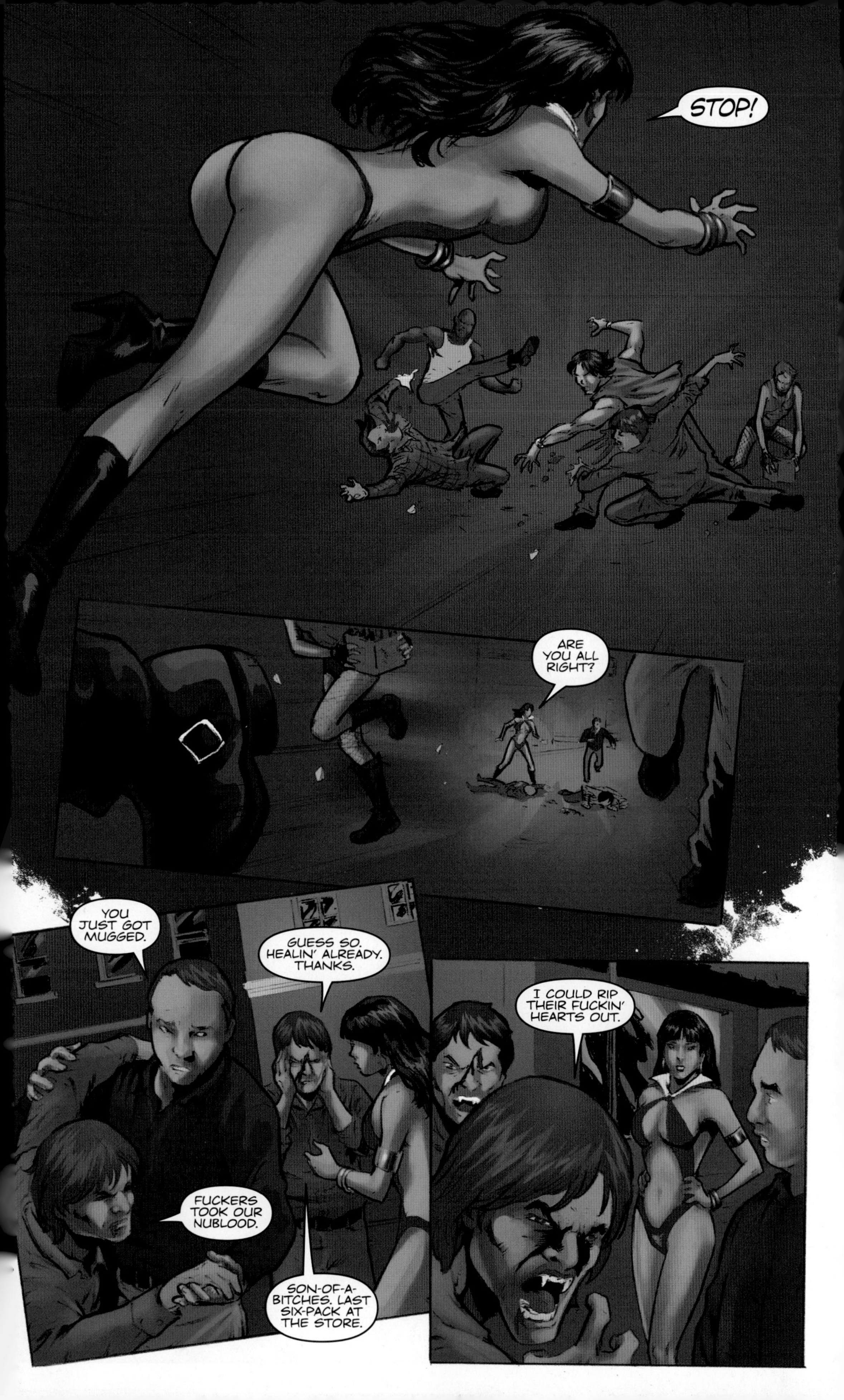
STOP!
ARE YOU ALL RIGHT?
YOU JUST GOT MUGGED.
FUCKERS TOOK OUR NUBLOOD.
GUESS SO. HEALIN' ALREADY. THANKS.
SON-OF-A-BITCHES. LAST SIX-PACK AT THE STORE.
I COULD RIP THEIR FUCKIN' HEARTS OUT.

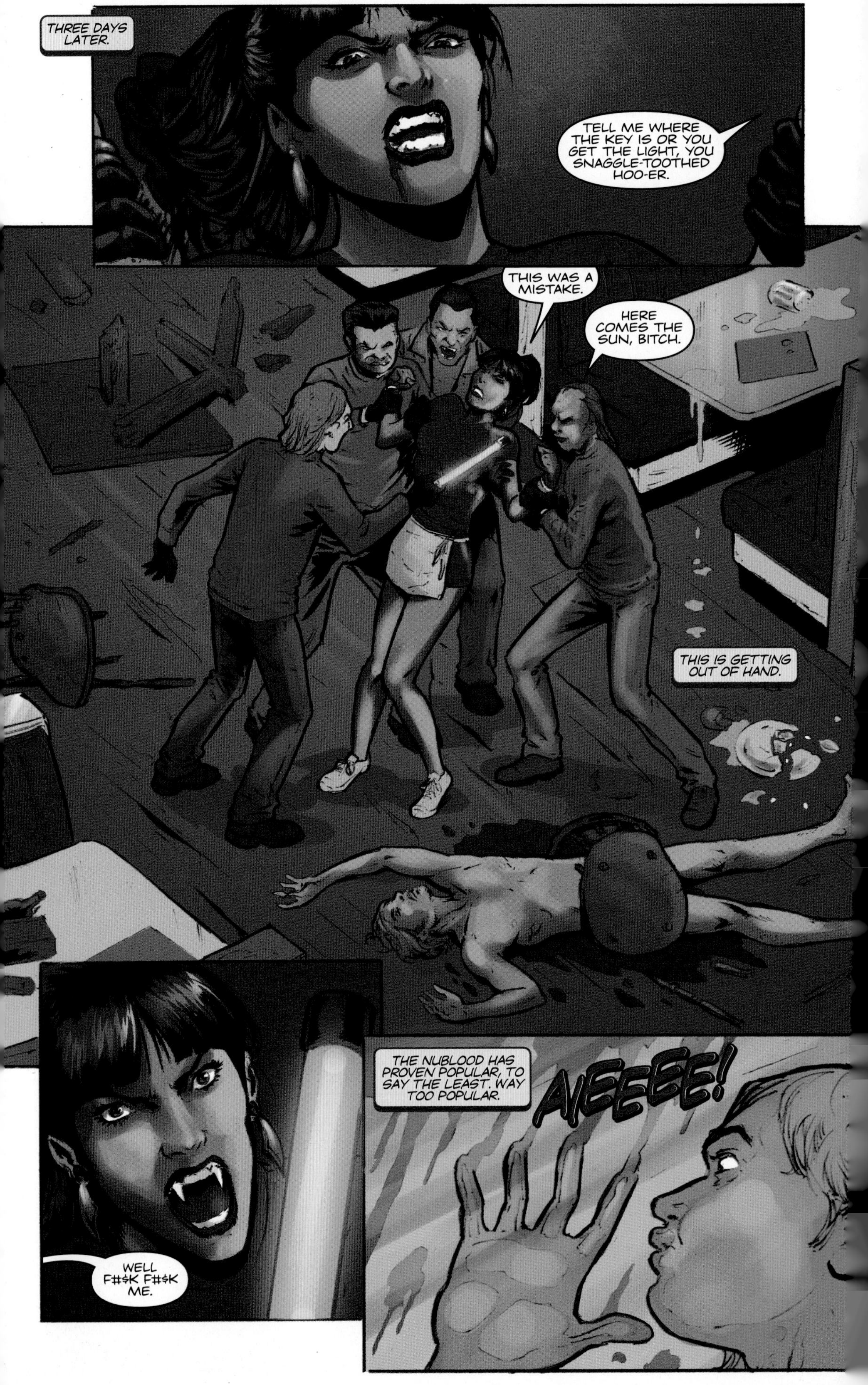
THREE DAYS LATER.
TELL ME WHERE THE KEY IS OR YOU GET THE LIGHT, YOU SNAGGLE-TOOTHED HOO-ER.
THIS WAS A MISTAKE.
HERE COMES THE SUN, BITCH.
THIS IS GETTING OUT OF HAND.
WELL F#$K F#$K ME.
THE NUBLOOD HAS PROVEN POPULAR, TO SAY THE LEAST. WAY TOO POPULAR.
AIEEEEE!

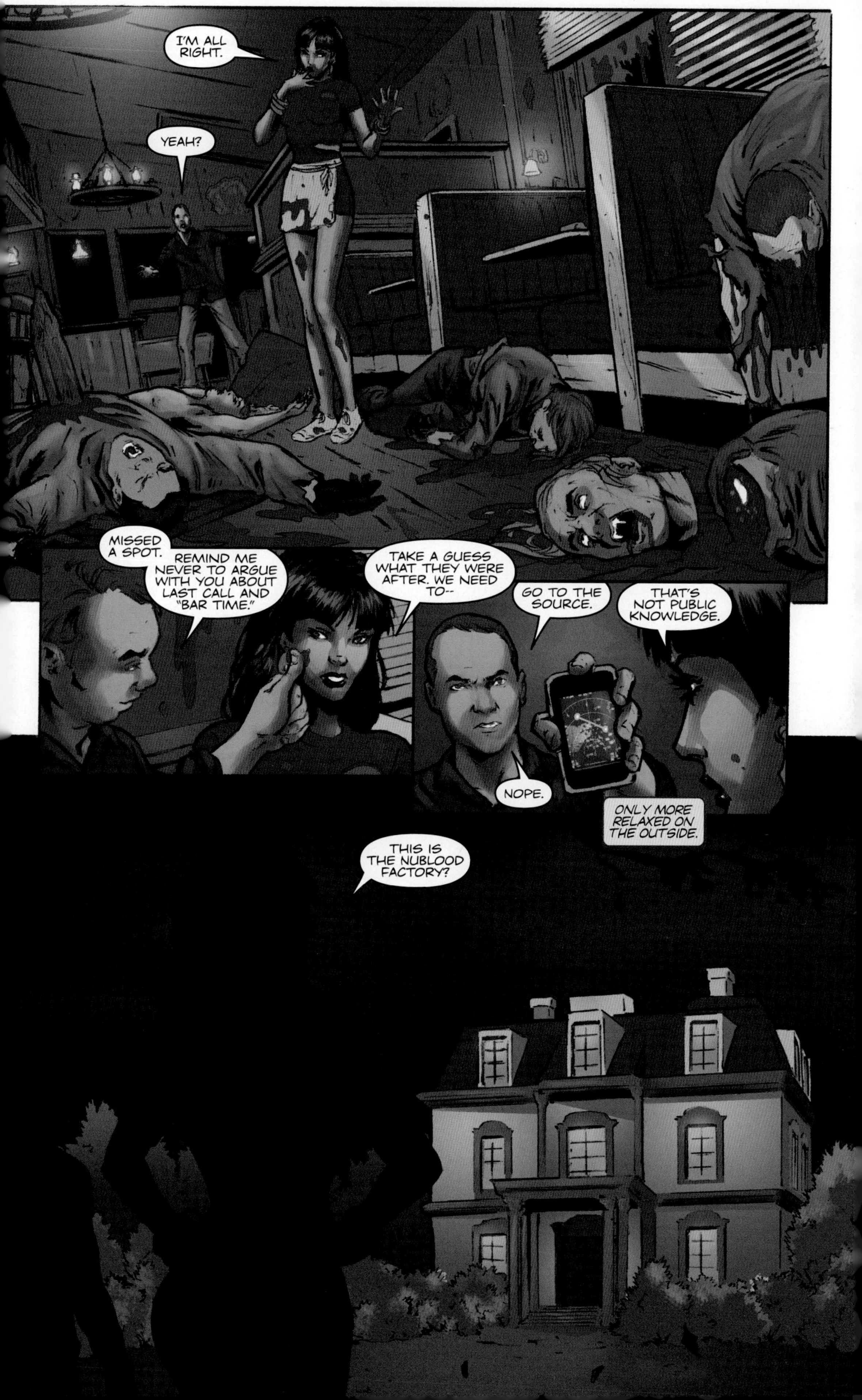
I'M ALL RIGHT.
YEAH?
MISSED A SPOT.
REMIND ME NEVER TO ARGUE WITH YOU ABOUT LAST CALL AND "BAR TIME."
TAKE A GUESS WHAT THEY WERE AFTER. WE NEED TO--
GO TO THE SOURCE.
THAT'S NOT PUBLIC KNOWLEDGE.
NOPE.
ONLY MORE RELAXED ON THE OUTSIDE.
THIS IS THE NUBLOOD FACTORY?

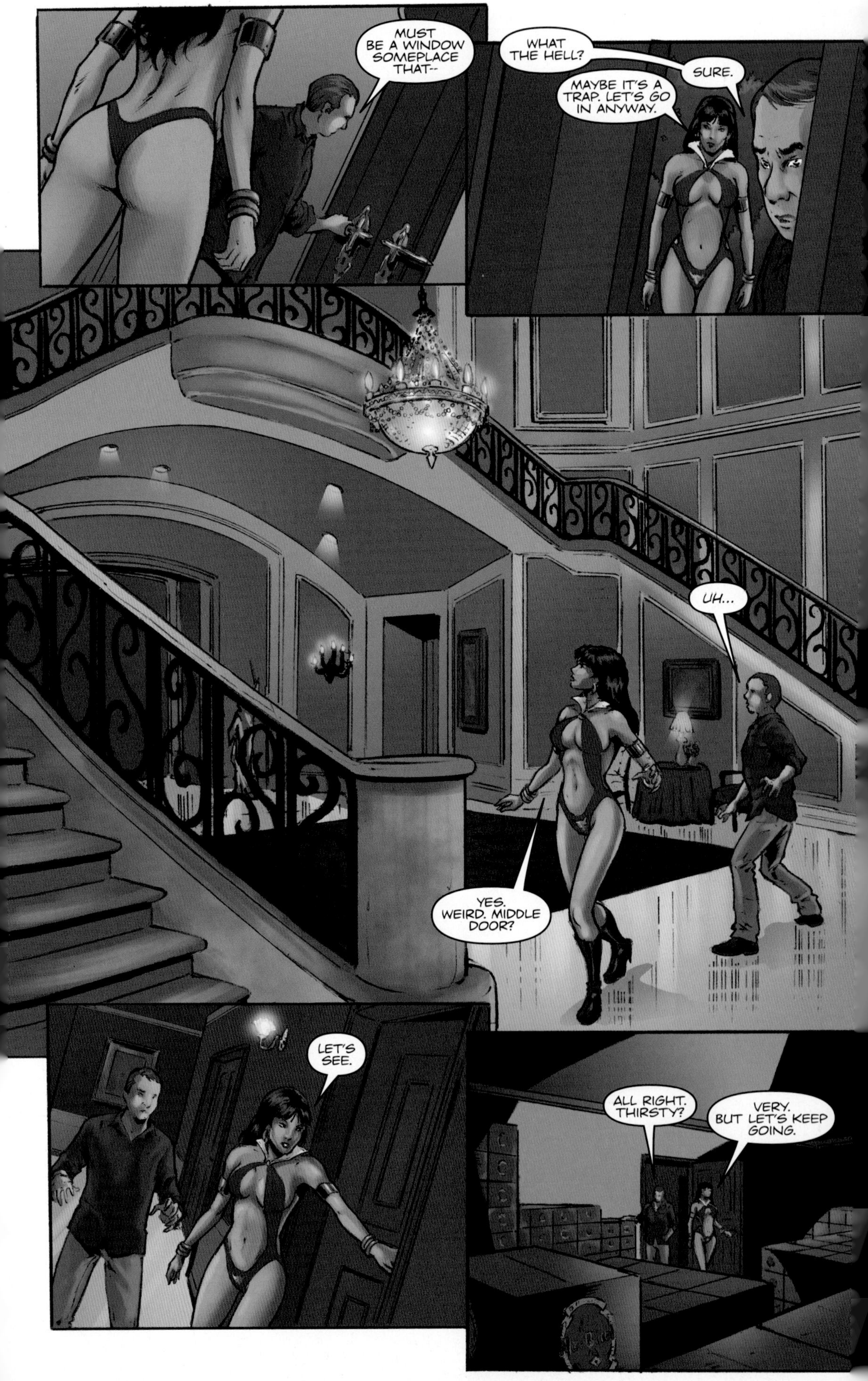
MUST BE A WINDOW SOMEPLACE THAT--
WHAT THE HELL?
MAYBE IT'S A TRAP. LET'S GO IN ANYWAY.
SURE.
UH...
YES. WEIRD. MIDDLE DOOR?
LET'S SEE.
ALL RIGHT. THIRSTY?
VERY. BUT LET'S KEEP GOING.

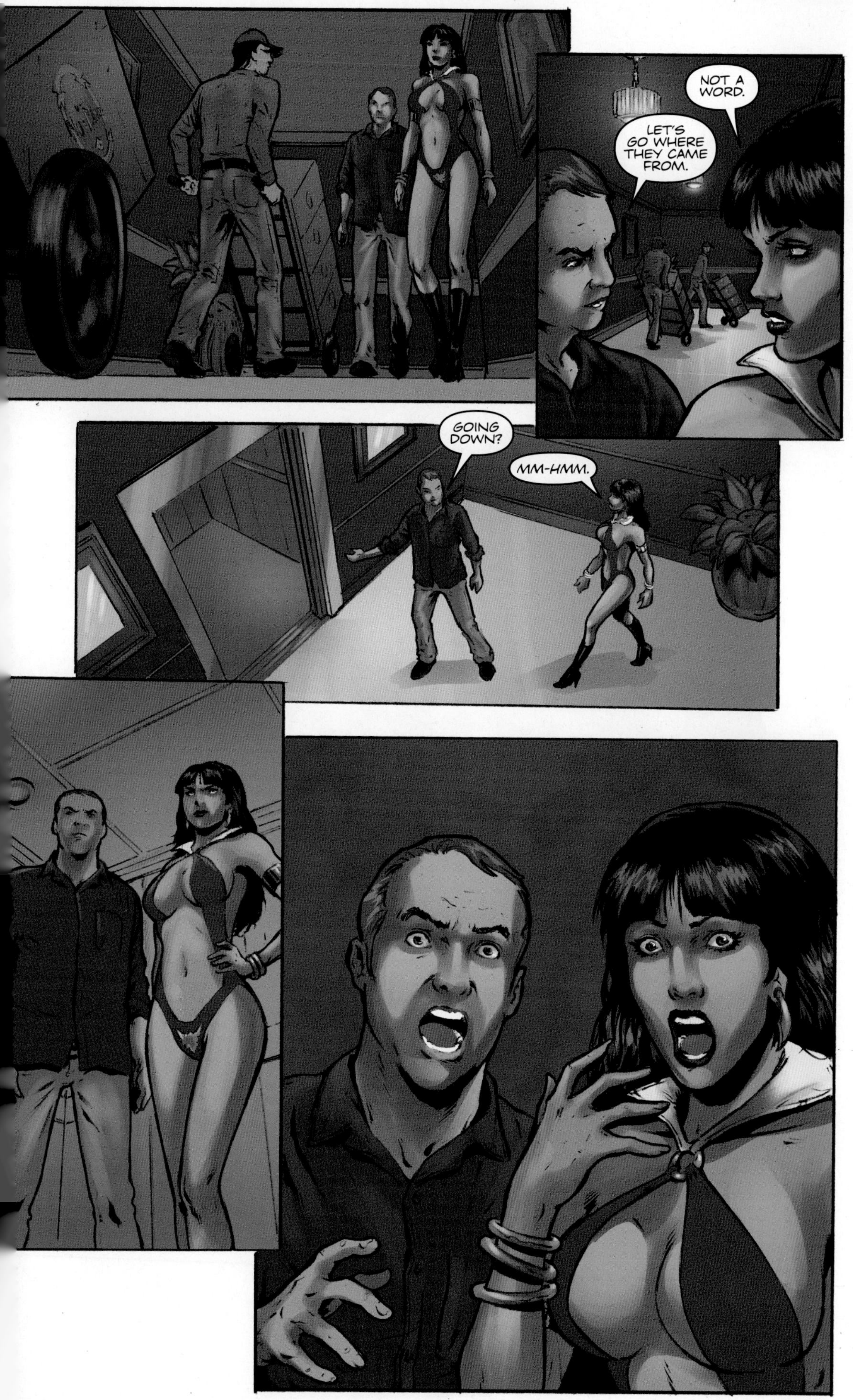
NOT A WORD.
LET'S GO WHERE THEY CAME FROM.
GOING DOWN?
MM-HMM.

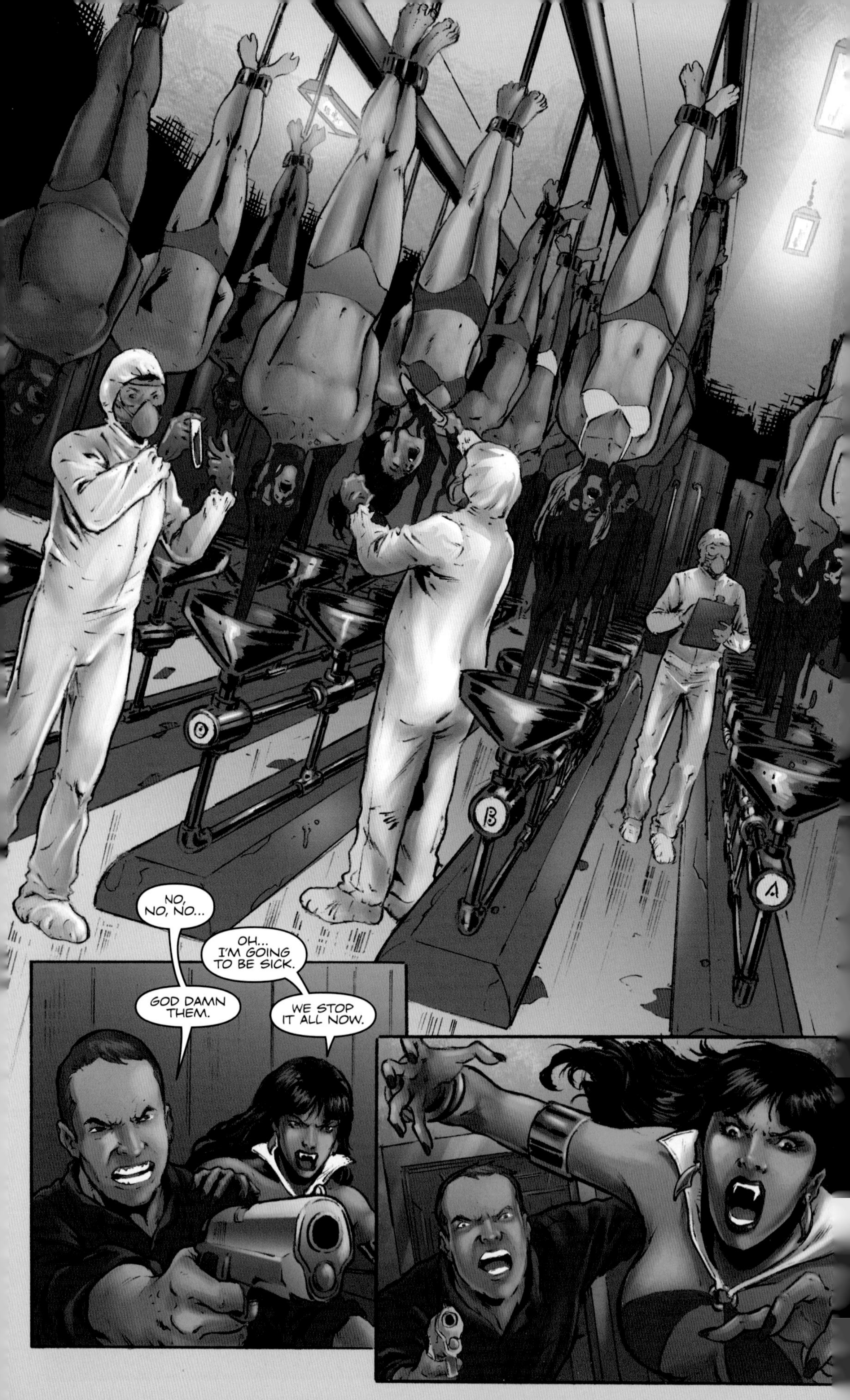
NO, NO, NO...
OH... I'M GOING TO BE SICK.
GOD DAMN THEM.
WE STOP IT ALL NOW.

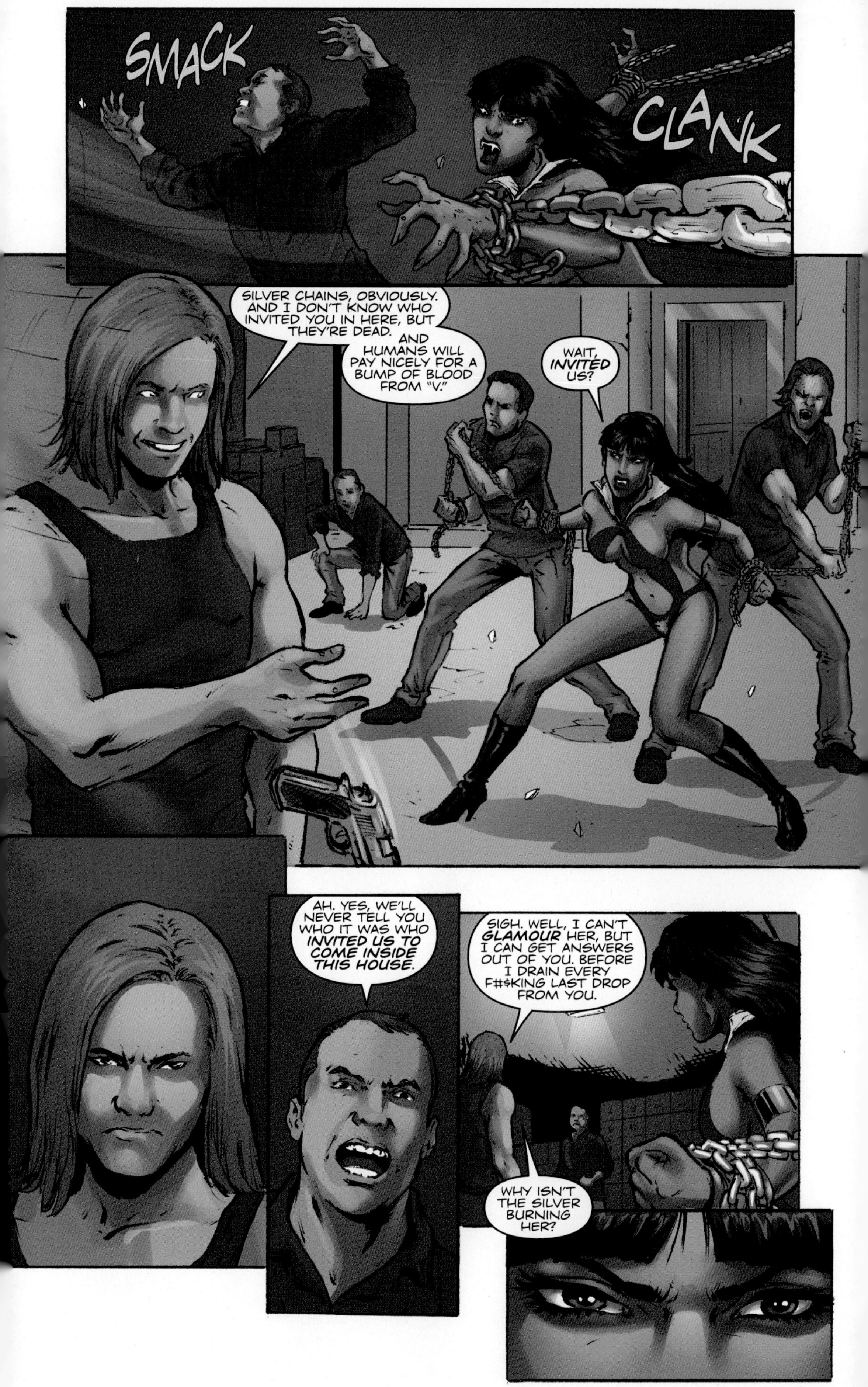
SMACK
CLANK
SILVER CHAINS, OBVIOUSLY. AND I DON'T KNOW WHO INVITED YOU IN HERE, BUT THEY'RE DEAD.
AND HUMANS WILL PAY NICELY FOR A BUMP OF BLOOD FROM "V."
WAIT, INVITED US?
AH. YES, WE'LL NEVER TELL YOU WHO IT WAS WHO INVITED US TO COME INSIDE THIS HOUSE.
SIGH. WELL, I CAN'T GLAMOUR HER, BUT I CAN GET ANSWERS OUT OF YOU. BEFORE I DRAIN EVERY F#$KING LAST DROP FROM YOU.
WHY ISN'T THE SILVER BURNING HER?

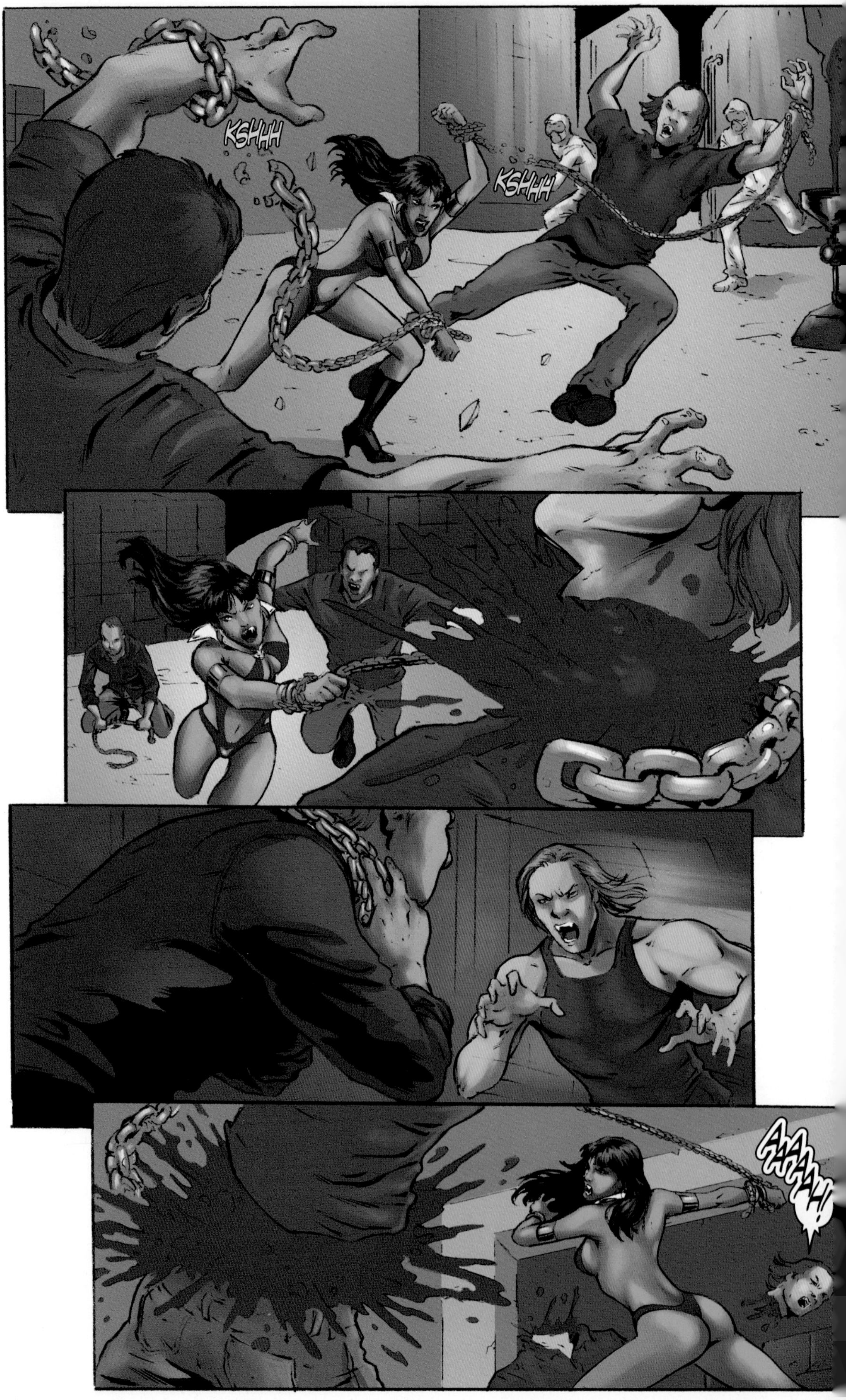
KSHHH
KSHHH
AAAAAAAH!

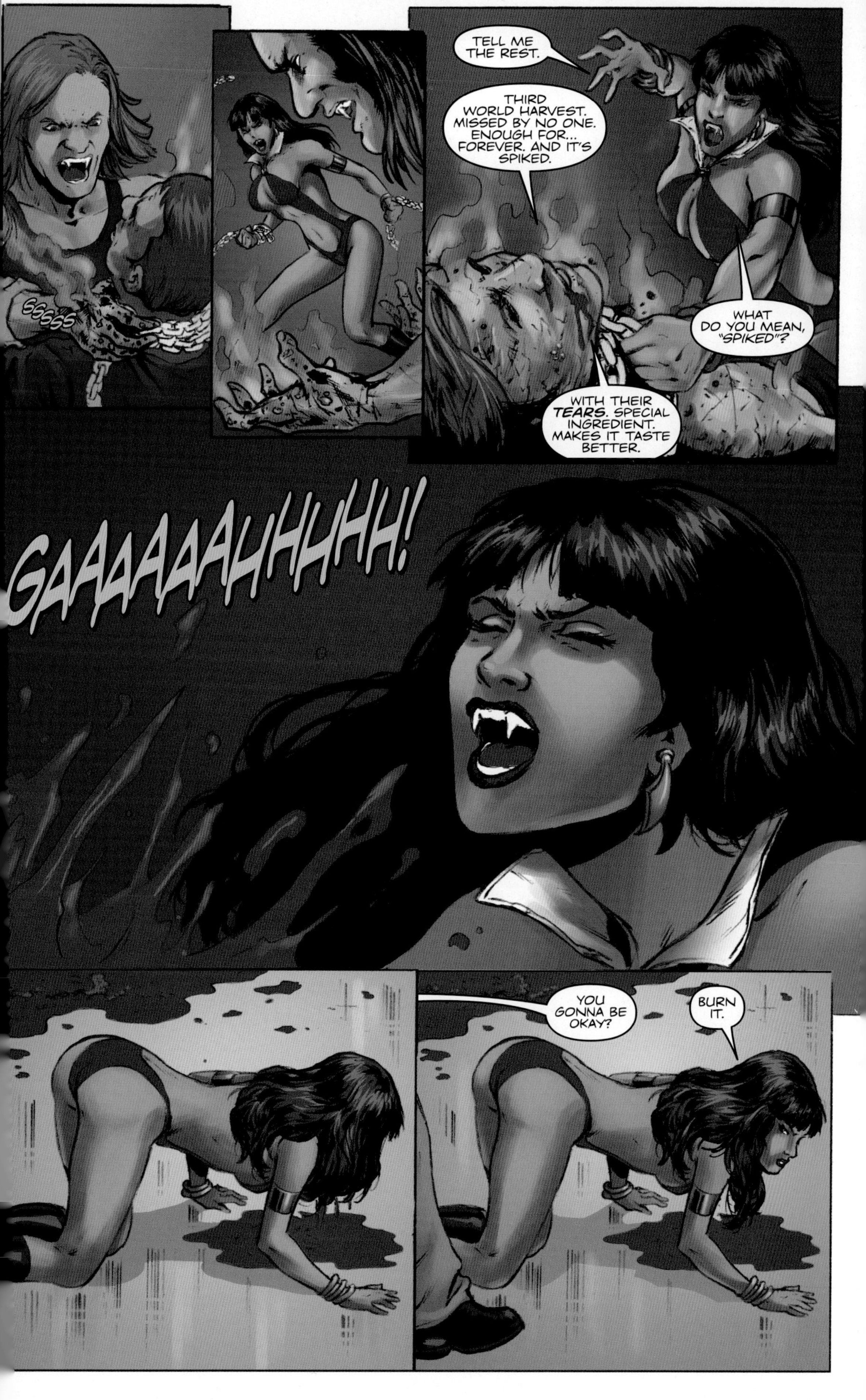
SSSSSS
TELL ME THE REST.
THIRD WORLD HARVEST. MISSED BY NO ONE. ENOUGH FOR... FOREVER. AND IT'S SPIKED.
WHAT DO YOU MEAN, "SPIKED"?
WITH THEIR TEARS. SPECIAL INGREDIENT. MAKES IT TASTE BETTER.
GAAAAAAHHHHH!
YOU GONNA BE OKAY?
BURN IT.

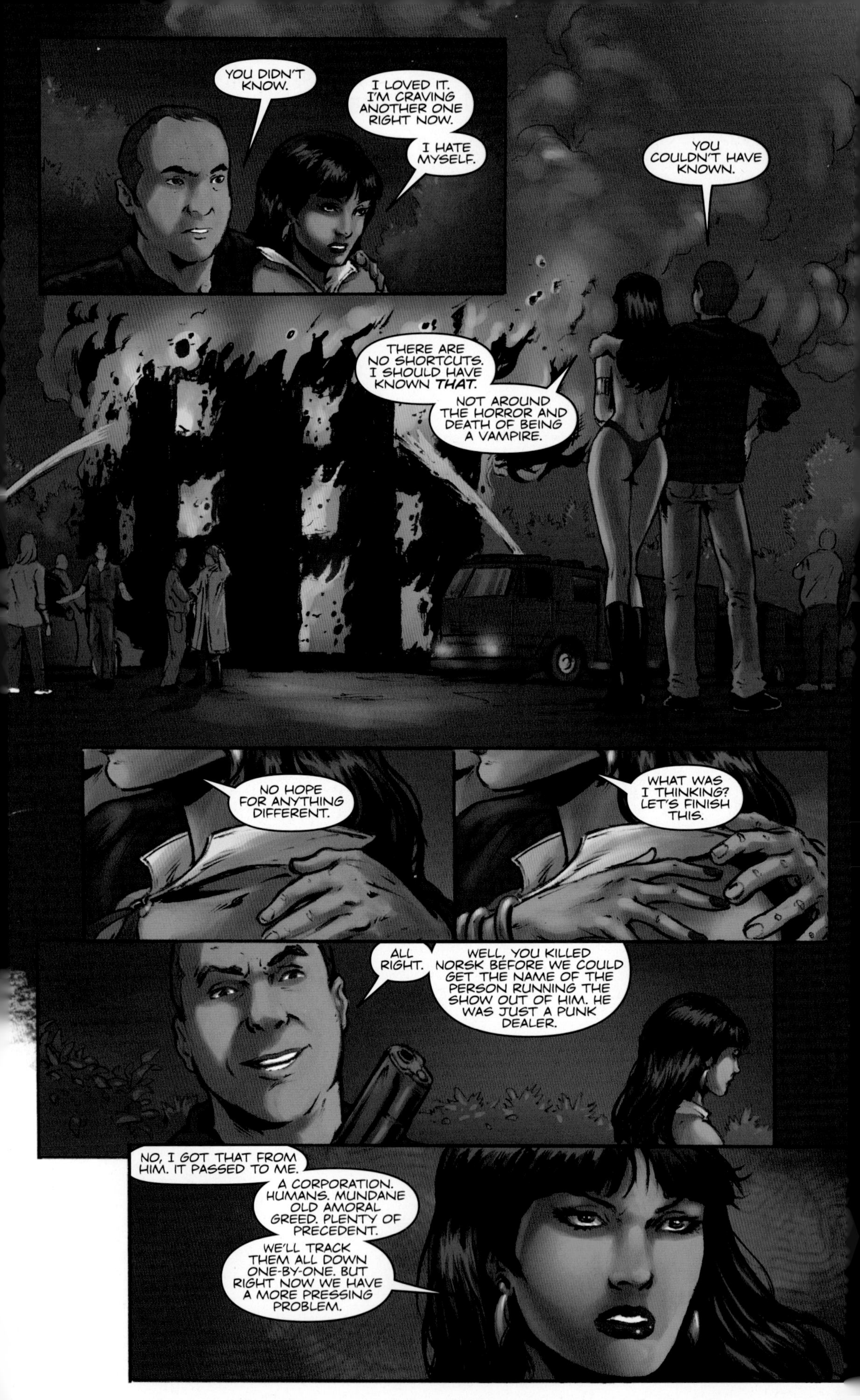
YOU DIDN'T KNOW.
I LOVED IT. I'M CRAVING ANOTHER ONE RIGHT NOW.
I HATE MYSELF.
YOU COULDN'T HAVE KNOWN.
THERE ARE NO SHORTCUTS. I SHOULD HAVE KNOWN *THAT*.
NOT AROUND THE HORROR AND DEATH OF BEING A VAMPIRE.
NO HOPE FOR ANYTHING DIFFERENT.
WHAT WAS I THINKING? LET'S FINISH THIS.
ALL RIGHT.
WELL, YOU KILLED NORSK BEFORE WE COULD GET THE NAME OF THE PERSON RUNNING THE SHOW OUT OF HIM. HE WAS JUST A PUNK DEALER.
NO, I GOT THAT FROM HIM. IT PASSED TO ME.
A CORPORATION. HUMANS. MUNDANE OLD AMORAL GREED. PLENTY OF PRECEDENT.
WE'LL TRACK THEM ALL DOWN ONE-BY-ONE. BUT RIGHT NOW WE HAVE A MORE PRESSING PROBLEM.

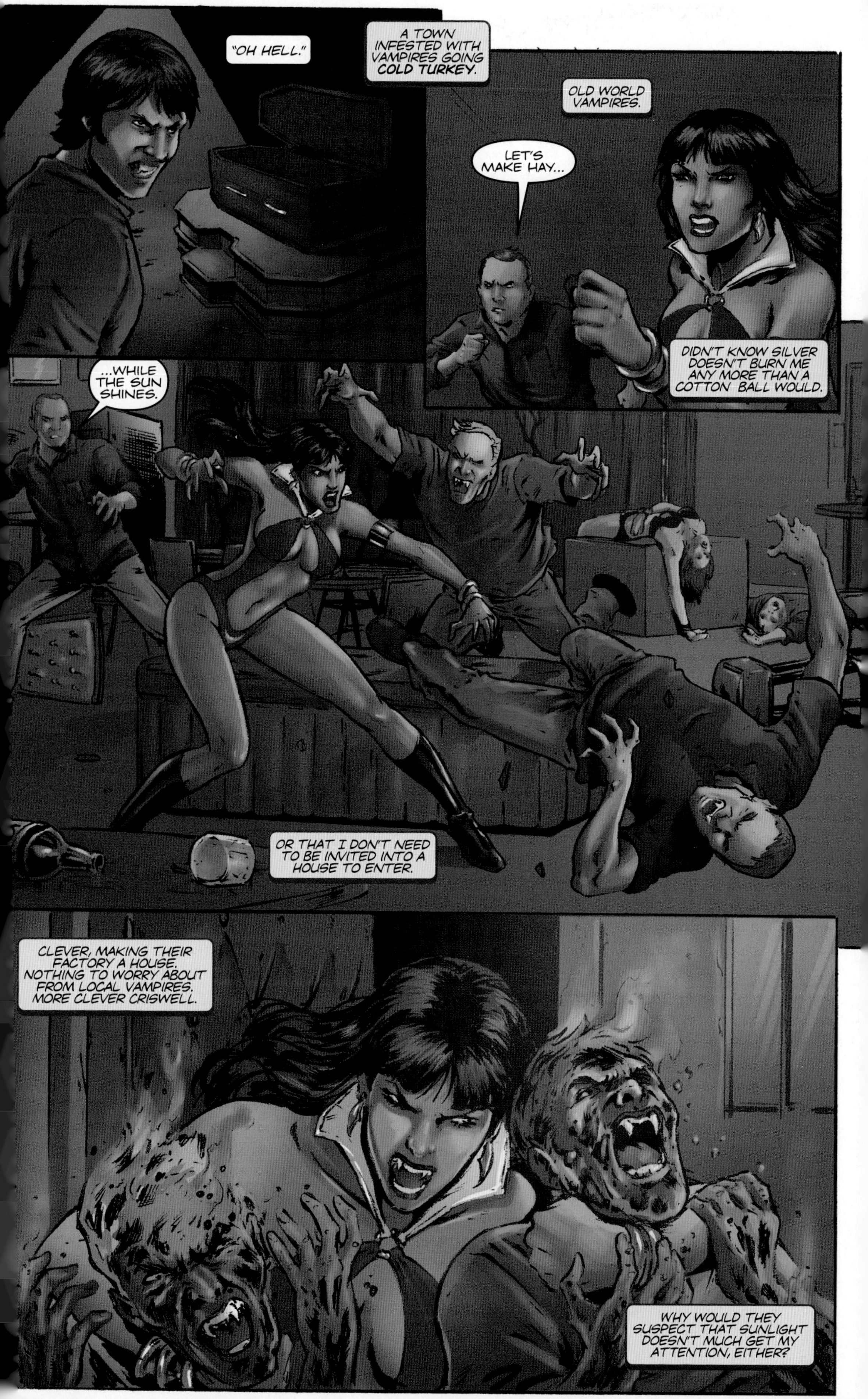
"OH HELL."
A TOWN INFESTED WITH VAMPIRES GOING COLD TURKEY.
OLD WORLD VAMPIRES.
LET'S MAKE HAY...
DIDN'T KNOW SILVER DOESN'T BURN ME ANY MORE THAN A COTTON BALL WOULD.
...WHILE THE SUN SHINES.
OR THAT I DON'T NEED TO BE INVITED INTO A HOUSE TO ENTER.
CLEVER, MAKING THEIR FACTORY A HOUSE. NOTHING TO WORRY ABOUT FROM LOCAL VAMPIRES. MORE CLEVER CRISWELL.
WHY WOULD THEY SUSPECT THAT SUNLIGHT DOESN'T MUCH GET MY ATTENTION, EITHER?

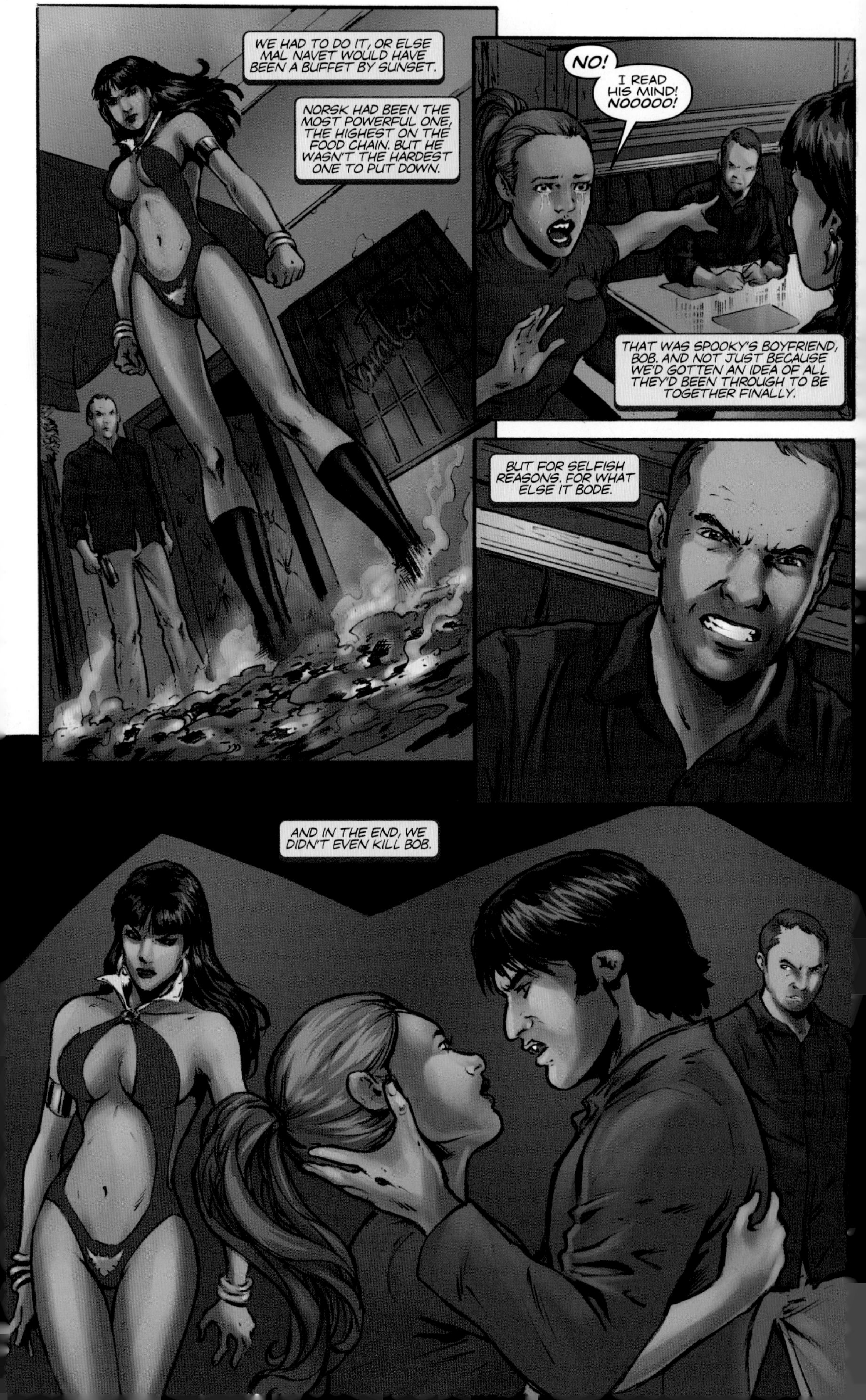
WE HAD TO DO IT, OR ELSE MAL NAVET WOULD HAVE BEEN A BUFFET BY SUNSET.
NORSK HAD BEEN THE MOST POWERFUL ONE, THE HIGHEST ON THE FOOD CHAIN. BUT HE WASN'T THE HARDEST ONE TO PUT DOWN.
NO!
I READ HIS MIND! NOOOOO!
THAT WAS SPOOKY'S BOYFRIEND, BOB. AND NOT JUST BECAUSE WE'D GOTTEN AN IDEA OF ALL THEY'D BEEN THROUGH TO BE TOGETHER FINALLY.
BUT FOR SELFISH REASONS. FOR WHAT ELSE IT BODE.
AND IN THE END, WE DIDN'T EVEN KILL BOB.

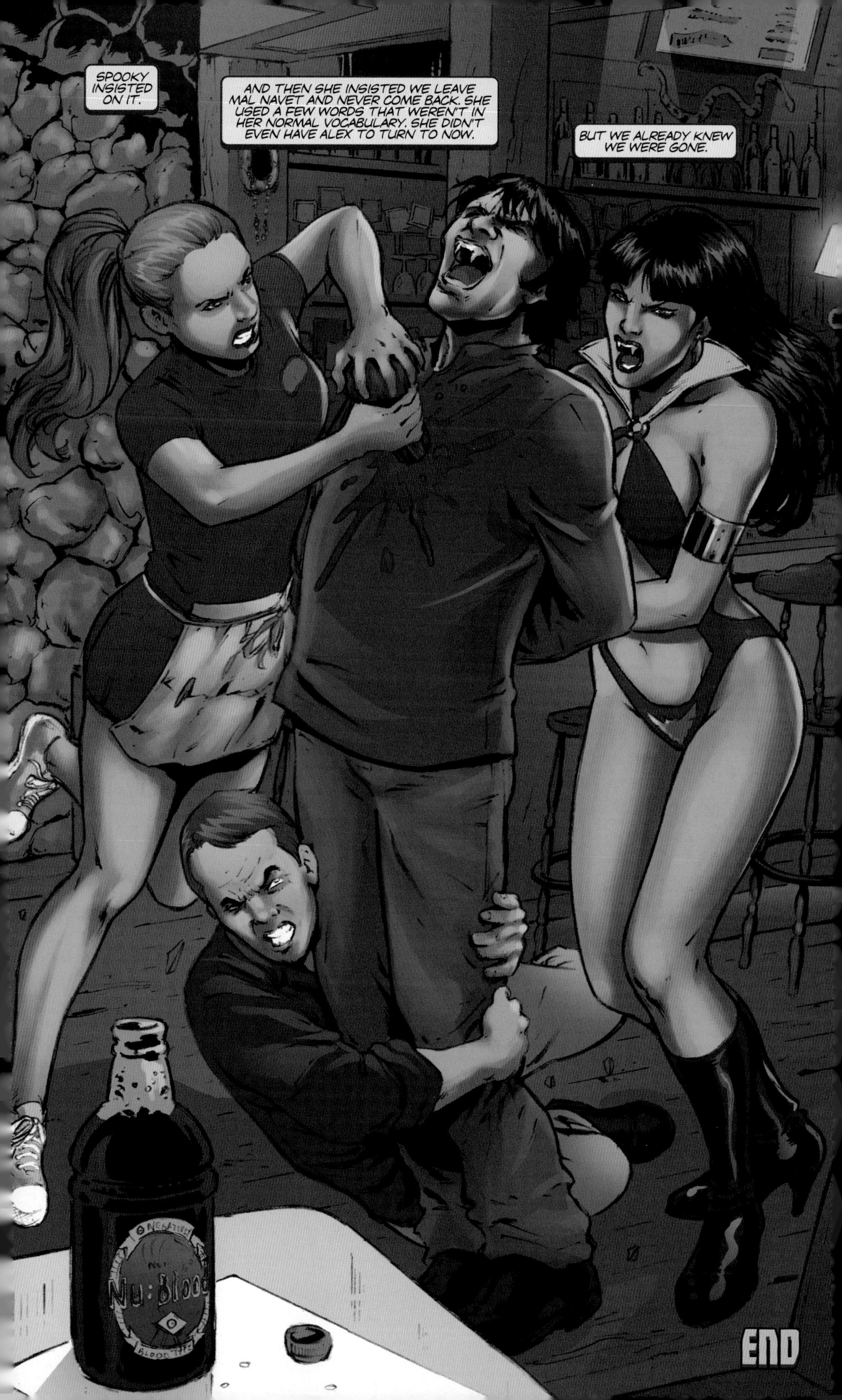
SPOOKY INSISTED ON IT.
AND THEN SHE INSISTED WE LEAVE MAL NAVET AND NEVER COME BACK. SHE USED A FEW WORDS THAT WEREN'T IN HER NORMAL VOCABULARY. SHE DIDN'T EVEN HAVE ALEX TO TURN TO NOW.
BUT WE ALREADY KNEW WE WERE GONE.
NEGATIVE
Nu:Blood
BLOOD TYPE
END

VAMPIRELLA ANNUAL 2013: VAMPI MEETS BAXTER

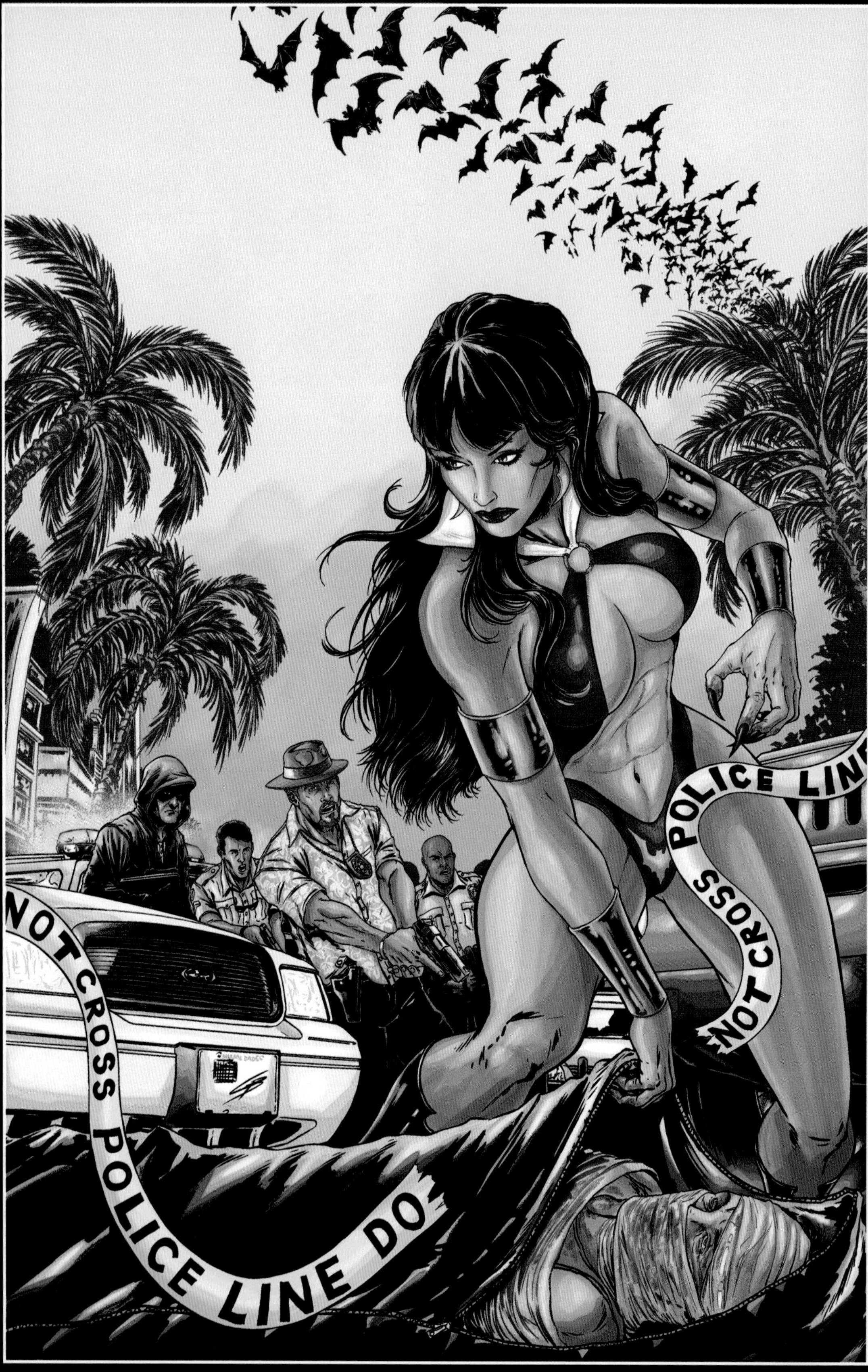
POLICE LINE DO NOT CROSS
NOT CROSS POLICE LINE DO

cover art by CHRIS BOLSON

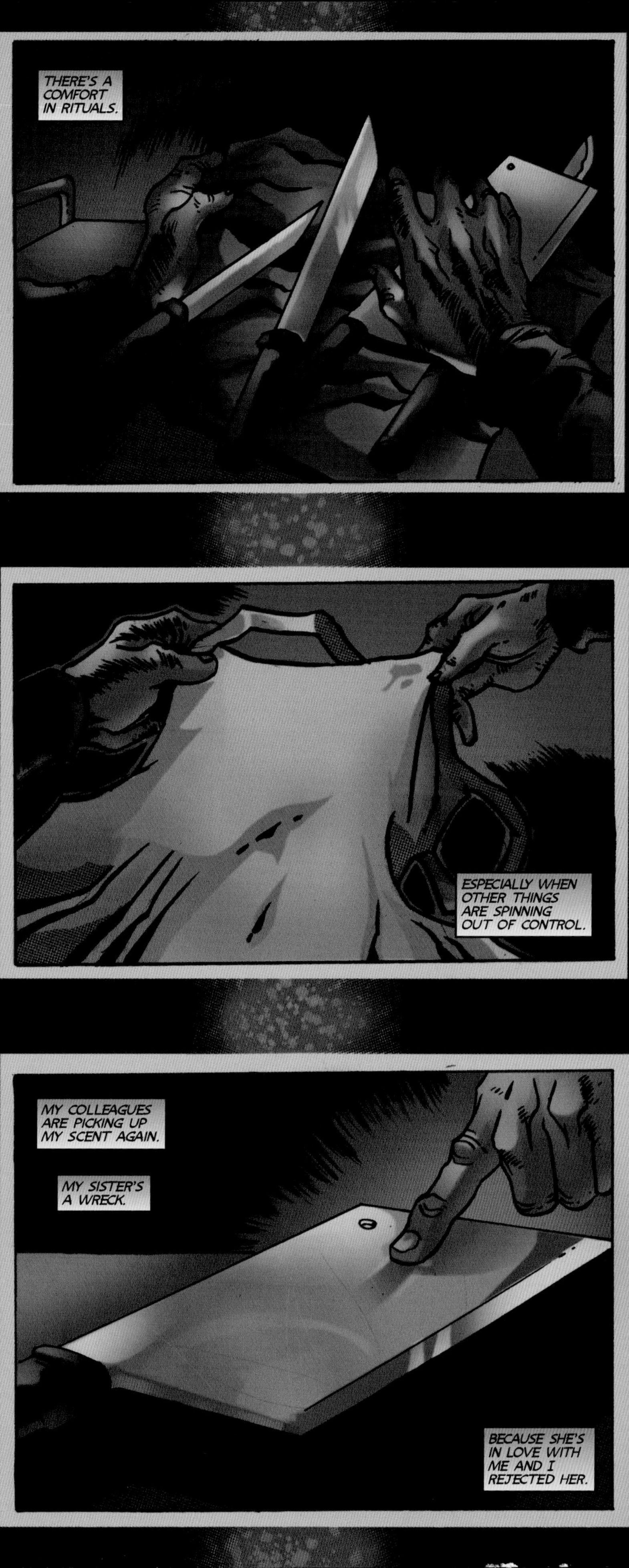
THERE'S A COMFORT IN RITUALS.
ESPECIALLY WHEN OTHER THINGS ARE SPINNING OUT OF CONTROL.
MY COLLEAGUES ARE PICKING UP MY SCENT AGAIN.
MY SISTER'S A WRECK.
BECAUSE SHE'S IN LOVE WITH ME AND I REJECTED HER.

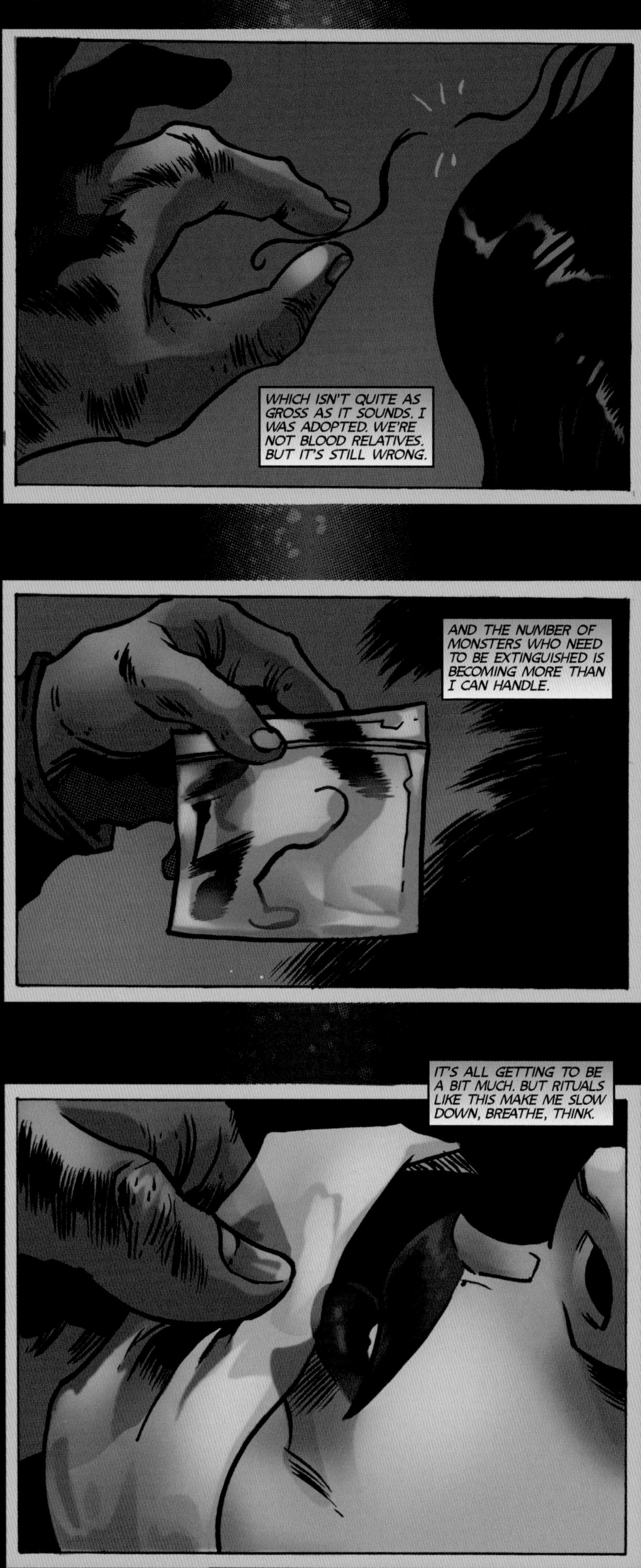
WHICH ISN'T QUITE AS GROSS AS IT SOUNDS. I WAS ADOPTED. WE'RE NOT BLOOD RELATIVES. BUT IT'S STILL WRONG.
AND THE NUMBER OF MONSTERS WHO NEED TO BE EXTINGUISHED IS BECOMING MORE THAN I CAN HANDLE.
IT'S ALL GETTING TO BE A BIT MUCH. BUT RITUALS LIKE THIS MAKE ME SLOW DOWN, BREATHE, THINK.

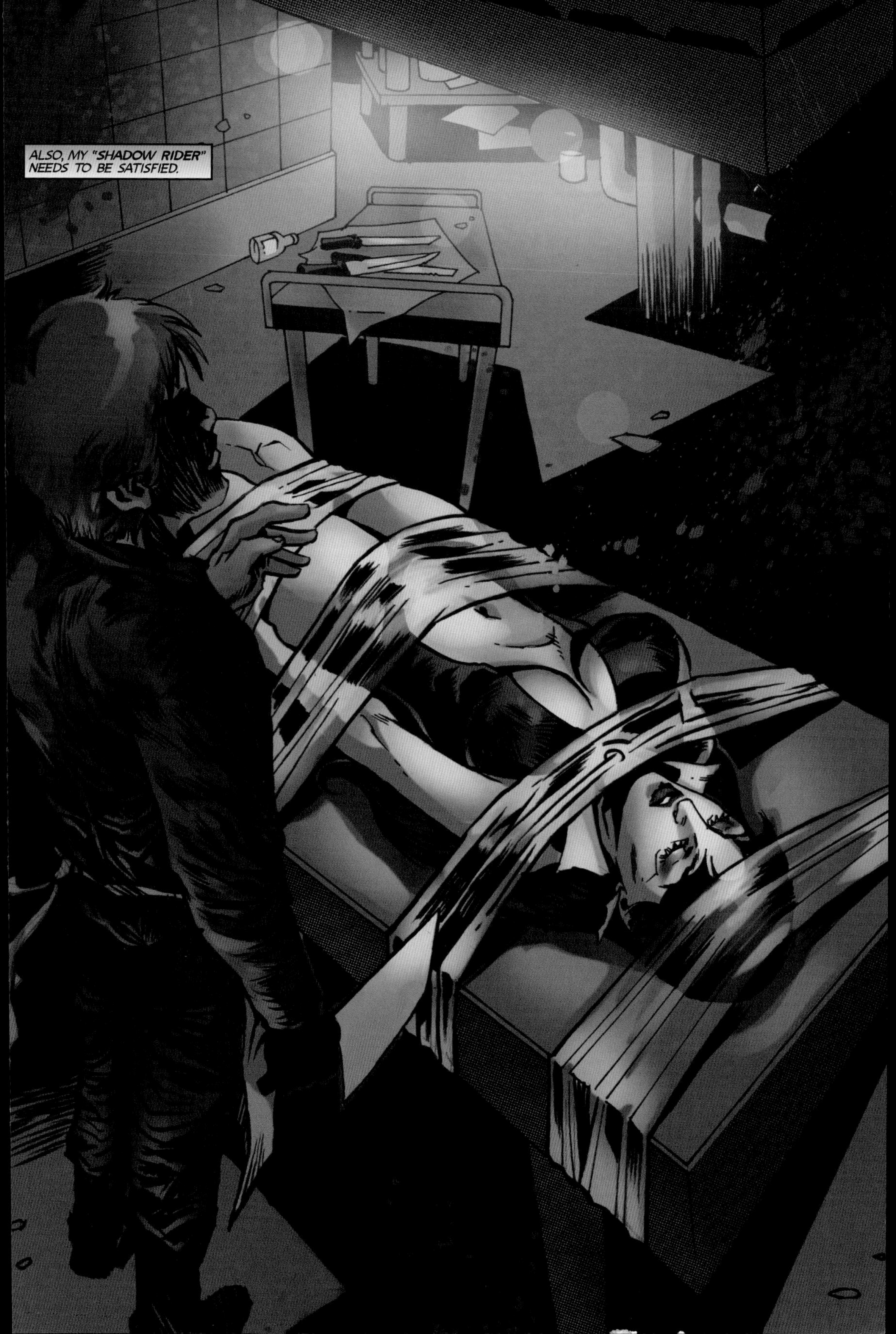
ALSO, MY "SHADOW RIDER" NEEDS TO BE SATISFIED.

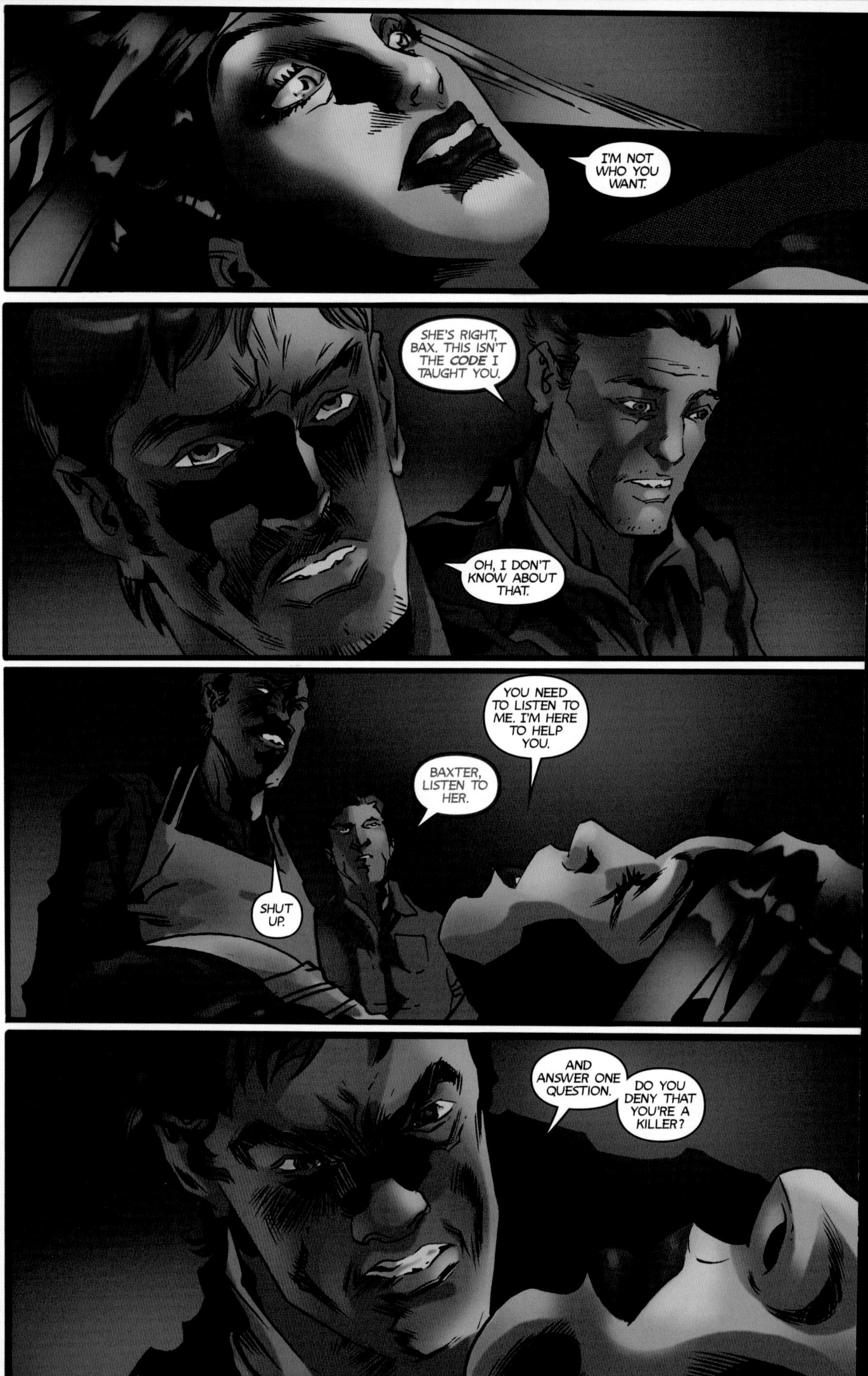
I'M NOT WHO YOU WANT.
SHE'S RIGHT, BAX. THIS ISN'T THE CODE I TAUGHT YOU.
OH, I DON'T KNOW ABOUT THAT.
YOU NEED TO LISTEN TO ME. I'M HERE TO HELP YOU.
BAXTER, LISTEN TO HER.
SHUT UP.
AND ANSWER ONE QUESTION.
DO YOU DENY THAT YOU'RE A KILLER?

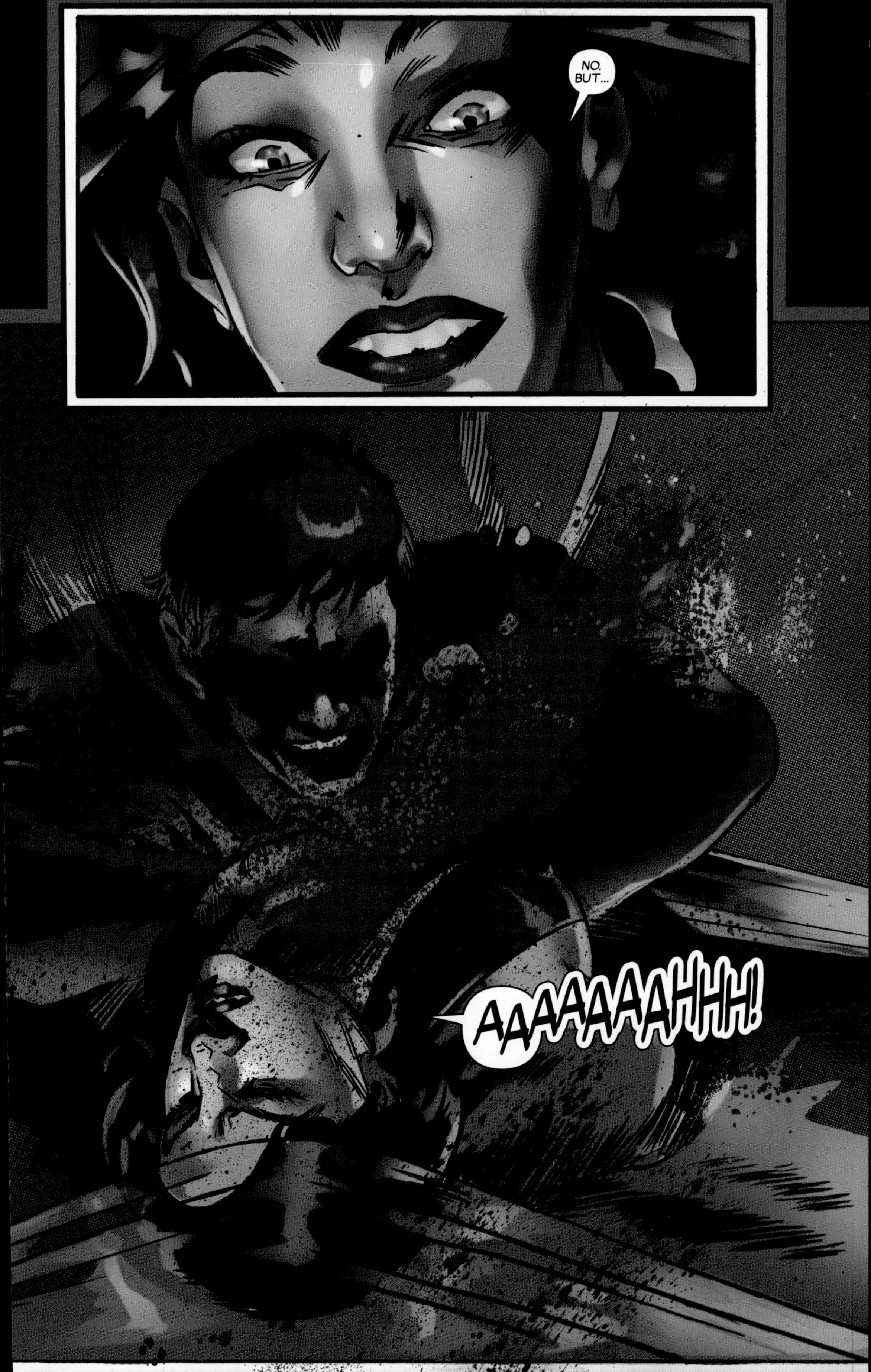
NO. BUT...
AAAAAAAHHH!

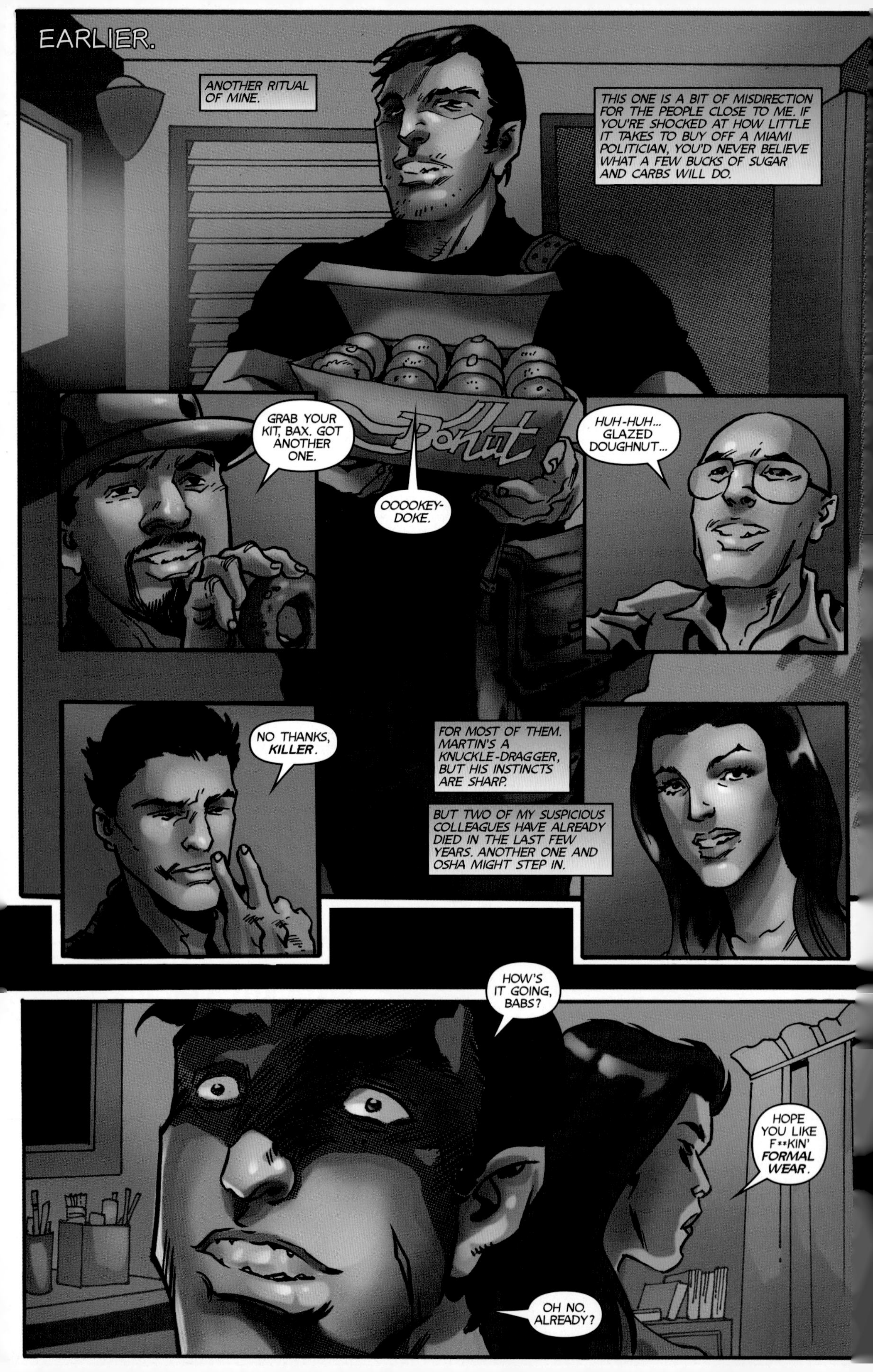
EARLIER.
ANOTHER RITUAL OF MINE.
THIS ONE IS A BIT OF MISDIRECTION FOR THE PEOPLE CLOSE TO ME. IF YOU'RE SHOCKED AT HOW LITTLE IT TAKES TO BUY OFF A MIAMI POLITICIAN, YOU'D NEVER BELIEVE WHAT A FEW BUCKS OF SUGAR AND CARBS WILL DO.
GRAB YOUR KIT, BAX. GOT ANOTHER ONE.
Donut
OOOOKEY-DOKE.
HUH-HUH... GLAZED DOUGHNUT...
NO THANKS, KILLER.
FOR MOST OF THEM. MARTIN'S A KNUCKLE-DRAGGER, BUT HIS INSTINCTS ARE SHARP.
BUT TWO OF MY SUSPICIOUS COLLEAGUES HAVE ALREADY DIED IN THE LAST FEW YEARS. ANOTHER ONE AND OSHA MIGHT STEP IN.
HOW'S IT GOING, BABS?
HOPE YOU LIKE F**KIN' FORMAL WEAR.
OH NO. ALREADY?

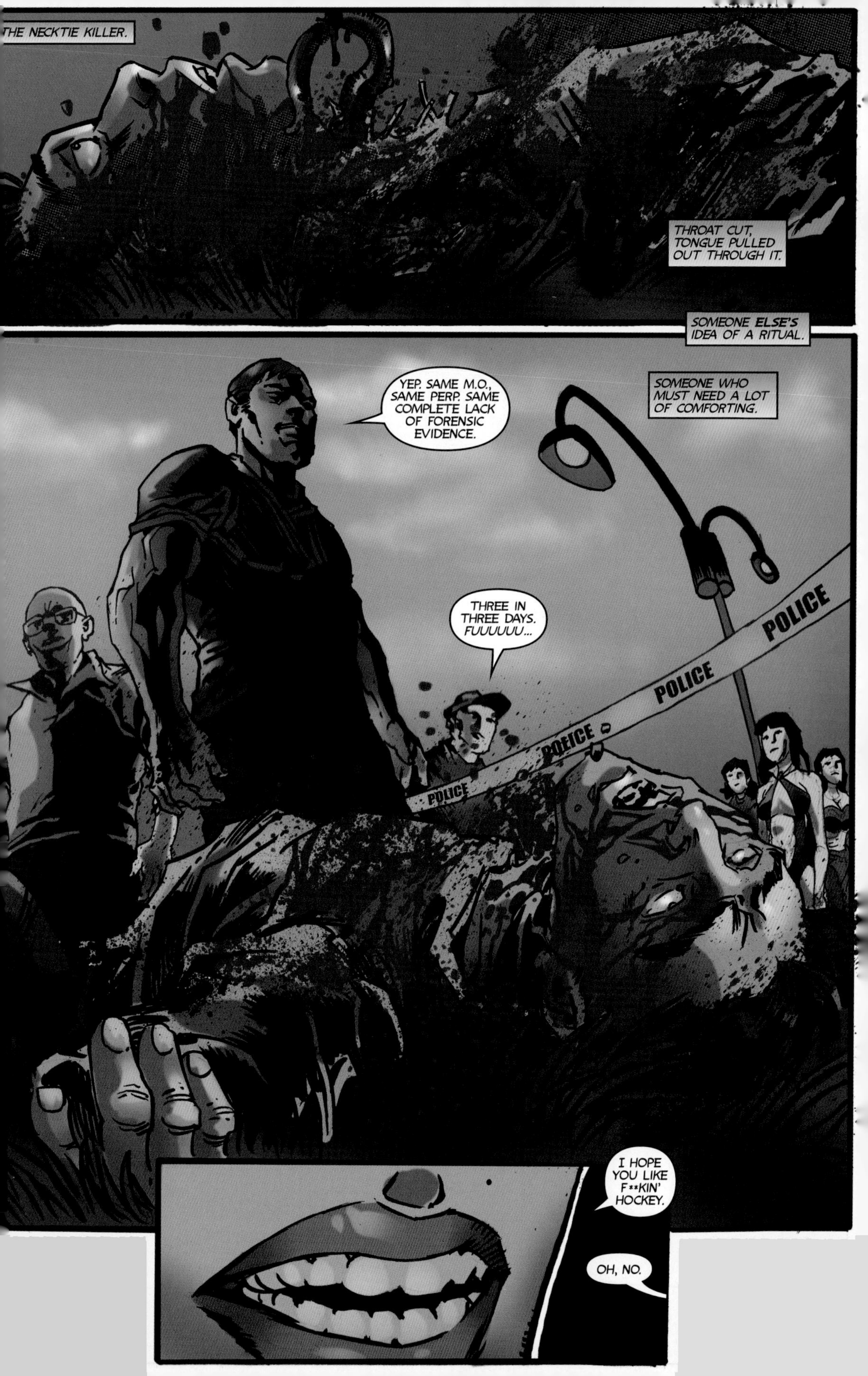
THE NECKTIE KILLER.
THROAT CUT, TONGUE PULLED OUT THROUGH IT.
SOMEONE ELSE'S IDEA OF A RITUAL.
YEP. SAME M.O., SAME PERP. SAME COMPLETE LACK OF FORENSIC EVIDENCE.
SOMEONE WHO MUST NEED A LOT OF COMFORTING.
THREE IN THREE DAYS. FUUUUUU...
POLICE
POLICE
POLICE
POLICE
I HOPE YOU LIKE F**KIN' HOCKEY.
OH, NO.

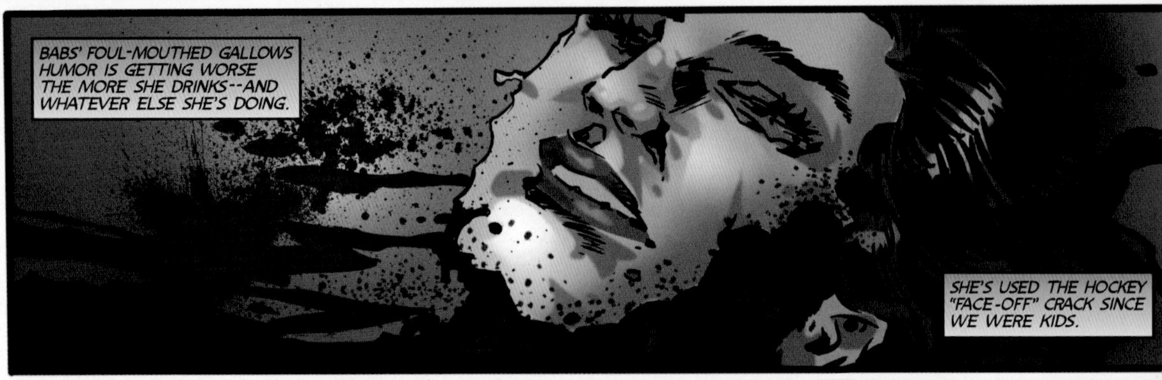
BABS' FOUL-MOUTHED GALLOWS HUMOR IS GETTING WORSE THE MORE SHE DRINKS--AND WHATEVER ELSE SHE'S DOING.
SHE'S USED THE HOCKEY "FACE-OFF" CRACK SINCE WE WERE KIDS.

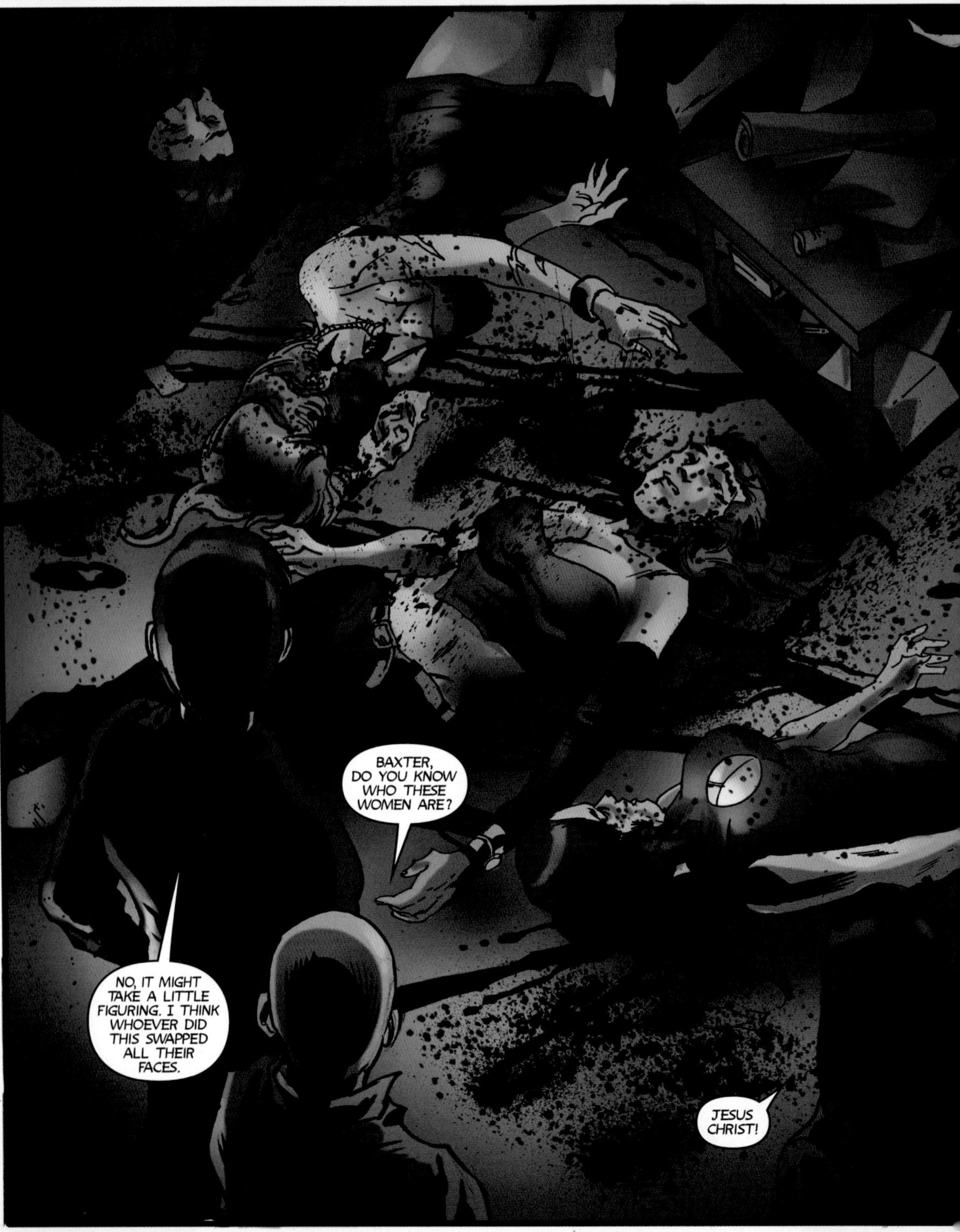
BAXTER, DO YOU KNOW WHO THESE WOMEN ARE?
NO, IT MIGHT TAKE A LITTLE FIGURING. I THINK WHOEVER DID THIS SWAPPED ALL THEIR FACES.
JESUS CHRIST!

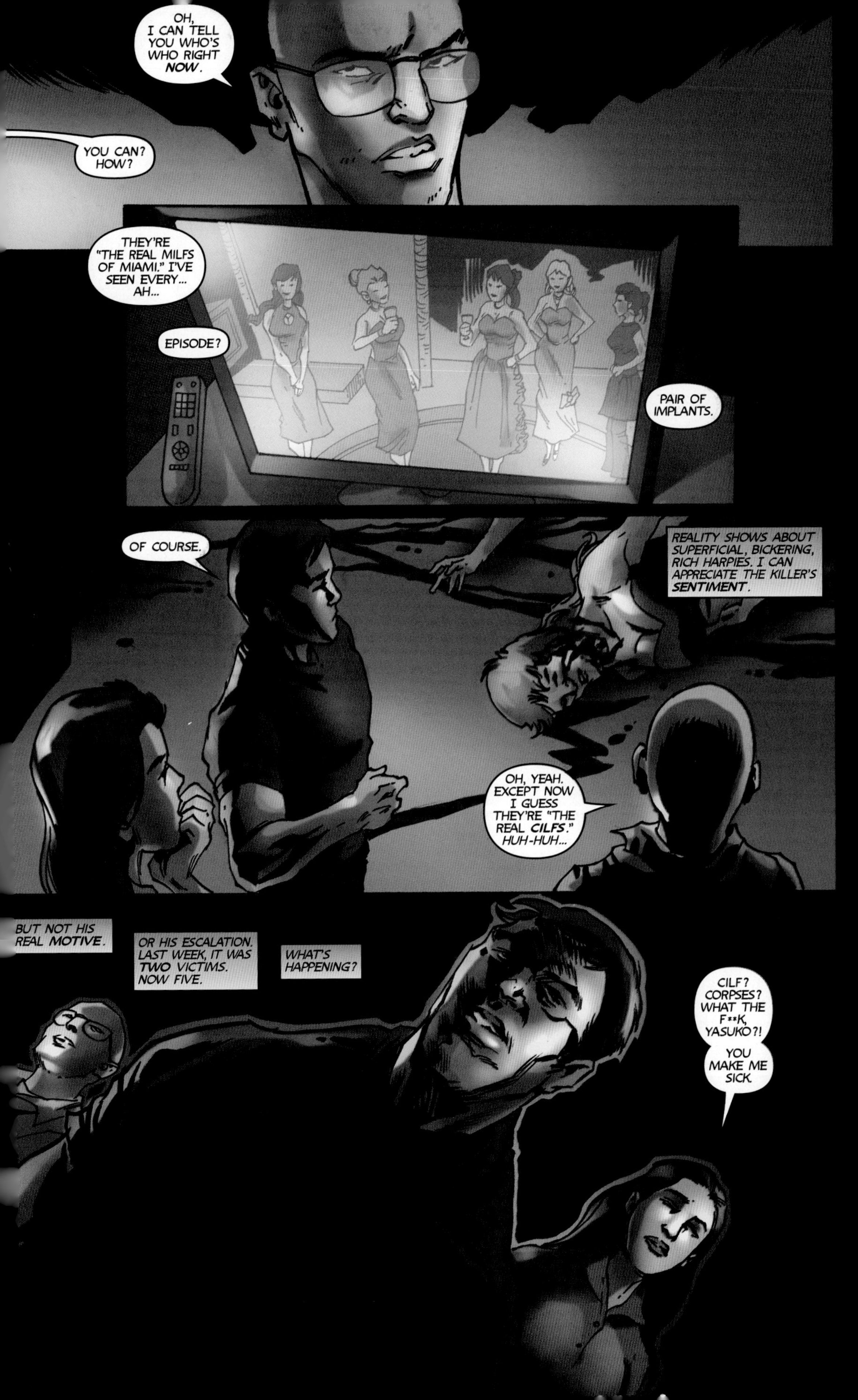
OH, I CAN TELL YOU WHO'S WHO RIGHT NOW.
YOU CAN? HOW?
THEY'RE "THE REAL MILFS OF MIAMI." I'VE SEEN EVERY... AH...
EPISODE?
PAIR OF IMPLANTS.
OF COURSE.
REALITY SHOWS ABOUT SUPERFICIAL, BICKERING, RICH HARPIES. I CAN APPRECIATE THE KILLER'S SENTIMENT.
OH, YEAH. EXCEPT NOW I GUESS THEY'RE "THE REAL CILFS." HUH-HUH...
BUT NOT HIS REAL MOTIVE.
OR HIS ESCALATION. LAST WEEK, IT WAS TWO VICTIMS. NOW FIVE.
WHAT'S HAPPENING?
CILF? CORPSES? WHAT THE F**K, YASUKO?!
YOU MAKE ME SICK.

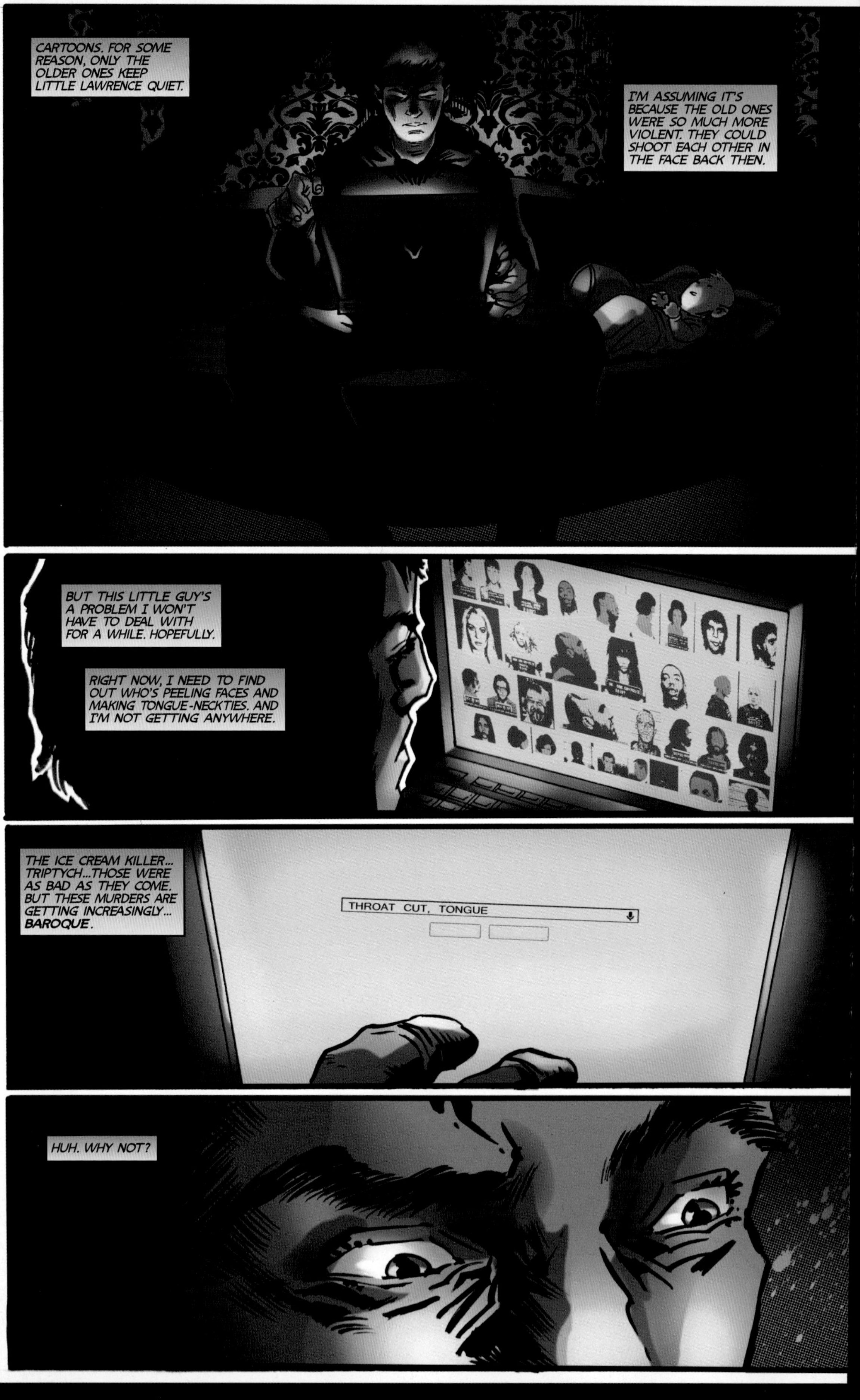
CARTOONS. FOR SOME REASON, ONLY THE OLDER ONES KEEP LITTLE LAWRENCE QUIET.
I'M ASSUMING IT'S BECAUSE THE OLD ONES WERE SO MUCH MORE VIOLENT. THEY COULD SHOOT EACH OTHER IN THE FACE BACK THEN.
BUT THIS LITTLE GUY'S A PROBLEM I WON'T HAVE TO DEAL WITH FOR A WHILE. HOPEFULLY.
RIGHT NOW, I NEED TO FIND OUT WHO'S PEELING FACES AND MAKING TONGUE-NECKTIES. AND I'M NOT GETTING ANYWHERE.
THE ICE CREAM KILLER... TRIPTYCH...THOSE WERE AS BAD AS THEY COME. BUT THESE MURDERS ARE GETTING INCREASINGLY... **BAROQUE**.
THROAT CUT, TONGUE
HUH. WHY NOT?

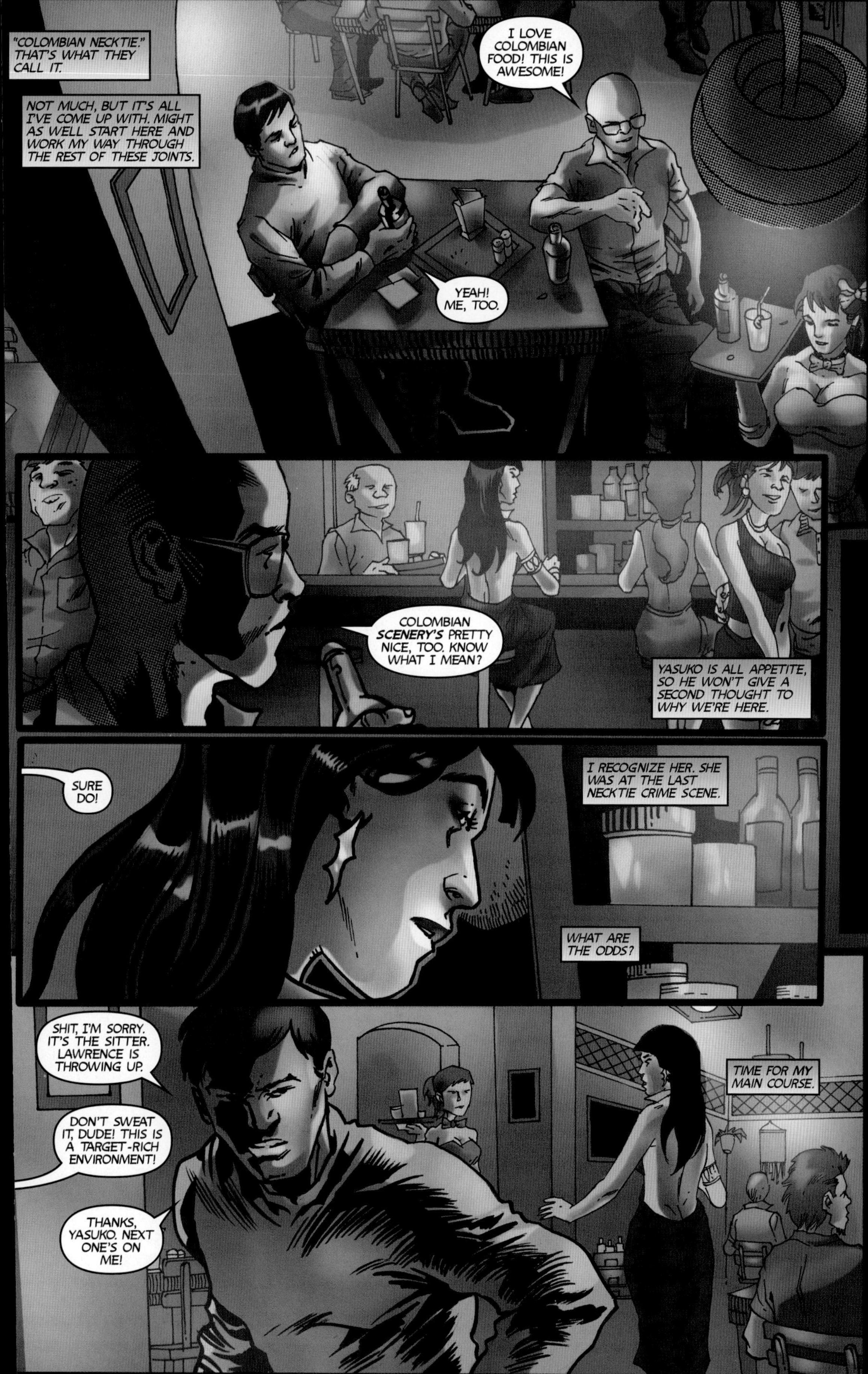
"COLOMBIAN NECKTIE." THAT'S WHAT THEY CALL IT.
NOT MUCH, BUT IT'S ALL I'VE COME UP WITH. MIGHT AS WELL START HERE AND WORK MY WAY THROUGH THE REST OF THESE JOINTS.
I LOVE COLOMBIAN FOOD! THIS IS AWESOME!
YEAH! ME, TOO.
COLOMBIAN SCENERY'S PRETTY NICE, TOO. KNOW WHAT I MEAN?
YASUKO IS ALL APPETITE, SO HE WON'T GIVE A SECOND THOUGHT TO WHY WE'RE HERE.
SURE DO!
I RECOGNIZE HER. SHE WAS AT THE LAST NECKTIE CRIME SCENE.
WHAT ARE THE ODDS?
SHIT, I'M SORRY. IT'S THE SITTER. LAWRENCE IS THROWING UP.
DON'T SWEAT IT, DUDE! THIS IS A TARGET-RICH ENVIRONMENT!
THANKS, YASUKO. NEXT ONE'S ON ME!
TIME FOR MY MAIN COURSE.

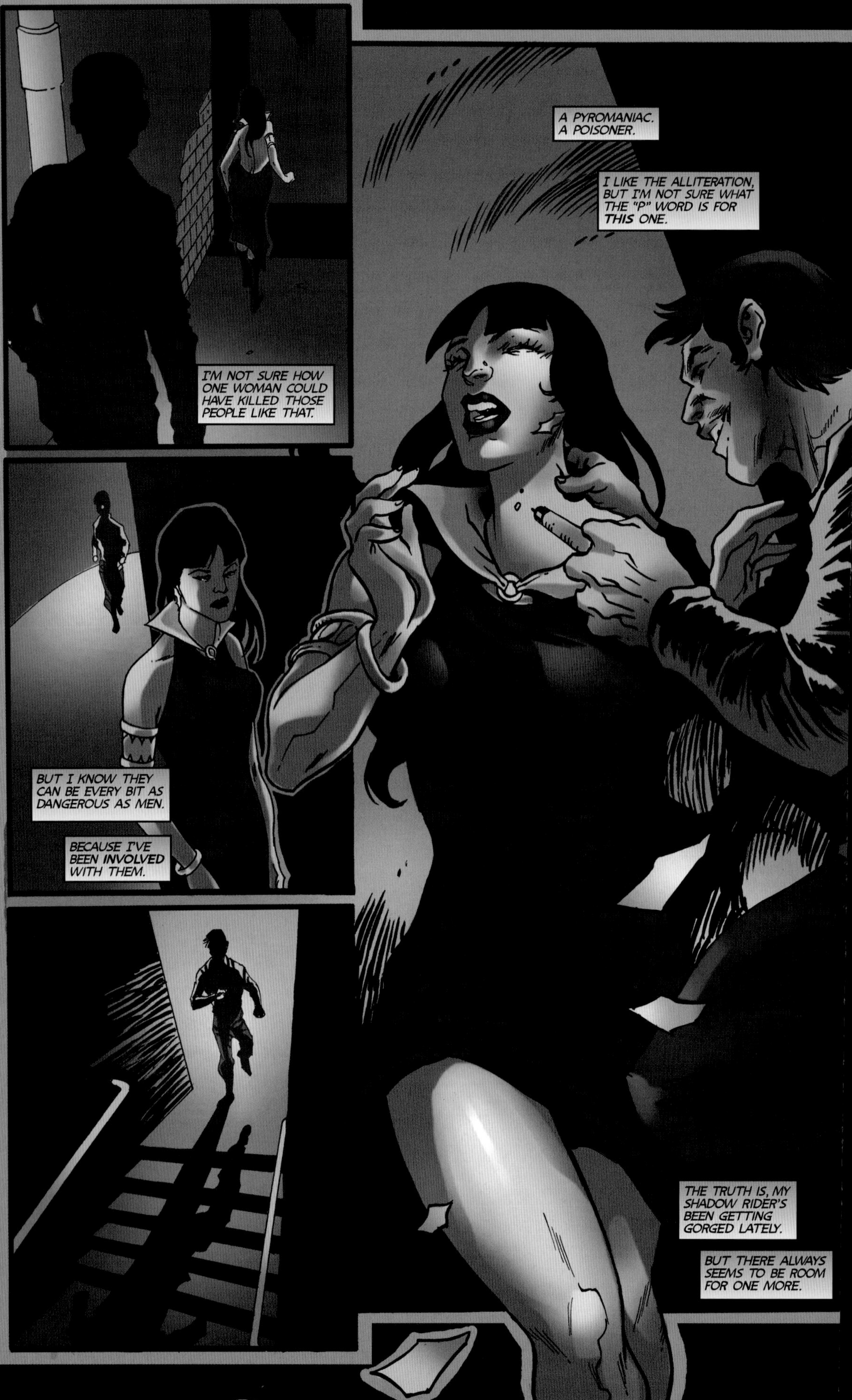
I'M NOT SURE HOW ONE WOMAN COULD HAVE KILLED THOSE PEOPLE LIKE THAT.
BUT I KNOW THEY CAN BE EVERY BIT AS DANGEROUS AS MEN.
BECAUSE I'VE BEEN INVOLVED WITH THEM.
A PYROMANIAC. A POISONER.
I LIKE THE ALLITERATION, BUT I'M NOT SURE WHAT THE "P" WORD IS FOR THIS ONE.
THE TRUTH IS, MY SHADOW RIDER'S BEEN GETTING GORGED LATELY.
BUT THERE ALWAYS SEEMS TO BE ROOM FOR ONE MORE.

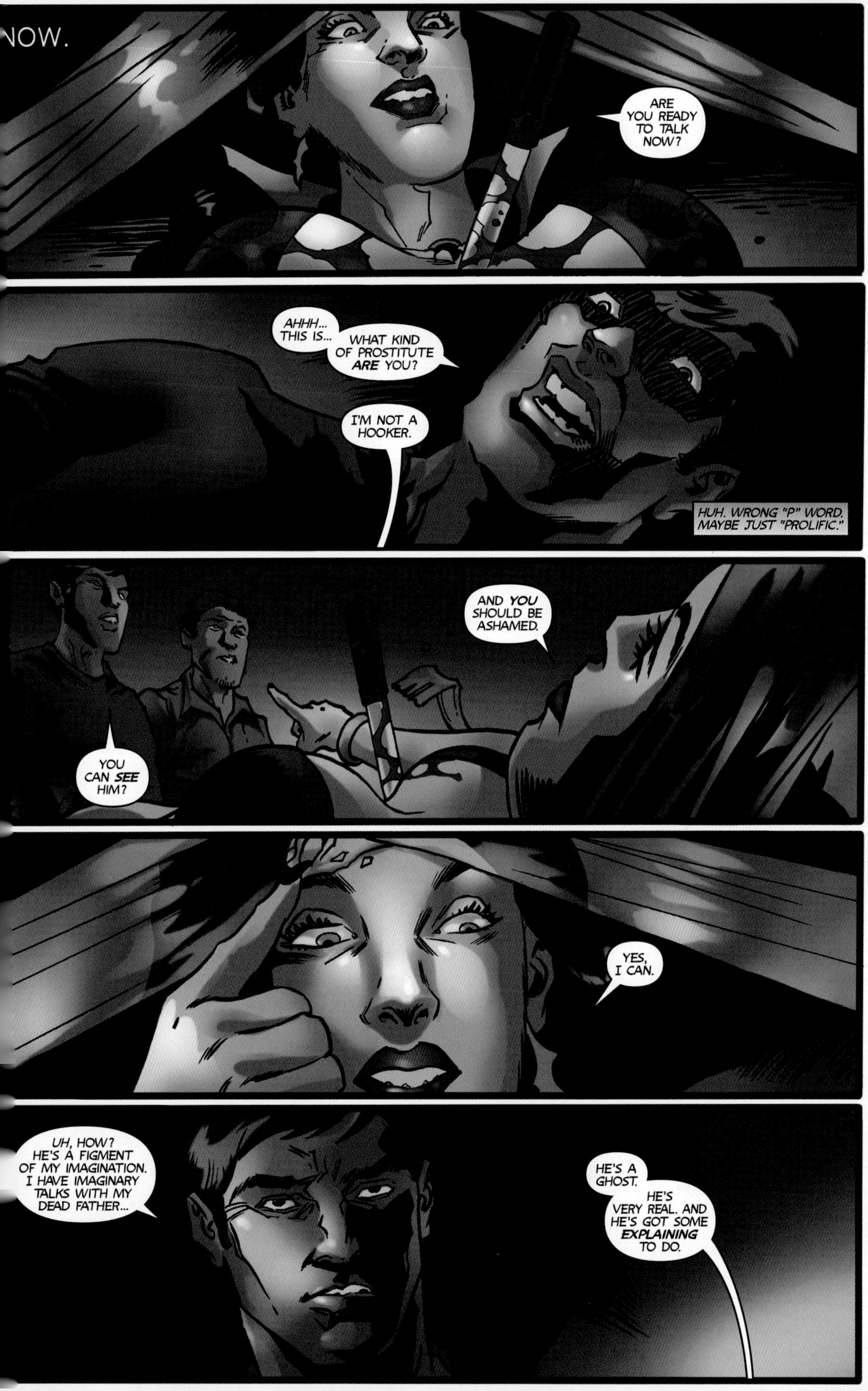
NOW.
ARE YOU READY TO TALK NOW?
AHHH... THIS IS...
WHAT KIND OF PROSTITUTE ARE YOU?
I'M NOT A HOOKER.
HUH. WRONG "P" WORD. MAYBE JUST "PROLIFIC."
AND YOU SHOULD BE ASHAMED.
YOU CAN SEE HIM?
YES, I CAN.
UH, HOW? HE'S A FIGMENT OF MY IMAGINATION. I HAVE IMAGINARY TALKS WITH MY DEAD FATHER...
HE'S A GHOST.
HE'S VERY REAL. AND HE'S GOT SOME EXPLAINING TO DO.

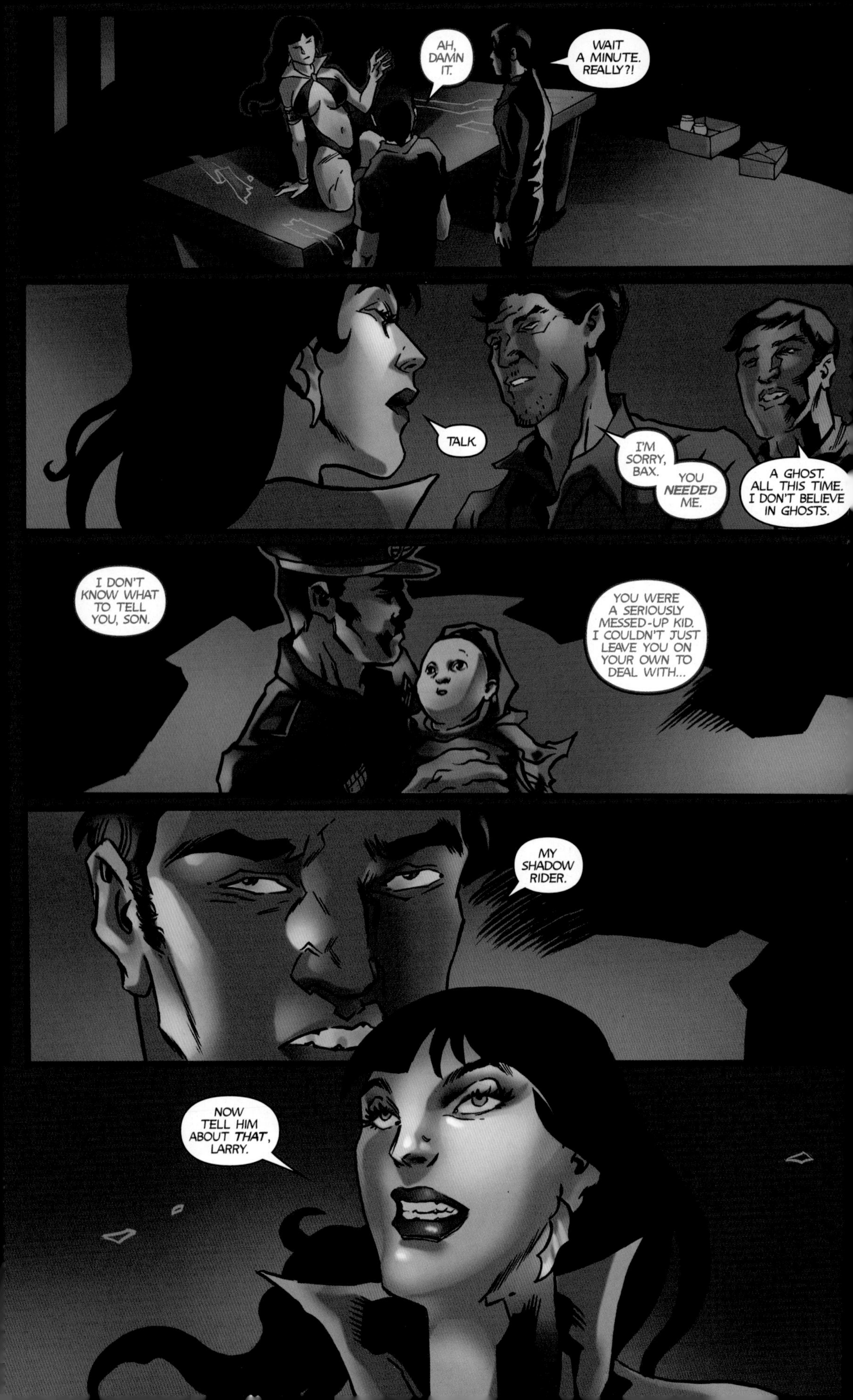
AH, DAMN IT.
WAIT A MINUTE. REALLY?!
TALK.
I'M SORRY, BAX.
YOU NEEDED ME.
A GHOST. ALL THIS TIME. I DON'T BELIEVE IN GHOSTS.
I DON'T KNOW WHAT TO TELL YOU, SON.
YOU WERE A SERIOUSLY MESSED-UP KID. I COULDN'T JUST LEAVE YOU ON YOUR OWN TO DEAL WITH...
MY SHADOW RIDER.
NOW TELL HIM ABOUT THAT, LARRY.

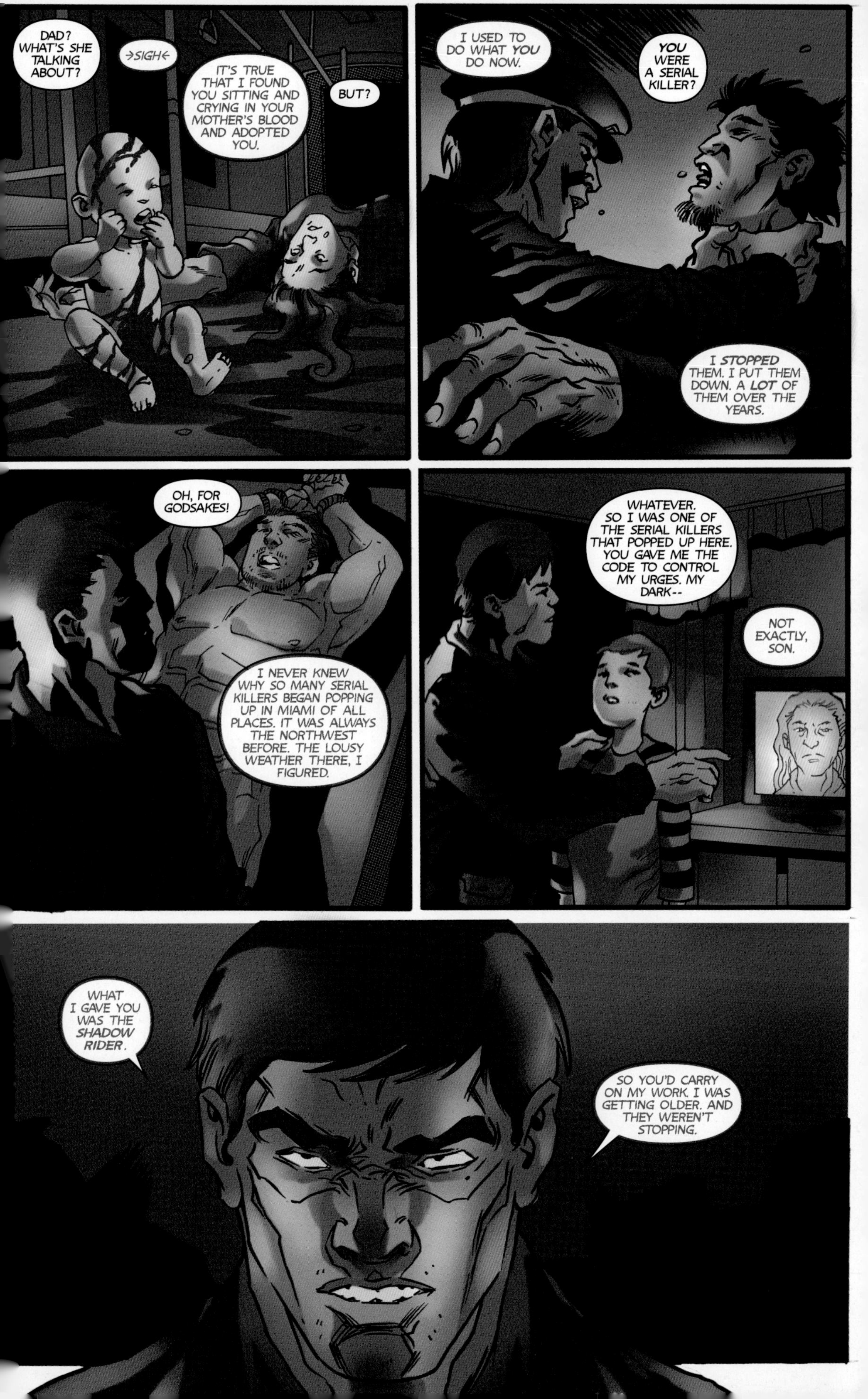
DAD? WHAT'S SHE TALKING ABOUT?
→SIGH←
IT'S TRUE THAT I FOUND YOU SITTING AND CRYING IN YOUR MOTHER'S BLOOD AND ADOPTED YOU.
BUT?
I USED TO DO WHAT YOU DO NOW.
YOU WERE A SERIAL KILLER?
I STOPPED THEM. I PUT THEM DOWN. A LOT OF THEM OVER THE YEARS.
OH, FOR GODSAKES!
I NEVER KNEW WHY SO MANY SERIAL KILLERS BEGAN POPPING UP IN MIAMI OF ALL PLACES. IT WAS ALWAYS THE NORTHWEST BEFORE. THE LOUSY WEATHER THERE, I FIGURED.
WHATEVER. SO I WAS ONE OF THE SERIAL KILLERS THAT POPPED UP HERE. YOU GAVE ME THE CODE TO CONTROL MY URGES. MY DARK--
NOT EXACTLY, SON.
WHAT I GAVE YOU WAS THE SHADOW RIDER.
SO YOU'D CARRY ON MY WORK. I WAS GETTING OLDER. AND THEY WEREN'T STOPPING.

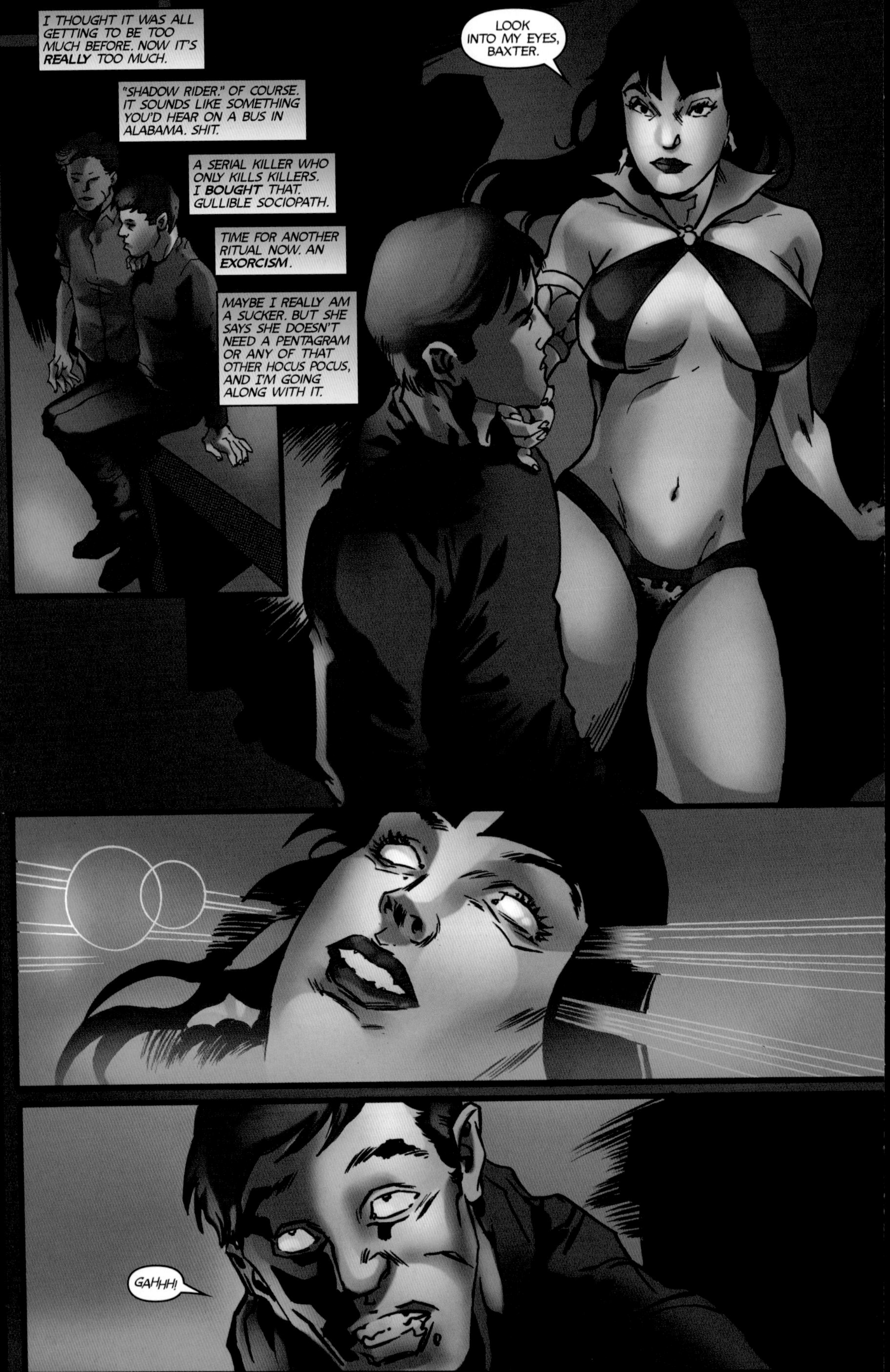
I THOUGHT IT WAS ALL GETTING TO BE TOO MUCH BEFORE. NOW IT'S REALLY TOO MUCH.
"SHADOW RIDER." OF COURSE. IT SOUNDS LIKE SOMETHING YOU'D HEAR ON A BUS IN ALABAMA. SHIT.
A SERIAL KILLER WHO ONLY KILLS KILLERS. I BOUGHT THAT. GULLIBLE SOCIOPATH.
TIME FOR ANOTHER RITUAL NOW. AN EXORCISM.
MAYBE I REALLY AM A SUCKER. BUT SHE SAYS SHE DOESN'T NEED A PENTAGRAM OR ANY OF THAT OTHER HOCUS POCUS, AND I'M GOING ALONG WITH IT.
LOOK INTO MY EYES, BAXTER.
GAHHH!

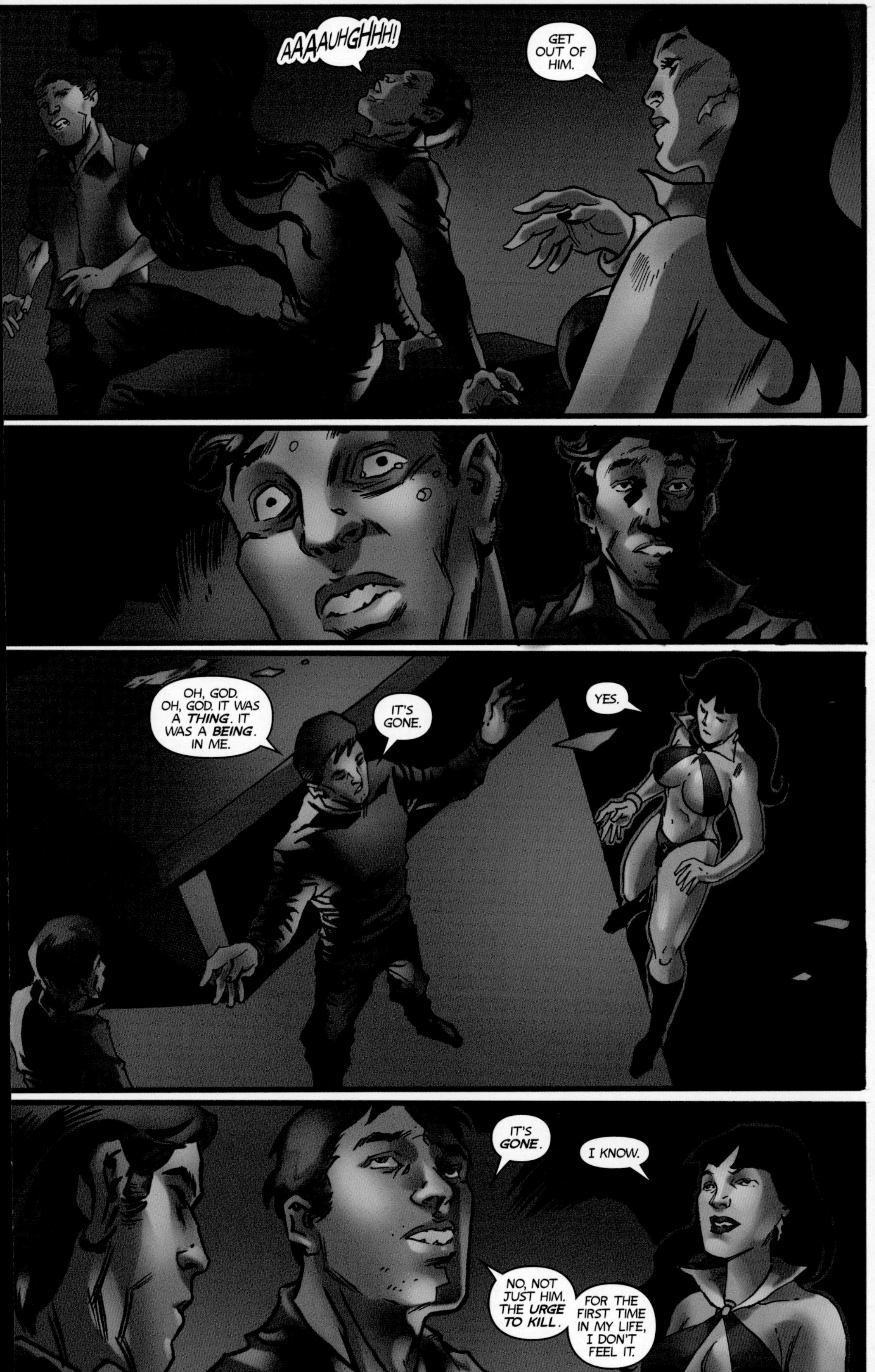
AAAAUHGHHH!
GET OUT OF HIM.
OH, GOD. OH, GOD. IT WAS A *THING*. IT WAS A *BEING*. IN ME.
IT'S GONE.
YES.
IT'S *GONE*.
I KNOW.
NO, NOT JUST HIM. THE ***URGE TO KILL***.
FOR THE FIRST TIME IN MY LIFE, I DON'T FEEL IT.

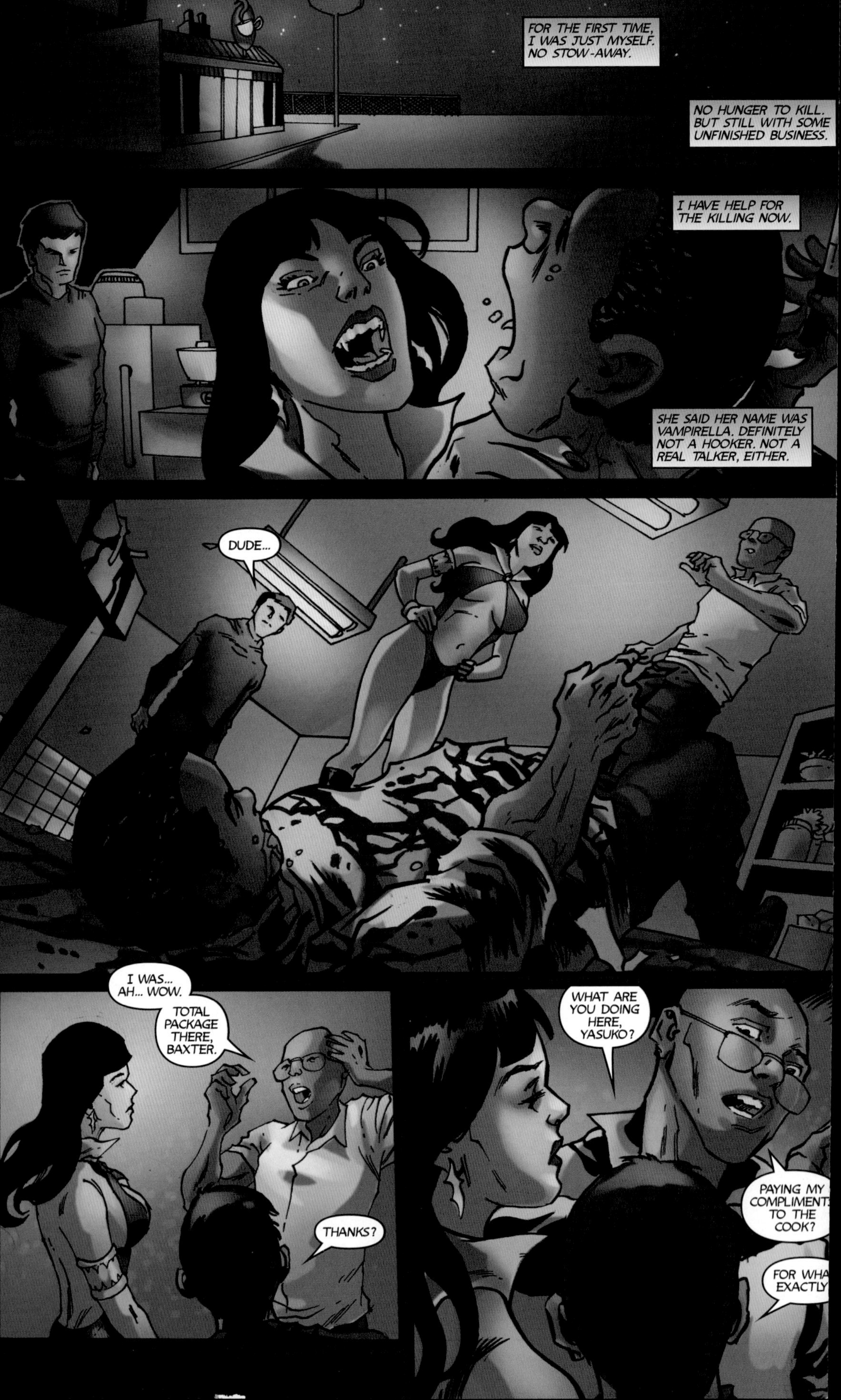
FOR THE FIRST TIME, I WAS JUST MYSELF. NO STOW-AWAY.
NO HUNGER TO KILL. BUT STILL WITH SOME UNFINISHED BUSINESS.
I HAVE HELP FOR THE KILLING NOW.
SHE SAID HER NAME WAS VAMPIRELLA. DEFINITELY NOT A HOOKER. NOT A REAL TALKER, EITHER.
DUDE...
I WAS... AH... WOW.
TOTAL PACKAGE THERE, BAXTER.
THANKS?
WHAT ARE YOU DOING HERE, YASUKO?
PAYING MY COMPLIMENT TO THE COOK?
FOR WHA EXACTLY

THERE'S SOMETHING VERY *DIFFERENT* ABOUT YOU.

HE'S A HUGE PERV.

VERY *DIFFERENT*.

YOU WILL TELL ME.

SHIIIIT.

YYYYAAAA!

I DON'T KNOW, I'M SOME SORT OF *EARTH-ELEMENTAL*, AND I WAS ALWAYS INTO THE *SEX* PART, BUT I NEVER HAD THE STOMACH FOR THE *KILLING*...

...BUT THAT ENERGY HAD TO GO SOMEWHERE, AND IT SEEPED INTO OTHER PEOPLE WHO WERE RECEPTIVE...

...AND IT'S BEEN GETTING STRONGER...

...AND SOME OF THE EROS-ENERGY HAS GOTTEN OUT OF CONTROL LATELY, TOO, AND THAT'S PROBABLY WHY BABS WANTS TO HOOK UP WITH HER OWN BROTHER...

...AND I'VE BEEN *COVERING FOR YOU FOR YEARS*, BECAUSE HOW THE HELL ELSE DO YOU THINK YOU'VE NEVER GOTTEN CAUGHT BY THE PEOPLE YOU WORK WITH WHO ARE ALL *POLICE DETECTIVES*?

...AND *WOW, MAMA!!!* THERE'S SOMETHING VERY DIFFERENT ABOUT *YOU*, TOO!

YASUKO, WHEN WERE YOU BORN? AND BAXTER, WHEN DID LARRY START THE FAMILY BUSINESS?

ZZZZT ZZZZT

THAT'S US, MAN.

YEP.

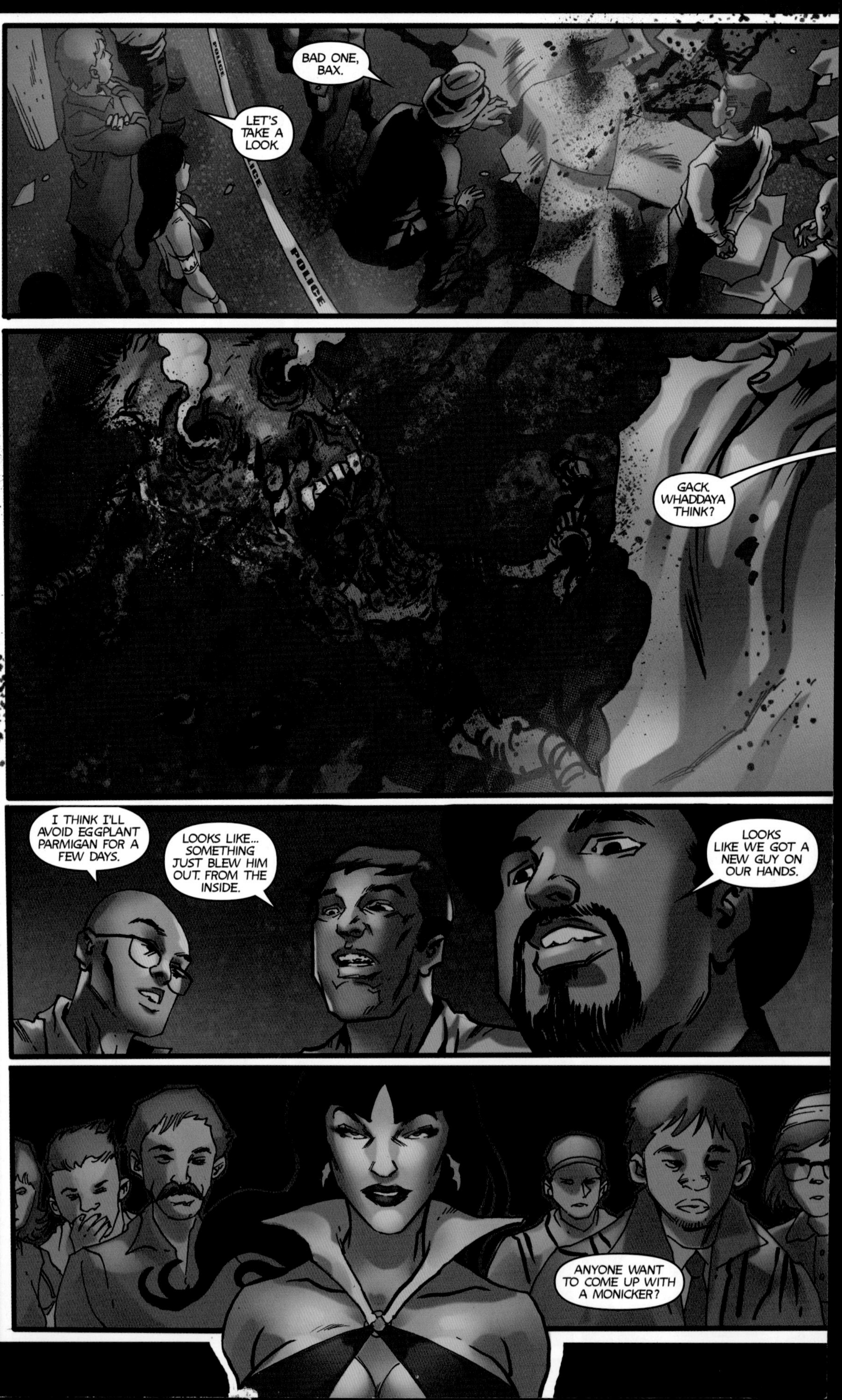

POLICE
BAD ONE, BAX.
LET'S TAKE A LOOK.
POLICE
GACK. WHADDAYA THINK?
I THINK I'LL AVOID EGGPLANT PARMIGAN FOR A FEW DAYS.
LOOKS LIKE... SOMETHING JUST BLEW HIM OUT. FROM THE INSIDE.
LOOKS LIKE WE GOT A NEW GUY ON OUR HANDS.
ANYONE WANT TO COME UP WITH A MONICKER?

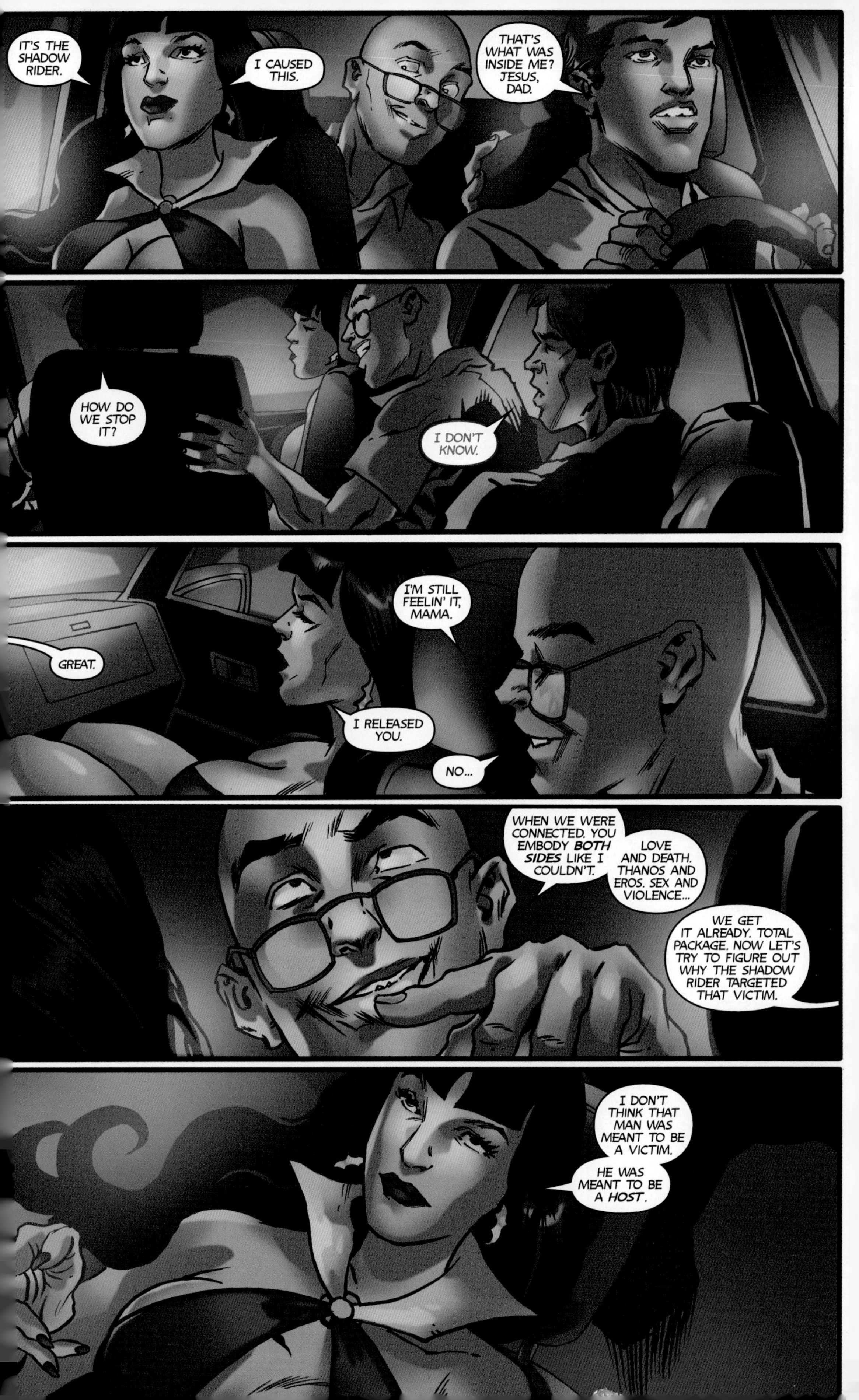
IT'S THE SHADOW RIDER.
I CAUSED THIS.
THAT'S WHAT WAS INSIDE ME? JESUS, DAD.
HOW DO WE STOP IT?
I DON'T KNOW.
I'M STILL FEELIN' IT, MAMA.
GREAT.
I RELEASED YOU.
NO...
WHEN WE WERE CONNECTED. YOU EMBODY **BOTH SIDES** LIKE I COULDN'T.
LOVE AND DEATH. THANOS AND EROS. SEX AND VIOLENCE...
WE GET IT ALREADY. TOTAL PACKAGE. NOW LET'S TRY TO FIGURE OUT WHY THE SHADOW RIDER TARGETED THAT VICTIM.
I DON'T THINK THAT MAN WAS MEANT TO BE A VICTIM.
HE WAS MEANT TO BE A ***HOST***.

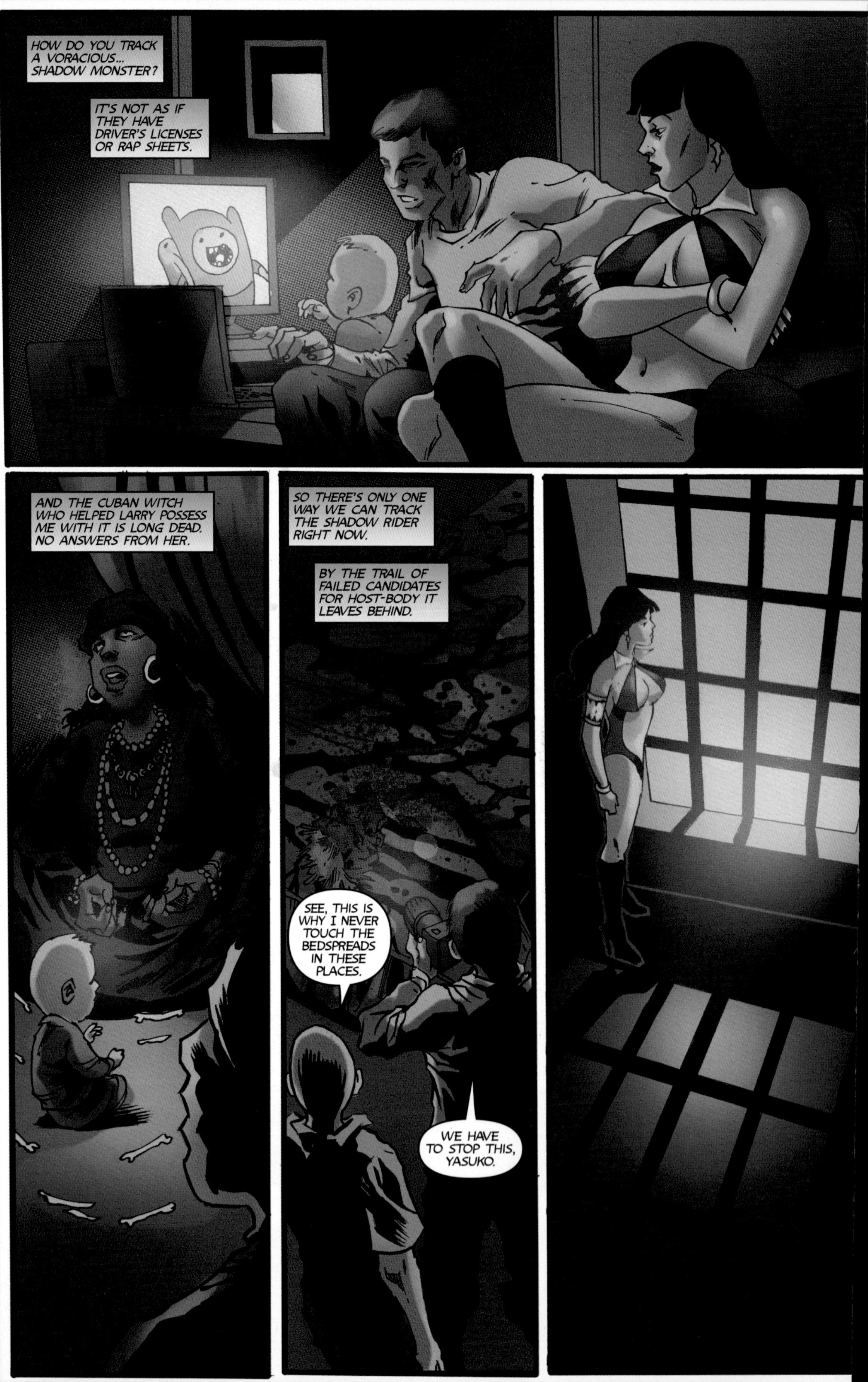
HOW DO YOU TRACK A VORACIOUS... SHADOW MONSTER?
IT'S NOT AS IF THEY HAVE DRIVER'S LICENSES OR RAP SHEETS.
AND THE CUBAN WITCH WHO HELPED LARRY POSSESS ME WITH IT IS LONG DEAD. NO ANSWERS FROM HER.
SO THERE'S ONLY ONE WAY WE CAN TRACK THE SHADOW RIDER RIGHT NOW.
BY THE TRAIL OF FAILED CANDIDATES FOR HOST-BODY IT LEAVES BEHIND.
SEE, THIS IS WHY I NEVER TOUCH THE BEDSPREADS IN THESE PLACES.
WE HAVE TO STOP THIS, YASUKO.

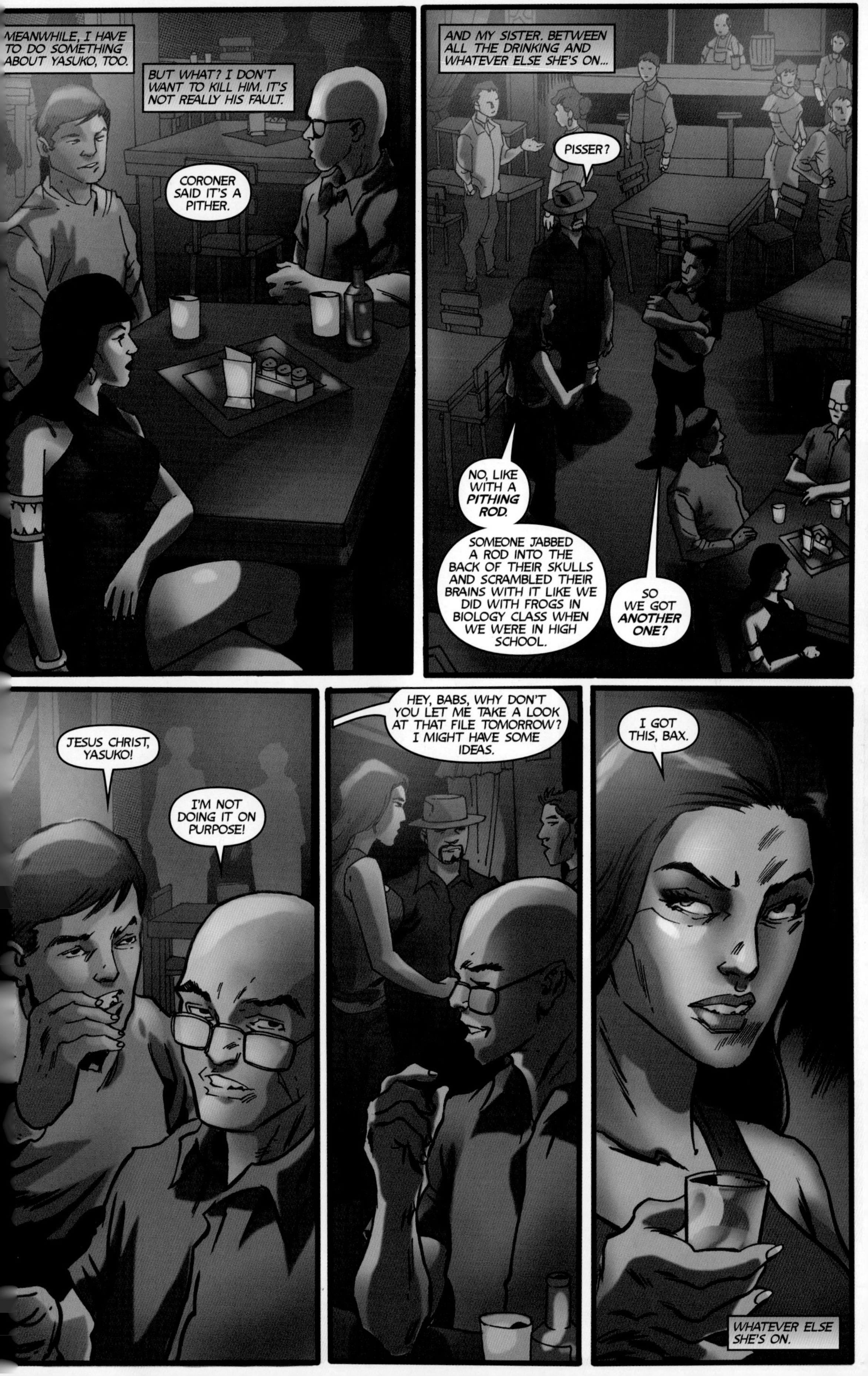

MEANWHILE, I HAVE TO DO SOMETHING ABOUT YASUKO, TOO.
BUT WHAT? I DON'T WANT TO KILL HIM. IT'S NOT REALLY HIS FAULT.
CORONER SAID IT'S A PITHER.
AND MY SISTER. BETWEEN ALL THE DRINKING AND WHATEVER ELSE SHE'S ON...
PISSER?
NO, LIKE WITH A PITHING ROD.
SOMEONE JABBED A ROD INTO THE BACK OF THEIR SKULLS AND SCRAMBLED THEIR BRAINS WITH IT LIKE WE DID WITH FROGS IN BIOLOGY CLASS WHEN WE WERE IN HIGH SCHOOL.
SO WE GOT ANOTHER ONE?
JESUS CHRIST, YASUKO!
I'M NOT DOING IT ON PURPOSE!
HEY, BABS, WHY DON'T YOU LET ME TAKE A LOOK AT THAT FILE TOMORROW? I MIGHT HAVE SOME IDEAS.
I GOT THIS, BAX.
WHATEVER ELSE SHE'S ON.

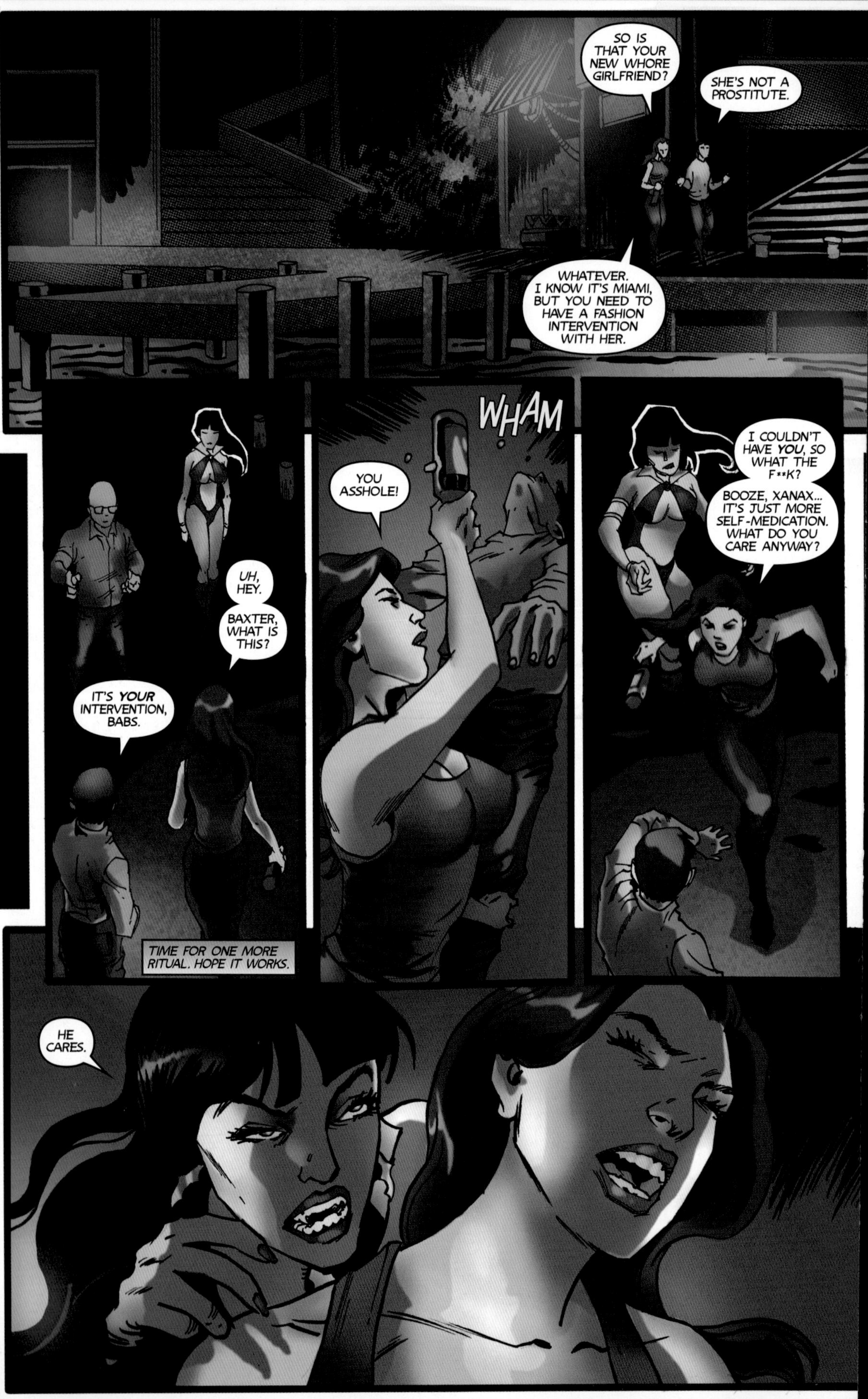
SO IS THAT YOUR NEW WHORE GIRLFRIEND?
SHE'S NOT A PROSTITUTE.
WHATEVER. I KNOW IT'S MIAMI, BUT YOU NEED TO HAVE A FASHION INTERVENTION WITH HER.
UH, HEY.
BAXTER, WHAT IS THIS?
IT'S YOUR INTERVENTION, BABS.
TIME FOR ONE MORE RITUAL. HOPE IT WORKS.
WHAM
YOU ASSHOLE!
I COULDN'T HAVE YOU, SO WHAT THE F**K?
BOOZE, XANAX... IT'S JUST MORE SELF-MEDICATION. WHAT DO YOU CARE ANYWAY?
HE CARES.

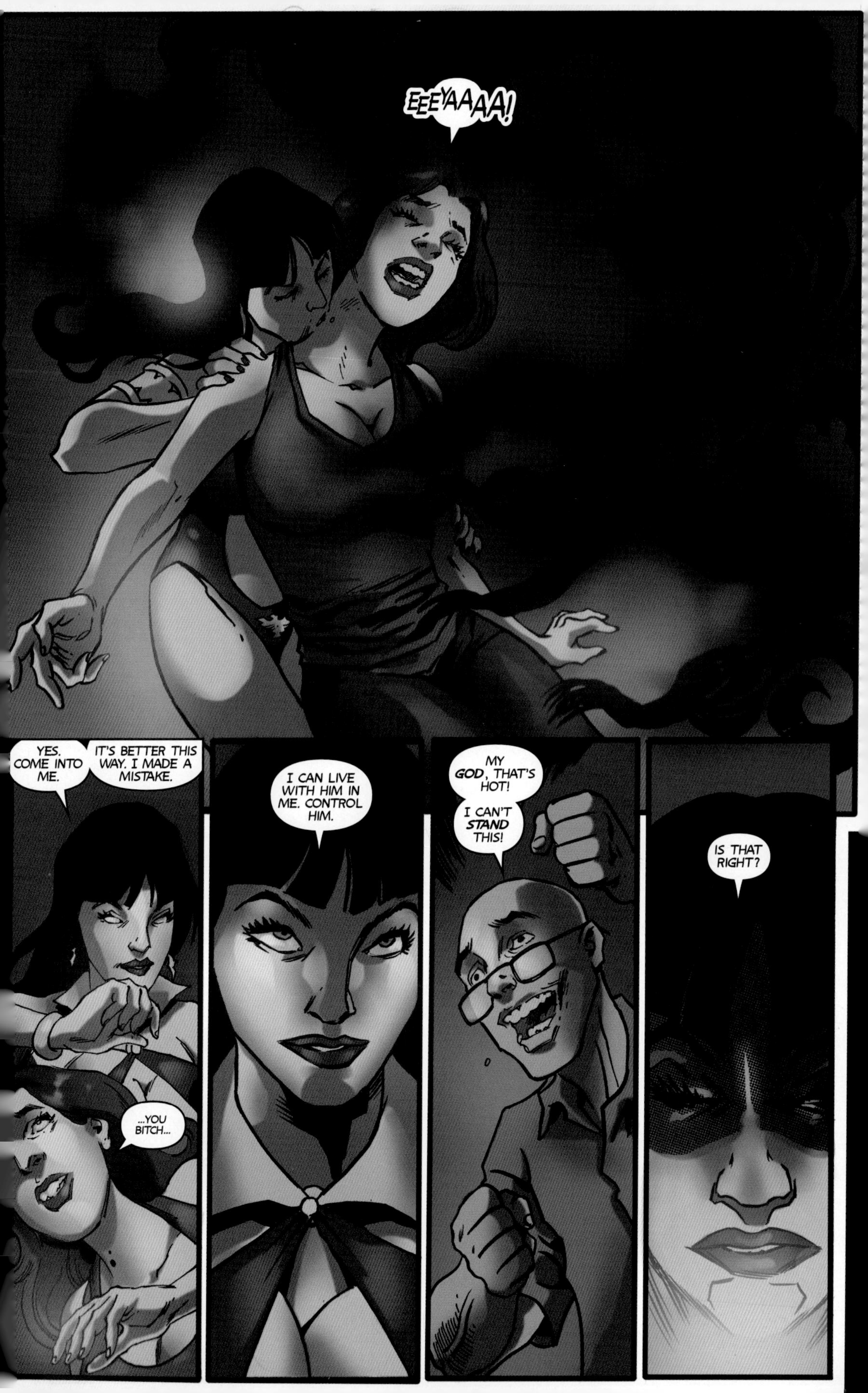
EEEYAAAA!
YES. COME INTO ME.
IT'S BETTER THIS WAY. I MADE A MISTAKE.
...YOU BITCH...
I CAN LIVE WITH HIM IN ME. CONTROL HIM.
MY GOD, THAT'S HOT!
I CAN'T STAND THIS!
IS THAT RIGHT?

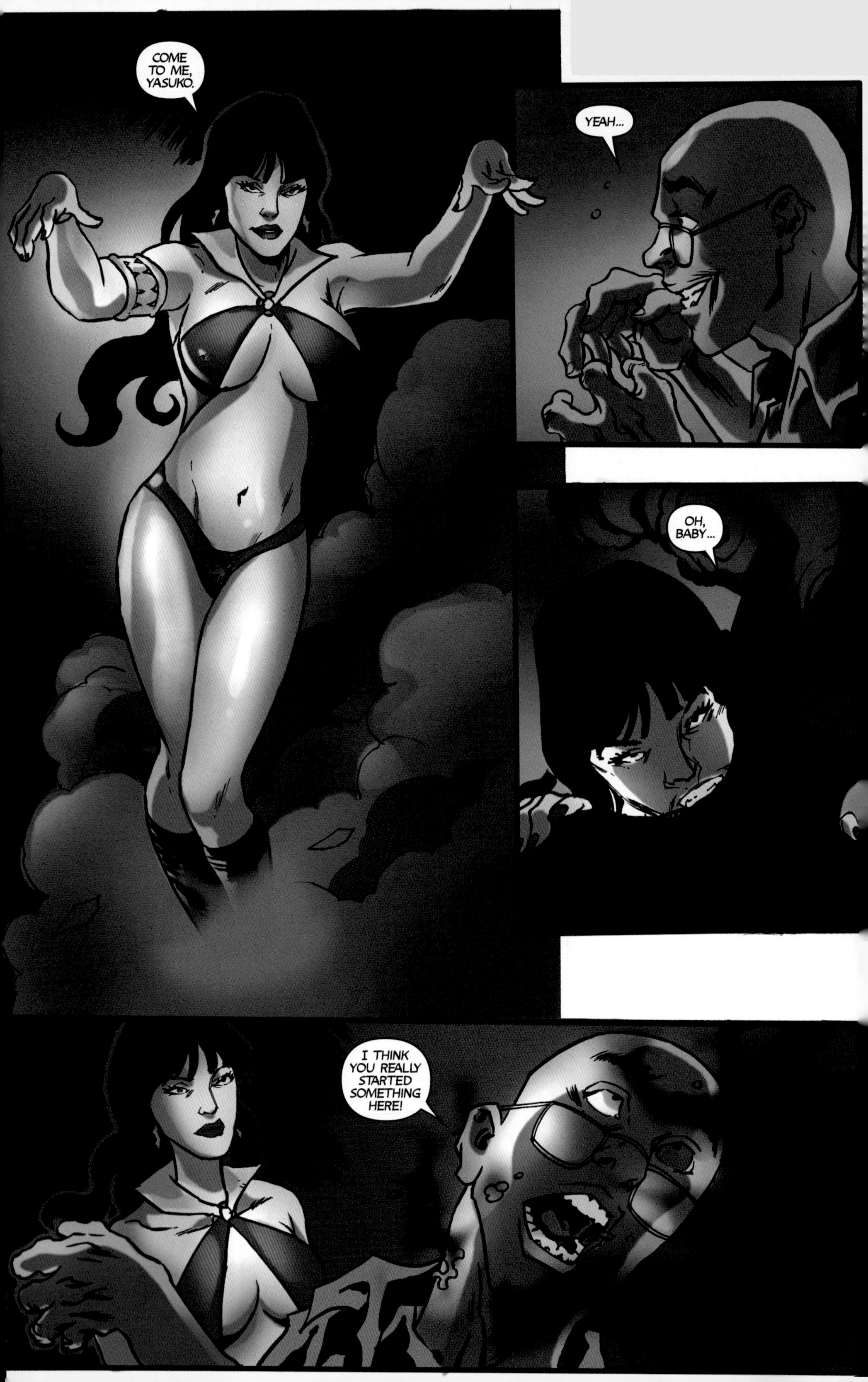
COME TO ME, YASUKO.
YEAH...
OH, BABY...
I THINK YOU REALLY STARTED SOMETHING HERE!

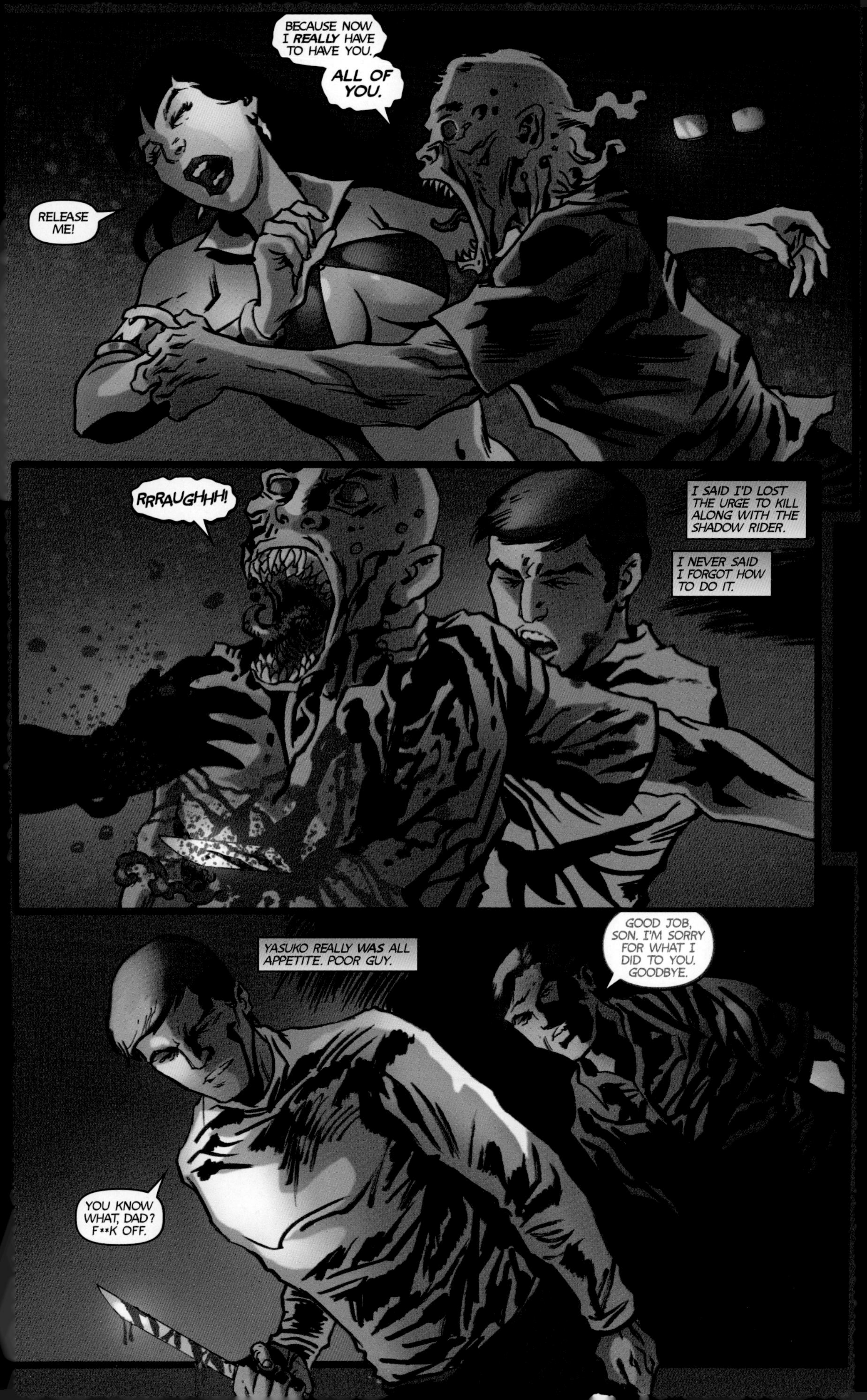
BECAUSE NOW I REALLY HAVE TO HAVE YOU.
ALL OF YOU.
RELEASE ME!
RRRAUGHHH!
I SAID I'D LOST THE URGE TO KILL ALONG WITH THE SHADOW RIDER.
I NEVER SAID I FORGOT HOW TO DO IT.
YASUKO REALLY WAS ALL APPETITE. POOR GUY.
GOOD JOB, SON. I'M SORRY FOR WHAT I DID TO YOU. GOODBYE.
YOU KNOW WHAT, DAD? F**K OFF.

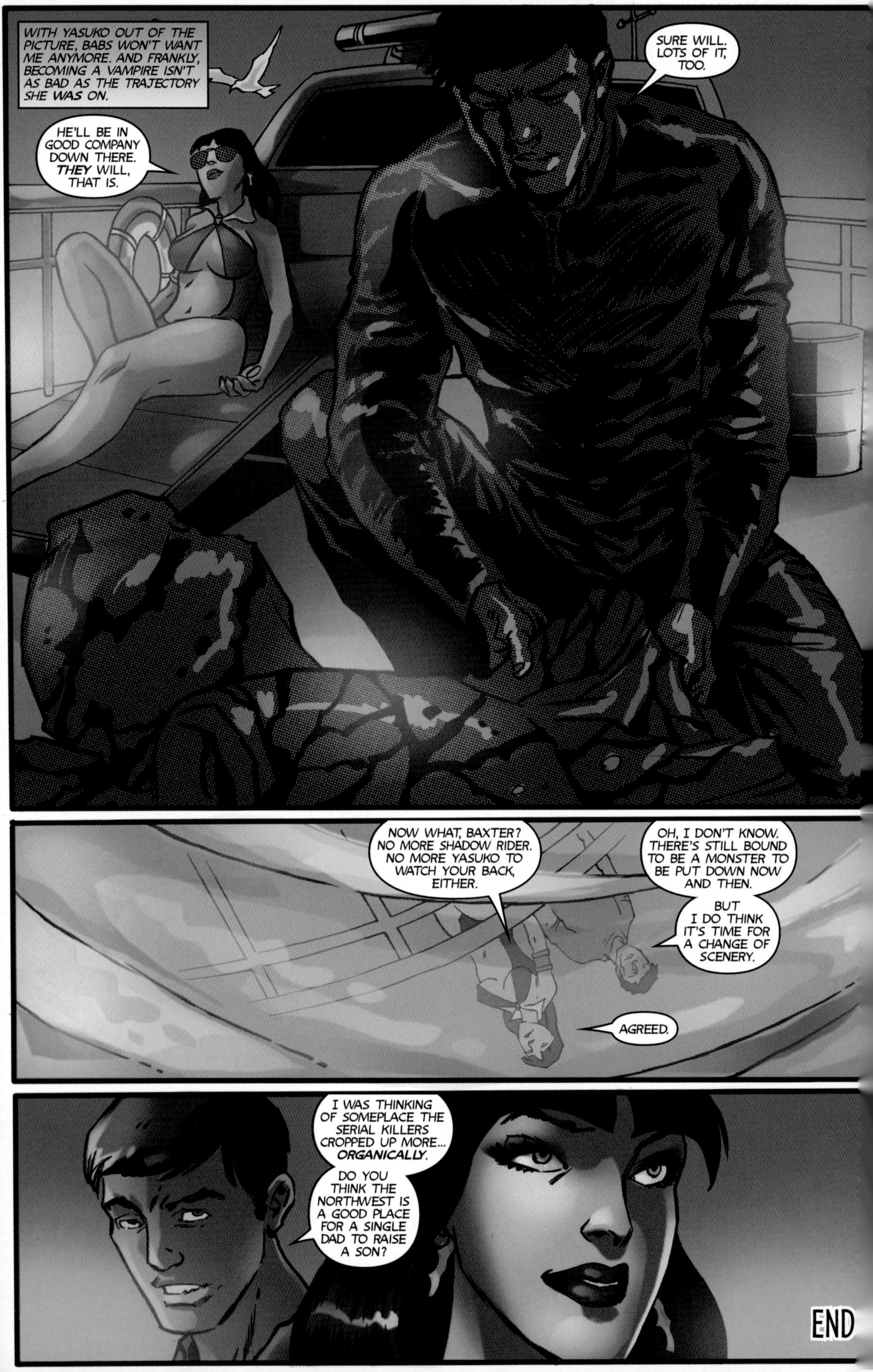
WITH YASUKO OUT OF THE PICTURE, BABS WON'T WANT ME ANYMORE. AND FRANKLY, BECOMING A VAMPIRE ISN'T AS BAD AS THE TRAJECTORY SHE *WAS* ON.
SURE WILL. LOTS OF IT, TOO.
HE'LL BE IN GOOD COMPANY DOWN THERE. ***THEY*** WILL, THAT IS.
NOW WHAT, BAXTER? NO MORE SHADOW RIDER. NO MORE YASUKO TO WATCH YOUR BACK, EITHER.
OH, I DON'T KNOW. THERE'S STILL BOUND TO BE A MONSTER TO BE PUT DOWN NOW AND THEN.
BUT I DO THINK IT'S TIME FOR A CHANGE OF SCENERY.
AGREED.
I WAS THINKING OF SOMEPLACE THE SERIAL KILLERS CROPPED UP MORE... ***ORGANICALLY***.
DO YOU THINK THE NORTHWEST IS A GOOD PLACE FOR A SINGLE DAD TO RAISE A SON?
END

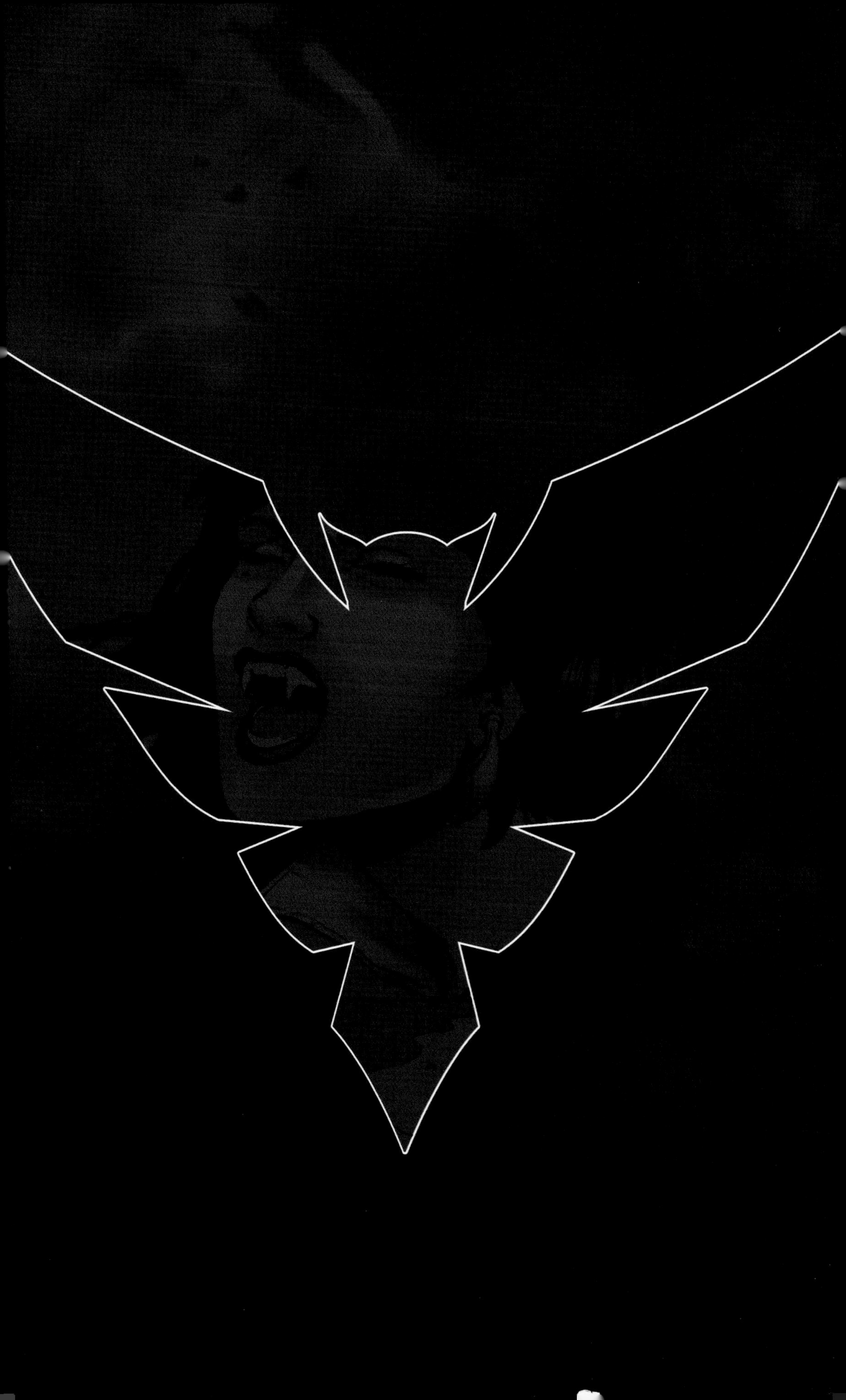

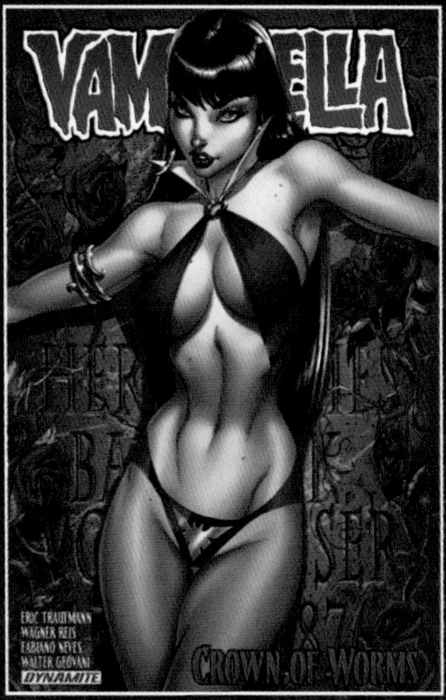
VAMPIRELLA
ERIC TRAUTMANN
WAGNER REIS
FABIANO NEVES
WALTER GEOVANI
DYNAMITE
CROWN OF WORMS
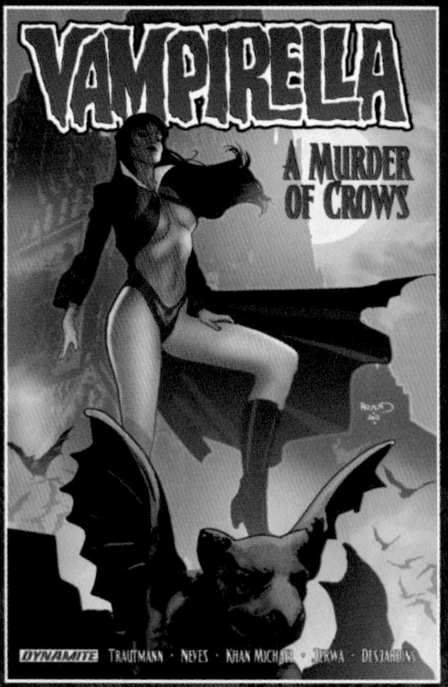
VAMPIRELLA
A MURDER OF CROWS
DYNAMITE TRAUTMANN · NEVES · KHAN MICHAEL · JERWA · DESJARDINS
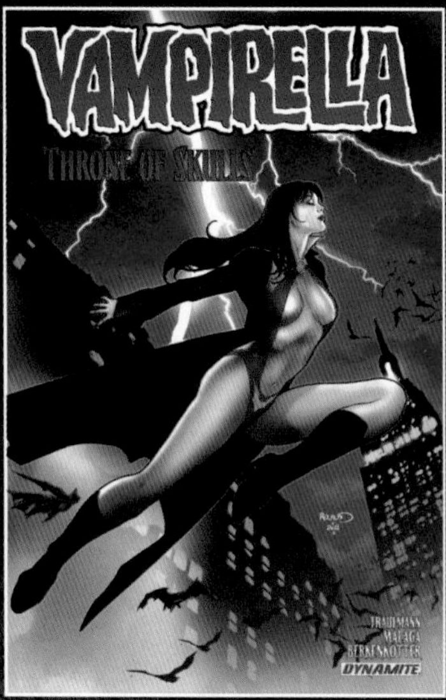
VAMPIRELLA
THRONE OF SKULLS
TRAUTMANN
MALAGA
BERKENKOTTER
DYNAMITE
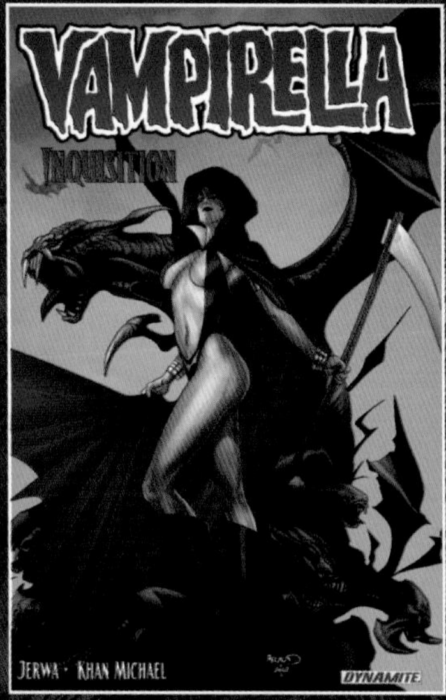
VAMPIRELLA
INQUISITION
JERWA · KHAN MICHAEL
DYNAMITE
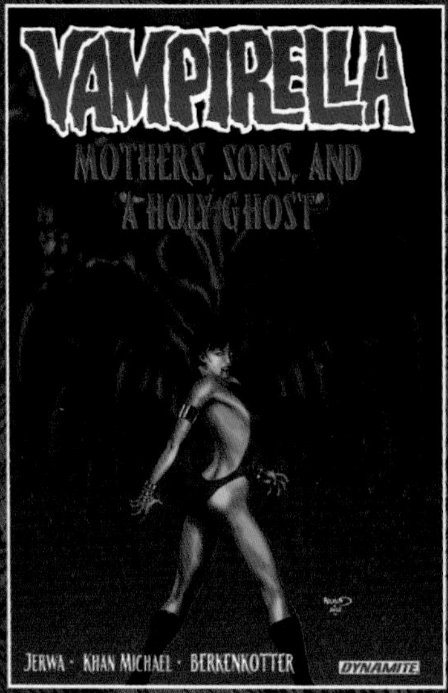
VAMPIRELLA
MOTHERS, SONS, AND "A HOLY GHOST"
JERWA · KHAN MICHAEL · BERKENKOTTER
DYNAMITE
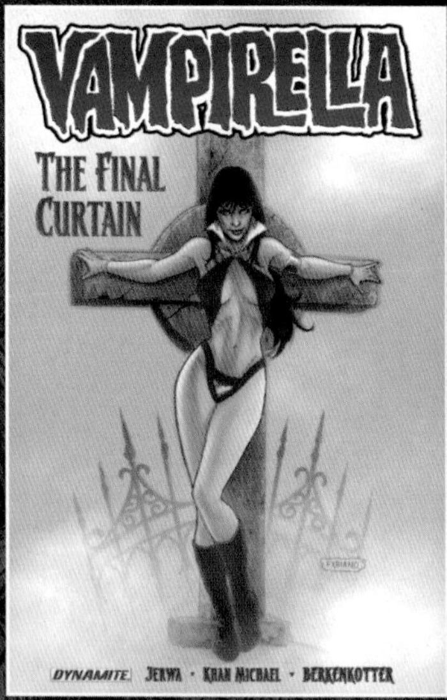
VAMPIRELLA
THE FINAL CURTAIN
DYNAMITE JERWA · KHAN MICHAEL · BERKENKOTTER

VAMPIRELLA VOL. ONE: "CROWN OF WORMS"
written by ERIC TRAUTMANN art by WAGNER REIS & WALTER GEOVANI

VAMPIRELLA VOL. TWO: "A MURDER OF CROWS"
written by ERIC TRAUTMANN & BRANDON JERWA
art by FABIANO NEVES, HEUBERT KHAN MICHAEL & JOHNNY DESJARDINS

VAMPIRELLA VOL. THREE: "THRONE OF SKULLS"
written by ERIC TRAUTMANN art by JOSE MALAGA & PATRICK BERKENKOTTER

VAMPIRELLA VOL. FOUR: "INQUISITION"
written by BRANDON JERWA art by HEUBERT KHAN MICHAEL

VAMPIRELLA VOL. FIVE: "MOTHERS, SONS, AND A HOLY GHOST"
written by BRANDON JERWA art by HEUBERT KHAN MICHAEL & PATRICK BERKENKOTTER

VAMPIRELLA VOL. SIX: "THE FINAL CURTAIN"
written by BRANDON JERWA art by HEUBERT KHAN MICHAEL & PATRICK BERKENKOTTER

WWW.DYNAMITE.COM FOLLOW US ON TWITTER: @DYNAMITECOMICS LIKE US ON FACEBOOK: /DYNAMITECOM

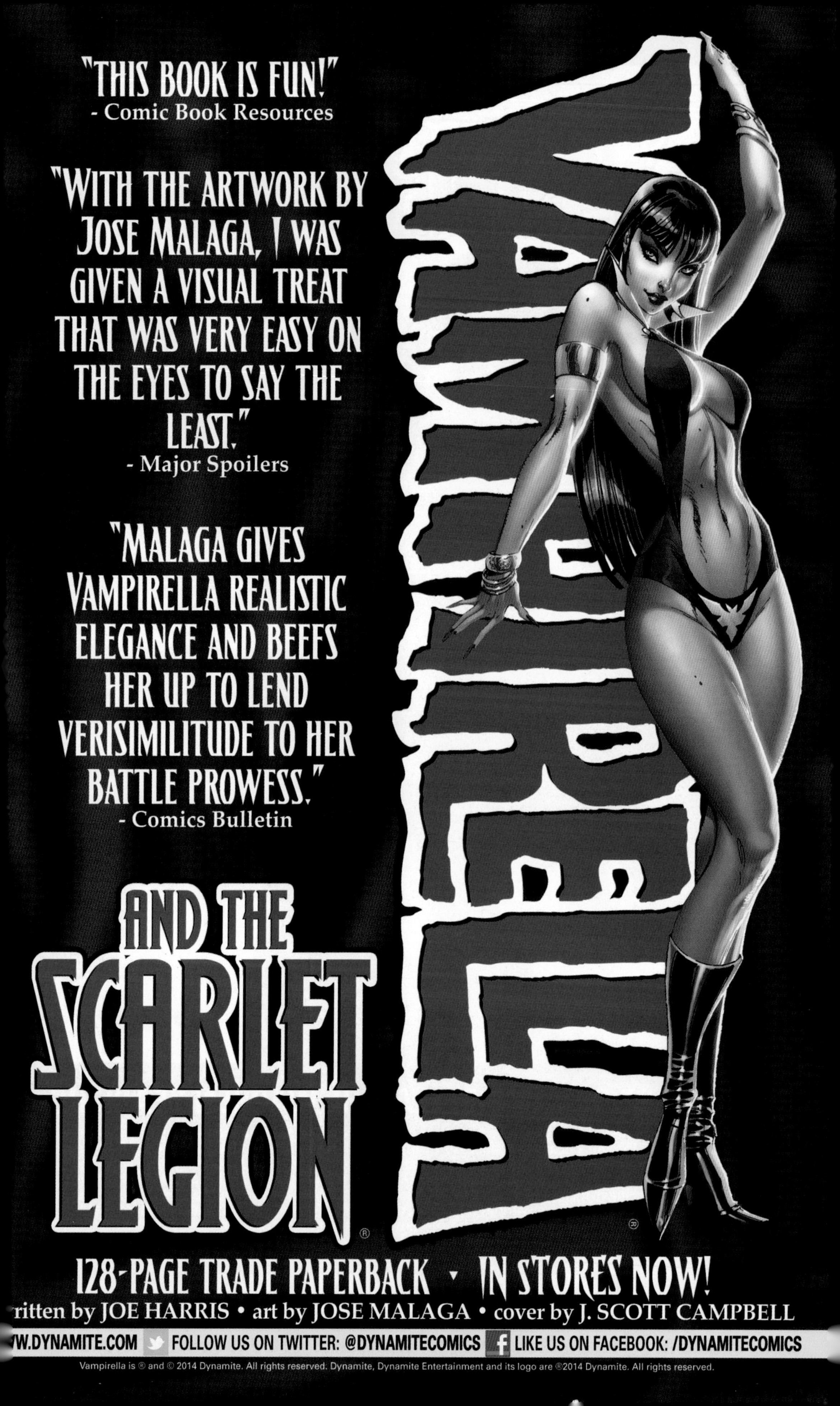
"THIS BOOK IS FUN!"
- Comic Book Resources
"WITH THE ARTWORK BY JOSE MALAGA, I WAS GIVEN A VISUAL TREAT THAT WAS VERY EASY ON THE EYES TO SAY THE LEAST."
- Major Spoilers
"MALAGA GIVES VAMPIRELLA REALISTIC ELEGANCE AND BEEFS HER UP TO LEND VERISIMILITUDE TO HER BATTLE PROWESS."
- Comics Bulletin
VAMPIRELLA®
AND THE SCARLET LEGION®
128-PAGE TRADE PAPERBACK • IN STORES NOW!
ritten by JOE HARRIS • art by JOSE MALAGA • cover by J. SCOTT CAMPBELL
W.DYNAMITE.COM
FOLLOW US ON TWITTER: @DYNAMITECOMICS
LIKE US ON FACEBOOK: /DYNAMITECOMICS
Vampirella is ® and © 2014 Dynamite. All rights reserved. Dynamite, Dynamite Entertainment and its logo are ®2014 Dynamite. All rights reserved.

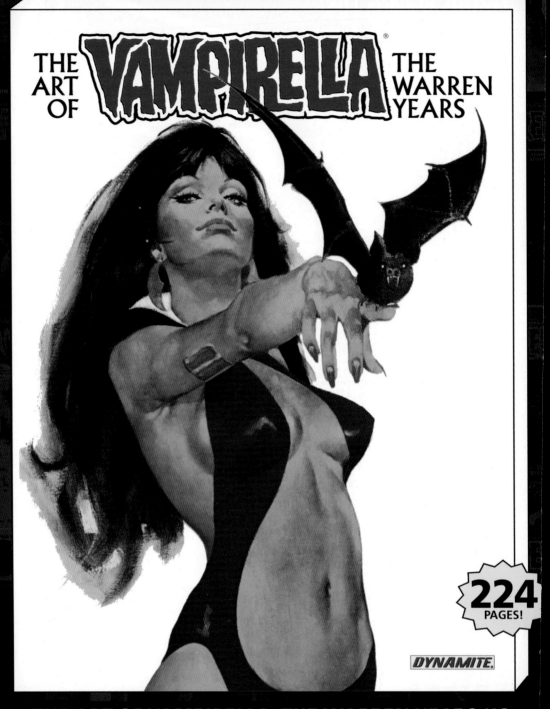

THE ART OF VAMPIRELLA: THE WARREN YEARS HC

In 1969 an iconic image of a mysterious female and the backdrop of an alien moon popped up on America's newsstands and forever became the fantasy of millions of young adult males! Dynamite Entertainment is celebrating these classic images of the original Vampirella series by presenting fans with The Art of Vampirella: The Warren Years which will feature every image to grace the cover of the Vampirella magazine from issue 1 through 112 and the 1972 Annual. Showcased in their purest form, every cover presented in this volume will be without logos and cover type. This is the first time anywhere that fans can see how the original works of art looked before any design elements were placed over them. Featuring the art of Frank Frazetta, Sanjulian, Enrich, Ken Kelly along with photo covers of the beautiful Barbara Leigh dressed as Vampirella! This is sure to be one of the hottest collectibles in Vampirella history!

IN STORES NOW FROM DYNAMITE!

WWW.DYNAMITE.NET   FOLLOW US ON TWITTER: #DYNAMITECOMICS   LIKE US ON FACEBOOK: /DYNAMITECOM

Vampirella is ™ & © 2014 Dynamite. All rights reserved. Dynamite, Dynamite Entertainment and its logo are ® & © Dynamite 2014. All rights reserved.

PRAISE FOR GAIL SIMONE'S

Newsarama
"A strong and promising debut."

Comic Book Resources
"Sword and sorcery adventure
done right... Great fun!"

IGN
"This is a great comic book and it
deserves your attention."

Comic Vine
"5 stars out of 5."

Comic Book Therapy
"Lives up to the hype."

Comicosity
"A fun, action-packed, violent and
humorous adventure."

Unleash The Fanboy
"Absolutely spectacular to behold."

Geeks of Doom
"Comic fans, what are you waiting for?!"

Major Spoilers
"I'm desperate for the next installment."

RED SONJA VOL. 1:
"QUEEN OF PLAGUES" TRADE PAPERBACK
written by GAIL SIMONE
art by WALTER GEOVANI

**Collection in stores now!
Ongoing series in stores monthly!**

DYNAMITE. DYNAMITE.COM • TWITTER: @DYNAMITECOMICS • FACEBOOK: /DYNAMITECOMICS

Red Sonja ® & © 2014 Red Sonja, llc. Dynamite, Dynamite Entertainment and its logo are ® and © 2014 Dynamite. All rights reserved.